# Interviewing
## for
## Social Scientists

# Interviewing
## for
# Social Scientists

## An
## Introductory Resource
## with Examples

Hilary Arksey
and Peter Knight

SAGE Publications
London • Thousand Oaks • New Delhi

SAGE Publications Ltd
6 Bonhill Street
London EC2A 4PU

SAGE Publications Inc
2455 Teller Road
Thousand Oaks, California 91320

SAGE Publications India Pvt Ltd
32, M-Block Market
Greater Kailash – I
New Delhi 110 048

**British Library Cataloguing in Publication Data**

A catalogue record for this book is
available from the British Library

ISBN 0 7619 5869 X
ISBN 0 7619 5870 3 (pbk)

**Library of Congress catalog card number 99–72817**

Typeset by Keystroke, Jacaranda Lodge, Wolverhampton.
Printed in Great Britain by The Cromwell Press Ltd, Trowbridge, Wiltshire

# Contents

# List of Boxes

# List of Figures

# List of Tables

# Preface

This book emerged from our belief that there was a need for a text that encompassed the principles and techniques involved in conducting a wide variety of interviews. Types of interviewing which we discuss range from the formal and structured to the completely unstructured; from one-to-one to group interviews; and from face-to-face to telephone interviews. We have used most of these techniques ourselves at some time or another, as they seemed appropriate to the research problems on which we were working. We also mention some techniques that have caused us problems, along with suggestions for overcoming them. This is in the belief that, as researchers, we learn through experience and reflection. Our commentary is also based on our work teaching undergraduate and post-graduate students about social science research methods.

Writers on research methods often argue about the strengths and weaknesses of the various approaches available to answer different research questions. This is especially true of those within the social sciences, where there have been 'paradigm wars' between the devotees of structured survey work that produces data in a quantifiable form, on the one hand, and of the unstructured interview with its fluid agenda and open questions that seek to achieve rich, detailed, qualitative information, on the other. Activists in these wars have tended to argue that a particular method is better at investigating the extent to which people hold certain views, or for trying to understand certain perspectives, and have claimed that certain theoretical stances – phenomenology, ethnography, or social interactionism – are to be preferred. Our purpose is not to criticize these approaches or to propound the strengths of any one of them, although in our practice we incline towards phenomenological, qualitative, investigations of human experience. Rather, we claim that different approaches and stances are fit for different purposes, so we have set out to review some of those purposes, and to identify some of the potential strengths, weaknesses and uses of the various stances and interviewing methods. In this way, we are trying to help people who are coming fresh to social science research to appreciate that investigating social relationships, social phenomena and the workings of society is a creative, value-full, contested and dynamic activity.

The book is intended to be accessible, reader-friendly and comprehensive. It is aimed primarily at undergraduate and postgraduate students, although much of the material will also be useful to applied social researchers, academic researchers and methodology lecturers. Given the principal readership, however, we have looked at interviewing mainly within the context of small-scale enquiries that have to be completed within tight time and resource constraints. Because our focus is principally on the relatively small-scale study, where the same individual is both researcher and interviewer, we use these two terms interchangeably.

In terms of discipline areas, the book is designed to be suitable for those with a social science background, but it is also applicable to people involved in the fields of educational research, health and social care, oral history, social psychology, anthropology and so on. We have not assumed that you will have a detailed knowledge of the theoretical and methodological debates that surround and (sometimes!) inform the social science research process. While we have surveyed the extent of these debates, we have not been able to go into detail, which is why we have provided a limited set of references to more extensive treatments of the issues, inviting you to investigate areas of especial interest in greater depth. Generally, the book is organized in line with the various stages of the research process: design, administration, implementation and analysis. Although we have organized our chapters in that conventional sequence, we are not wanting to imply that the research process is, in practice, linear or sequential.

The book is completed with an interview checklist that pulls together the major themes and topics discussed in the body of the text, thereby giving a convenient summary of the main issues that need to be taken into account when conducting social research.

We are both grateful to Rhidian Hughes, Mary Maynard and Alan Warde for reading and commenting on the text. Bryony Beresford helped Hilary with useful comments about interviewing techniques for children and adolescents. Anne Corden, Michael Hirst and Ken Simons provided valuable advice in relation to interviewing people with learning disabilities. Peter acknowledges the help he received from colleagues in Canadian universities who talked to him about their experiences of using interview methods. A year's sabbatical leave from Lancaster University made it possible for him to contribute to the book. Our special thanks go to Teresa Frank and Sally Pulleyn for their excellent secretarial support.

# 1    Interviews and Research in the Social Sciences

... there is a very practical side to qualitative [research] methods that simply involves asking open-ended questions of people and observing matters of interest in real-world settings in order to solve problems. (Patton, 1990: 89)

This is a chapter about the theories behind interviewing, which is one, immensely popular research method in the social sciences. It is also a deceptive method, for, since we have read, seen and heard hundreds of interviews in the press, on radio and on television, it is easy to be blasé about them and to assume that interviewing is nothing more than common sense at work.

For that reason, and because this chapter deals in some complex, difficult and contested ideas, there may be a temptation to skip this chapter, a temptation that is both understandable and regrettable. Regrettable, because it is here we argue that interviewing is a family of research approaches that demand method more than common sense; and that approaches to interviewing are influenced by the purpose behind the research and by our often unvoiced assumptions about the nature of social science. Furthermore, choosing to interview might mean choosing not to use other research techniques, and that is a decision that needs to be justified.

Much of what we say in this chapter holds good for social science research in general. The same could be said of Chapter 2, in which we outline a common social science technique called triangulation and suggest that interviewing may be used in conjunction with other methods. Chapter 4, which is about the design of an interview study, also addresses issues that arise in designing any social science research.

In each of these chapters, for the sake of completeness, we have introduced some terms, such as reliability and validity, before dealing with them in depth. In those cases we have given references to the pages on which they receive fuller treatment.

Throughout, our position is that research methods may be, and often are, applied atheoretically. Their power is greater when methods, such as interviews, are chosen because they are the best for the purpose, and when that choice is consistent with an understanding of what social science is and is not. (We are not saying that there is only one understanding. We are saying that it is important to have an understanding of what social science can and cannot do.)

So, while we see the sense in what Patton is claiming, in this chapter we shall sketch the reasons why you need to be thoughtful as an interviewer. Our stance is that people's perceptions of the world are more or less individualistic and that different interviewing approaches are suitable for documenting perceptions that are widely shared from those used when exploring more personal, individualistic understandings. That involves a foray into the large debate about the nature of social science itself. Having surveyed this ground, we open a recurrent theme of this book, namely that interviews are one social science research method and will frequently be used alongside others. Since different methods have different strengths and different limitations, the choice of method(s) is a fundamental one in any social science enquiry. Just as you cannot drive a nail into wood using a screwdriver, so too the choice of methods in social science enquiry limits the types of conclusions you will be able to draw.

## Interviewing in the social sciences

Interviewing, we suggest, is not a research method but a family of research approaches that have only one thing in common – conversation between people in which one person has the role of researcher. We understand 'research' to be 'systematic enquiry', so there is no implication in the use of the term 'researcher' that the interviewer wears a white coat and horn-rimmed glasses, holds a clipboard, talks jargon, scribbles illegible notes and dominates proceedings. Rather, we claim that choosing the most appropriate interviewing approach is a skilled activity, one that involves taking a stance on some complex and important debates about the nature of research in the social sciences.

Interviewing has a lot in common with questionnaire-based methods[1] and, taken together, they dominate social science research. Interviews are also widely used in other disciplines and for other purposes. Some historians of modern times use them in oral history work. Interviews are also used in helping and caring professions for diagnostic and counselling purposes, although we will not give systematic attention to therapeutic and diagnostic interviewing.

We do not see interviewing as a straightforward activity, although there are dissenting voices in the research community:

> The overwhelming majority who have thought about [interviewing as a research method] have concluded that interviewing is overwhelmingly based on common-sense activities and therefore, we might as well accept the inevitable and do it without thinking much about how we do it, just as everyone does common-sensically. (Douglas, 1985: 12)

However, we argue that research has most power when the choice of methods is deliberate and, where interviews are one of the chosen methods, where full thought has been given to our goals and to the type of interviews that we will use: these are complex decisions that shape the potential meanings of our findings.

### Similarity and difference in human affairs

Interviews may provide data on understandings, opinions, what people remember doing, attitudes, feelings and the like that people have in common (survey interviews). They may be more exploratory and qualitative (qualitative[2] inter-views), concentrating on the distinctive features of situations and events, and upon the beliefs of individuals or sub-cultures. This continuum from convergence to divergence is represented by the increasing depth of shading in Figure 1.1.

Underlying that figure is a constructivist view of knowledge. The claim is that perception, memory, emotion and understanding are human constructs, not objective things. Yet, this construction is not a chaotic process because it takes place within cultural and sub-cultural settings that provide a strong framework for meaning-making. So, we share similar (but not identical) understandings of things that are common experiences and subject to society-wide interpretations. We have similar understandings within our society of law, school and work. However, we also bring to each of these an understanding that has personal elements. Nevertheless, in the lower right-hand corner of the grid, meanings are more even and predictable. Consequently, it is often appropriate to use surveys to investigate their incidence and salience. As we move to more personal events, such as falling in love, then understandings and the meanings that go with them, although they are still socially shaped, are likely to become more diverse. Furthermore, if we encounter a fresh situation, then the understandings we construct are less governed by social rules, social norms and social conventions, and are more likely to be more individualistic. Here, we would need to use more qualitative approaches to try to understand the nature and effects of these meanings.

| | Level | | |
|---|---|---|---|
| | Personal | Sub-cultural | Society-wide |
| *Context* | | | |
| Unusual contexts | | | |
| New contexts with clear, familiar features | | | |
| Routine social contexts | | | |

FIGURE 1.1  *The sequence from light to dark shading indicates the continuum of understanding from individual and distinctive to more shared and communal. The same movement could also be described as one from relativist to positivist perspectives.*

Interviews can explore areas of broad cultural consensus and people's more personal, private and special understandings. However, different research designs will be needed to see how many people intend to vote for a particular political party (an example of what is called survey research) and to try to find out why so many young people have unprotected sex (which may need more qualitative research). In the first case, there is a wish to claim that what we have found out about the sample is likely to hold good for voters in general. This is called generalizing from a sample to the population and depends on carefully selecting a sample that reflects key characteristics of that population. This might also be described as quantitative research, since the intention is to collect data that can be analysed so as to give a numerical description of the sample's voting intentions. Quantitative research is designed to produce conclusions in the form of numerical data, and typically uses 'closed' questions. Box 1.1 contains examples of closed and open questions, and the topic is revisited in Chapter 7. Surveys are the most common form of quantitative interview research.

In the second case, the intention is to explore meanings, and the sample might be far smaller and generalization would not be the researcher's main goal. The sampling technique might be quite opportunistic, and involve asking one informant to nominate others who might be worth talking with (this is sometimes called 'snowball sampling'). The interviewer would be anxious to listen to informants' accounts of their behaviours, beliefs, feelings and actions and would probably ask open-ended questions, rather than ask questions that invite precise answers that can be tallied to provide numerical summaries. The data do not easily yield any conclusions that can be put in a precise numerical form and some workers in the qualitative research tradition go so far as to argue that numerical data should not be extracted from such qualitative research (for example, McCracken, 1988). The interviewers would probably complement their conclusions with recommendations about policy, or with suggestions about directions that future research might take. That further research might take the form of a survey involving a carefully designed sampling technique, with the intention of making general statements on the basis of the findings.

Table 1.1 illustrates the key, surface differences between survey and qualitative research. These differences can be exaggerated, and researchers often draw upon features of each approach when designing a study, even though the two approaches rest on very different assumptions about the social world and the nature of human understanding of it.

*Interviews and structure* While surveys tend to be highly structured, with a precise interview schedule that the researcher has to follow closely, qualitative interviews are less structured. Table 1.2 indicates the relationship between the type of research and the degree of structure imposed on the interviewer. Table 1.3 gives a more detailed picture of the differences between structured and unstructured interviews, while also identifying characteristics of semi-structured interviews.[3] These themes are also addressed in Chapter 7.

Structured interviews produce simple descriptive information very quickly. So, for instance, it would be relatively easy to find out how many people smoked,

---

**Box 1.1 Closed and open questions**

Survey research is intended to produce data that can be neatly and reliably summarized by numbers, tested for statistical significance and represented in charts.

*Closed questions* are normal. For example:

---

**1 In the last 12 months, have you visited your**      Yes      No
**doctor?**

**2 If you have answered 'yes' please say how many times you have visited**
Once   Twice   3, 4 or 5 times   6–10 times   More than 10 times

---

Qualitative research is less interested in measuring and more interested in describing and understanding complexity. Here, *open questions* are normal, although closed questions are often asked to collect background data (for example, about career, health history, attitudes, cognitive styles). Open questions let informants respond in their own words. For example:

---

**1 What have been the most interesting things about your new job?**

[If need be, prompt the informant to talk about why these are seen as the most interesting things.]

**2 Why do you say that?**

[If need be, prompt the informant to explain why she/he says that.]

---

what brand of cigarettes they used and to get an (under)estimate of how many cigarettes they smoked. (People tend to under-report their less socially acceptable behaviours and to over-report those that are more desirable.) However, points of interest explaining why people continued to smoke knowing that it was bad for their health, the significance and meaning smoking held for them, would not come to light. Structured interviewing is often used as a precursor to more open-ended discussion, or alternatively afterwards to ascertain whether hypotheses generated during qualitative interviews are statistically verifiable.

TABLE 1.1  *Data types and survey and qualitative interviewing approaches*

Research approach

| Type of data | Survey characteristics | Qualitative characteristics |
|---|---|---|
| *Quantitative*: data that can easily be put into clear categories and summarized by numbers, which can then be subject to statistical manipulation. The researcher is more interested in trends in the sample as a whole, than in the special features of any case within the sample | Most survey research is of this sort<br><br>Positivist approach (see page 10)<br><br>Set interview schedule, which interviewers must follow scrupulously<br><br>Respondents expected to answer only the questions asked and often have to choose from one of a set of pre-determined answers<br><br>Data analysed to produce numerical summaries<br><br>Statistical testing and inference often follow | Usually only used for collecting basic background data – age, years in the job, years of training, highest level of education etc.<br><br>Some researchers will also use attitude scales and other psychological or social measures within qualitative research in order to learn more about the informants |
| *Qualitative*: data in the form of complex stories, images, descriptions and such-like that cannot be easily put into categories or simplified. (Of course, the researcher can make connections between different accounts, but is also aware that the distinctiveness of each account must not be lost in the process of generalization) | Survey researchers may ask open-ended questions that provide qualitative data. However, the respondent is only in the position of explaining their perspective on the items chosen by the researcher. The respondents' perspectives are not explored, but only those which researchers have, in advance, selected | Most qualitative research will yield complex data<br><br>The assumptions are non-positivist, and there is an emphasis on subjectivity – on using subjective elements, such as warmth, empathy and spontaneity, to help to understand informants' subjective perceptions<br><br>Qualitative data are notoriously hard to analyse and the conclusions drawn from the data are more obviously open to criticism than those from quantitative surveys |

At the other extreme are unstructured interviews, also known as naturalistic, intensive, autobiographical, in-depth, narrative or non-directive (Holland and Ramazanoglu, 1994). With this form of interview, the researcher will have decided only in general terms upon the main themes and topic areas to be explored, but will be flexible in the approaches used to explore them. Instead, interviewees (or informants) are encouraged to be open and spontaneous, and to speak about the issue in question using language and ideas of their own, rather

TABLE 1.2  *Research purposes and interview structures*

| Research approach and purpose | Survey: purpose is to see to what extent a hypothesis or view can be sustained. | Qualitative: aim is to find out about people's perspectives, beliefs, attitudes etc. |
| --- | --- | --- |
| **Interview structure** | | |
| *Structured* (questions all agreed in advance. Interviewers *must* stick rigidly to a script) | Surveys are usually structured to provide for the most robust test of the hypothesis | Used only for collecting standard information about informants |
| *Semi-structured* (main questions and script are fixed, but interviewers are able to improvise follow-up questions and to explore meanings and areas of interest that emerge) | Commonest in qualitative work, where there is a desire to hear what informants have to say on the topics and areas identified by the researcher. However, survey interviews may sometimes also have room for the interviewer to improvise questions to clarify or extend answers | |
| *Unstructured* (the interviewer may have a list of broad topics or themes to explore, or may even have none. The direction is largely set by the informant) | Unusual. However, the interviewer may be allowed the discretion to ask questions at the end of the interview to explore things that come to be of interest | Although this approach may seem to be the epitome of qualitative approaches, it is most often used early in a study with the intention of generating a script for subsequent, semi-structured enquiries |

than any imposed by the researcher. From this point of view, the interviewer adopts a more passive, less directive role. Unstructured interviews produce a wealth of qualitative data; the findings can generate deep insights into people's understandings of their social world. However, at the analysis stage of the research, the time needed to do justice to all the data that have been collected is considerable. This is a very important consideration to bear in mind, and generally this type of interview is not suitable for projects that have to be completed when time is in short supply.

Semi-structured interviews are perhaps the commonest and most diverse of the three formats. They fall between the structured and unstructured format, but are more similar to the latter in the sense that they too generate qualitative data. The approach adopted is far less formal than that employed in a structured interview. Having said that, the interviewer does have a specific agenda to follow and will have selected beforehand the relevant topic areas and themes to pursue. The interview is loosely structured (thus allowing for some degree of comparability) around an interview guide (see Chapter 7), which contains key questions. Interviewers are free to follow up ideas, probe responses and ask for clarification or further elaboration. For their part, informants can answer the questions in terms of what they see as important; likewise, there is scope for them to choose what to say about a particular topic, and how much.

TABLE 1.3  *Characteristics of structured, semi-structured and unstructured interviews*

| Structured | Semi-structured | Unstructured |
|---|---|---|
| Quick to do | Can be longer, even very long | |
| Large samples possible and usual | Tend to be medium-sized samples | Time taken on interviewing and the complexity of transcription and analysis tend to restrict sample size |
| Sample obtained at random (telephone surveys); by intercepting people at events (football matches) or places (shopping centres) – sometimes known as clipboarding; by interviewing in a workplace or other setting | Can use the approaches of structured or qualitative interviews: the longer the interview is, the more advisable it is to sample in the manner of qualitative interviewing | The length of the interviews means that a greater commitment is needed from informants, making it harder to get them. Consequently, opportunity sampling and 'snowballing' are common. Possible to invite all people in an organization to volunteer, or to target those in positions that make them likely to be good 'key informants' |
| Interviewer follows a script or schedule exactly | Interviewer refers to a guide, which is usually a mix of closed and open questions. Interviewer will use judgement to improvise | Interviewer uses an *aide-mémoire* which is a list of topics of discussion, around which he or she will improvise |
| Interviewer is testing a theory – largely blind to things not covered by the schedule. So, the schedule defines what is discovered | Partly interviewer-led, partly informant-led | Interviewer seeks the informants' stories and perspectives. The informants govern what is discovered (see note 4)<br>Allows one to hear the voice of people who might not respond to written questions<br>Greater danger than with written questionnaires of mainly getting responses from the more confident members of the target group |
| Validity depends on the validity of the schedule. (See pages 51–2 for a discussion of validity) | Validity partly dependent on schedule, partly on interview dynamics (see under Unstructured to the right) | Validity depends on skill of the interviewer, time available, and the rapport that lets subjects be as informative as they know how |
| Reliability of data collection dependent upon interviewer training, supervision and strict rules of working. (See pages 52–4 for a discussion of reliability) | A mixture of the characteristics of the other two styles | Reliability takes second place to validity. Usually, evidence that the interviewer's actions were appropriate is a proxy for formal evidence of reliability |

TABLE 1.3 *continued*

| Structured | Semi-structured | Unstructured |
|---|---|---|
| No transcription problems, given the fixed-responses that are collected | A mixture of the characteristics of the other two styles | Full transcription desirable. Notes sometimes acceptable, with the taped record serving as a reference point. Very time-consuming |
| Easy to analyse | Some parts easy to analyse, some hard | Usually hard to analyse |
| Reliability of analysis seldom a problem, in the sense that there is seldom room for argument about whether the analysis is the best summary of the data. (See pages 166–7 for a discussion of reliability in data analysis) | Hard to achieve 'reliable' analysis of open-ended responses. Usually, less difficult though than for unstructured interviews, where it can be unclear what the question was, never mind what the answer means | Hard to analyse reliably. Can be difficult to decide what a section of conversation is about, let alone to agree on the key messages it contains Plausibility of analysis a better concept than reliability? |
| Tends to a positivist view of social science knowledge | A mixture of the characteristics of the other two styles | Non-positivist view of social science knowledge |
| Respondents' anonymity can be easily guaranteed in some survey styles (clipboarding) | Harder than clipboarding to ensure anonymity | Researcher tends to know the identity of the informant. This can lead informants to be more cautious about their responses than if they have anonymity |
| Little danger of individuals being identifiable in any report (this approach usually has large samples and collects data that could not easily be associated with any respondent) | Possibility that individuals might be identifiable in any report, even if no names – or false names – are used | Small sample size and distinctive features in the data can make it even harder to avoid identifying individuals in a report, so compromising any promise of anonymity |

### Interviews and assumptions about social research

Interview and other social research methods vary, we have suggested, according to whether we are studying essentially convergent or more individualistic social phenomena. There are also competing theories of being (ontology) and of knowledge (epistemology), with different theories having implications for the research methods that social scientists use. Fuller, although sometimes challenging, discussions of this are to be found in many social science texts, including Jacob (1987), Patton (1990), Denzin and Lincoln (1994) and Merriam (1998). Here we offer an outline of these competing theories.

Once, in Western society, the world was understood in religious terms. Explanations were based on exegesis of religious texts, on hermeneutics and on the authority of Aristotle and other writers of classical times. This was supplemented and eventually displaced by the scientific revolutions of the twelfth and seventeenth centuries and by the eighteenth century Enlightenment. All of these movements emphasized human power to understand reality through rational enquiry, and in natural science in particular, through experimentation. 'Positivism' is often used to describe the types of knowledge typically associated with the natural sciences. The central idea is that there are objective facts 'out there' to be discovered by rigorous enquiry, leading to laws or generalizations that describe the world and, ideally, allow good predictions to be made. Social scientists tended to try to find ways of taking the methods that had been so successful in natural science and to apply them to human affairs, for example, through disciplines such as psychology, linguistics and sociology; in fields such as educational studies and health policy research; and to the study of the past by historians.

Social science disciplines are concerned with the sentient experience of being human and have in common an interest in human thought, life, culture and action. However, even if we try to study human life with scrupulous rigour, people (except as biological systems) are different from quarks, leptons and muons: they have minds, feelings and – many would say – spirits or souls. Arguably, it is possible to see law-like regularities in the behaviour of millions of people over long periods of time, as Marx suggested. Yet, that is disputed, and when it comes to studying smaller groups in the shorter term, positivism has its limits. People respond to specific situations *as they see them* and they make values-led choices. Even where it seems to be possible to make law-like statements about human thought and behaviour, those statements tend to be very loose and general. And those statements do little to help us to understand *why* people act as they do. These limitations to positivism in social science matter far more with some enquiries than others, but they still incline many social scientists to be cautious about what McCracken called 'the winter of positivism' (1988: 14; see also Guba and Lincoln, 1994). In the words of one psychologist,

> Social scientists generally, and psychologists in particular, have modelled their work on physical sciences, aspiring to amass empirical generalizations, to restructure them into more general laws, and to weld scattered laws into coherent theory. That lofty aspiration is far from realization . . . enduring systematic theories about man [*sic*] in society are not likely to be achieved. (Cronbach, 1975: 125–6)

Alternative, qualitative,[5] approaches concentrate on understanding the thinking and behaviours of individuals and groups in specific situations. This approach directs attention to the differences and particularities in human affairs and prompts the social scientist to discover what people think, what happens and why. Such social research should give authentic accounts of human thought, feeling and actions, recognizing that those accounts do not apply to all people and that they do not allow predictions to be made in the way that they are made in the positivist natural sciences. These researchers often argue that capturing this complex, humanly created reality demanded that they become participants in the social setting, abandoning the detached observer status of the natural scientist. Box 1.2 shows what can be gained by being a participant researcher, and an elaboration of the differences between the perspective of the participant or insider

**Box 1.2   The value of being a participant researcher**

(This is based on an interview with an anthropologist who described several research studies she had done)

The researcher, a 26-year-old, apparently single and naive woman, was investigating fertility in a remote island fishing community, which was more or less cut off from the mainland for six months of the year.

Initially, she said, 'I didn't get a lot of answers' to interview questions. It seemed as if the women were trying to protect the innocent young researcher from the facts of life. She arranged for judiciously worded postcards to be sent from her physician husband, expecting them to be read by the postal workers and relayed to other members of the community. When it was realized that she too was at risk [of conception] women in the community began to see her differently and to open up. However, there were other barriers to rapport: she was an educated member of the professional classes and an off-comer. Here, it helped that an ancestral connection could be forged between her and the islanders, with genealogical work suggesting that she was possibly (probably?) related to one of the island families.

Another interview-based study of occupational health and safety in the fishing industry highlighted the significance of interviewer characteristics and also shows how these can be used to advantage *by a team* of interviewers. There were four interviewers: a woman with sailing knowledge, two older men with work and/or fishing knowledge, and a younger man who knew only about this work from books. As an interviewer, the young man failed, changing to the role of data analyst after four interviews. The fishermen thought that if he wanted to know about life at sea, he should don oilskins, sweater and boots and sail with them. His lack of familiarity with the trade meant that he was not treated with seriousness.

The woman, on the other hand, could take the role of the 'dumb broad' and ask naive questions that would expose answers that would be hidden by assumptions were the interviewer more expert-seeming. So, she could ask for more detailed descriptions of routines and procedures, in the process accessing tacit knowledge that could not have been exposed by someone who was treated on some measure of equal footing. So, a fuller story could be constructed by having the woman and one of the more experienced men interview the same people on different occasions. Where a fisherman might claim never to have had a serious injury (the culture being that serious injury disabled you from fishing again), the woman could ask about the scar on the arm (which had been the result of an accident that had nearly severed the arm – but to the fishermen, this was not 'serious').

When she went to sea with them, she had to unsex herself: to dress like them and to meet their expectations of sea-borne life in order to build the trust and rapport necessary for the research. As a semi-insider, she had access to answers that would have been denied a complete outsider.

Arguments about which was the best approach to social science research, positivism and its numbers, or qualitative research with its close descriptions of particular people, places and times, largely missed the important point that methods have to be fit for their purpose. For some purposes, quantitative approaches are the best. In other cases the choice will be qualitative methods. Furthermore, although qualitative and quantitative approaches rest on very different ontological and epistemological assumptions, they can be complementary in the hands of the thoughtful researcher and need not be incompatible (Donmoyer, 1996). Many studies would benefit from mindfully using each approach for different purposes at different stages of the research.

Furthermore, the realist assumption that better methods would give a better picture of the way things really are has been challenged by researchers who are under the sway of postmodern thinking. In essence, postmodernism emphasizes the diversity of meanings and their fluidity, and also insists that all accounts are not only created by their writer but also that all writings (or films, photographs or other 'texts') are interpreted by the reader, and not necessarily in the way the author intended. In short, the idea of a reality to be discovered is denied. There are just creations.

This can be illustrated by the discussion of Whyte's classic book *Street Corner Society* (1943) in the April 1992 edition of *Journal of Contemporary Ethnography*. The book is an ethnographic, qualitative depiction of groups of poor Italian youths. The *Journal* is given over to discussion of this seminal work. We are not concerned here with whether Whyte produced the only correct account of these groups. Instead we draw attention to two articles that debate whether there actually is a reality to be accurately captured. Richardson points to the role of the researcher who creates the account, observing that Whyte's race, class, gender, age, sexual orientation and religion all 'enter into and shape that which constitutes "knowledge"' (1992: 110). Researchers, she argues, invariably use the lens of their own selves when they examine human affairs – the objective researcher does not and cannot exist, so all accounts of 'reality' are, in fact visions of 'reality'.

Denzin rehearses a number of assumptions that are embedded in the realist view that the main issue is choosing the right methodology to uncover what is 'out there' and notes that there is a counter-view which we see as a manifestation of postmodernist thinking. That thinking 'undermines the realist agenda, contending that things do not exist independently of their representations in social texts' (1992: 126). Postmodernist and realist assumptions are summarized in Table 1.4.

For some, the value of this research approach is that it extends, complicates and challenges understandings, sensitizing policy-makers and practitioners to the complex dimensions of their work. Such expectations can support a view that it can be legitimate for the researcher not to try to generalize, as with studies of individuals or of cases: on that view, it is expected that the reader of the research will – and should – make his or her own generalizations. This matter is explored more fully in Chapter 4. Yet, policy-makers often want clear recommendations and we will show that social sciences have developed ways of demonstrating that research has been designed and carried out in ways that allow some confidence to be put in generalizations and recommendations ventured by the researchers.

TABLE 1.4  *'Realist' and post-structuralist assumptions*

| 'Realist' | Post-structuralist (postmodernist) |
| --- | --- |
| A 'camera theory' of research. | Multiple inscriptions of events are made, so . . . |
| Reality exists . . . | it is the text which creates the subjects . . . |
| and can be captured . . . | who may not know what they think, change their minds, perhaps mislead the researcher . . . |
| by skilled researchers . . . | and who are 'copies of already reproduced cultural standards and identities' . . . |
| who are sufficiently close to it . . . | besides which, language distorts experience . . . |
| to make literal transcripts | and so there are few facts to be established by researchers. |
| Research subjects' talk is a mirror of inner reality. | |

*Source*: after Denzin, 1992

A common objection to qualitative research has been that the findings cannot be tested but have to be taken on trust. The objection can be more forcefully made to research in a postmodern vein. However, this charge of relativism, of an embedded subjectivity which is contrasted to the supposed neutrality of positivist research, can be met, as we shall show in Chapter 4, where we examine ways in which the interviewer can warrant that the research *is* systematic enquiry, and that the picture that is presented is authentically grounded in a careful study of a social phenomenon or situation. Even so, in some disciplines (psychology is a common example) and in some parts of the world (the USA, for example), you would expect to have to defend your approach if you chose to use qualitative methods.

Here, our intention has been to show that different research and interviewing methods are not just responses to different research needs but also embody quite different ontological and epistemological perspectives. Different methods may represent different understandings of the social world and of fair ways of portraying that world. Where that is appreciated, it is possible to combine interview methods, and research methods generally, to get a richer picture of how that world might be.

Before developing our analysis of approaches to interviewing, we need to take the criterion of fitness for purpose seriously enough to consider the value of interview methods in comparison to other social research methods.

## Interviews and other research methods in social research

Interviews are one method by which the human world may be explored, although it is the world of beliefs and meanings, not of actions, that is clarified by interview research. Since what people claim to think, feel or do does not necessarily align well with their actions, it is important to be clear that interviews get at what people say, however sincerely, rather than at what they do. Is this still true if we interview people about what they have done? Probably. The longer ago, the less personally important or striking an event, the more discreditable or sensitive the behaviour, the less likely it is that the deed and the story will match up. But even a question about yesterday's actions might produce responses that differ from what observers might have noticed had they watched the action in question. The interviewee works with a memory that remembers some aspects and not others; which orders memory in the light of what happened subsequently and in the light of the interview situation; which tends to neaten things up; and which tends to put the interviewee in a socially acceptable light.

One implication is that in order to know about what people do, *observational methods* should be preferred over interview methods, although observational methods are no more free of problems of interpretation and bias than other methods. Indeed, ethnographers, who are dedicated to understanding cultures, are likely to think that they can best understand cultural meanings by becoming participants in the culture. That is likely to involve observation, study of texts and artefacts *and interviews*: Pat Barker's novel *The Ghost Road* (1996) contains a good account of these techniques in action. Clearly, in these circumstances, claims to objectivity are very fragile. That may help to account for the attraction that postmodernist theories, with their denial of the possibility of objectivity, have for modern anthropologists and ethnographers.

Some psychologists would see *experimental methods* as their main, or even as their only, research tool. There is a seductive parsimony to this scientific method. The first step is to measure subjects on a rating scale. Suppose we were interested to know whether yoga helped to reduce feelings of depression amongst self-critical people. Two rating scales would be needed, one to identify self-critical people and the other to gauge their level of depression. Experimental subjects are then divided into two groups, either at random or, where numbers are small, in a way designed to form matched groups where each group contains people with a similar range of scores on the depression rating scale. One group does yoga and the other, the control group, does not (but should do something else for the same amount of time as the experimental group spends on yoga). Afterwards, the depression tests are done again. If there is a change in the experimental group's score, then it can be said that yoga is the cause. Only experiments allow researchers to claim *this* is a cause of *that*, which is their greatest attraction. However, it can be hard to get people to participate in experiments, and for this reason the intervention (yoga, in this case) is often far shorter and more hurried than we should like. Questions arise as to whether we can generalize from what can often be quite artificial experimental situations to the messy, meaning-saturated contexts of daily life and it must be remembered that experiments show relationships but may give little insight into the meanings and motivations that pervade people's actions. Lastly, they are neither suitable for, nor possible in, many social science enquiries.

Where researchers wish to know about how widely a view, attitude or belief is held, or whether a situation is perceived in a particular way by people at large, or whether many people explain a certain set of actions in the same way, then *self-administered questionnaires* (which may include psychometric instruments) are often the preferred method. The reasons why they are used so much are mainly practical. Making claims about large groups of people involves drawing data from large samples. Even survey interviewing of large samples has been seen as expensive, although this is changing as telephone interviewing becomes more acceptable. However, while self-administered questionnaires and interviews are both useful for survey research, such questionnaires are markedly inferior as a way of exploring the world of informants. Social interaction is important here, as is the scope to explore informants' answers with them. There are further discussions of this in Chapters 3 and 6.

In a similar vein, there is a host of *psychometric instruments*, such as attitude and rating scales, that can be and frequently are used to categorize people – into extroverts and introverts; into those who believe that they have a lot of control in their lives and those who do not; and into holist or serial thinkers, for example. They tend to be too long and complex to be used in interviews. However, they can be useful adjuncts to some interview approaches, especially where surveys are designed to explore the relationship between things such as attitudes, mental or motivational styles, dispositions to study and people's self-reported behaviours.

*Reports, documents and statistics* are widely used in social research. Despite their authoritative appearance, these sources are not objective. Equally, even official statistics are bias-ridden. They are still valuable and very usable sources, as long as the researcher is clear about their limitations and shares that awareness with readers. So, before using British figures for the number of people seeking work, it is important to realize that they are notoriously unreliable *as measures of unemployment* because certain conditions have to be met before an unemployed person can claim state benefit, and the number of claimants of state benefit is what gets reported as the number of people seeking work. Similarly, definitions of suicide vary from country to country and from time to time, making these figures difficult to work with. Again, it is well known that much crime is either not reported or not recorded by police agencies, making official crime figures untrustworthy measures of the incidence of crime. They can be even less reliable as records of changes in the incidence of certain types of crime over time – for example, what was formerly counted as indecent assault might now be counted as rape.

Documents are created for a purpose and may mislead the enquirer who has different questions in mind. For example, the minutes of meetings say what was discussed and what was decided. However, they say little about the context of the meetings, nor do they indicate who took what stance and why certain stances prevailed over others. So, when one of us was investigating the work of two professional associations, interviews with key players in the associations revealed extensive micro-political activity that was not evident from the minutes of meetings. That said, it is possible to compare documents one with another to try to get a better picture, and when they are used with other research methods documents can be invaluable as sources of background knowledge and for cross-checking the data.

In social science research, the trend is to design research that draws upon *multiple methods*. For example, a questionnaire might be used to get an indication

of attitudes, reasoning or behaviour in the target group at large and then interviews might be used to explore what lay behind the findings of the questionnaire
study. Here, interviews are being used to understand the meanings of the questionnaire responses. Researchers might then try to check the link between the
interview and questionnaire findings and behaviour in different settings. The use
of multiple methods in this way is generally regarded as a strength in a research
design, although there can be severe problems if different methods produce
different results. There is an example of the use of multiple methods in Box 3.2
and in the discussion of triangulation in Chapter 2. A very good and full account
of the variety of qualitative research methods is provided by Murphy et al. (1998).

A related research approach is called 'progressive focusing'. This means that
the researcher starts with a general area of interest, a topic of concern or a puzzle,
and investigates it quite generally to begin with. This 'orienting phase' will often
involve immersion in relevant research literature. Early in the enquiry, time
would be well spent in the research setting, getting a feel for what happens and
how it happens. Equally, the researcher might use documents and interviews
and perhaps more structured observation as ways of getting ideas about how to
focus the research – on what lines to follow through, with whom and how. The
experienced researcher spends time on a relatively unfocused enquiry (which is
what beginners do as well) and then concentrates on a pivotal aspect that has the
power to illuminate the larger question (which is what new researchers are far less
skilled at doing). So, the experienced researcher progressively focuses. In the case
of interviews, some open-ended conversations with people might follow. They
are likely to be unstructured or semi-structured interviews. The aim is to hear
about the problem area in the words of the people in the situation, to try to
understand things in their terms. Analysis, which involves a great deal of thought,
discussion and time (see Chapter 11), might then suggest key questions to be
asked and, taken with a good knowledge of the literature and relevant documents,
could lead to the production of a much more formal and structured set of interview questions. The process of focusing may continue, as it becomes evident
which people are the most significant informants about the issue, which are the
key questions and central ideas, attitudes and feelings. It may lead to survey work,
done by highly structured interviews or by questionnaires, with the aim of finding
out how widely the findings emerging from the research are a fair representation
of matters in the wider community.

So, not only is there a range of interviewing approaches, but it is increasingly
common to use interviews as one method within multiple-method research
designs that often use a progressive focusing approach.

### Conclusions

As people, we share understandings with others and also bring something
quite distinctively personal to them. Different interviewing approaches are best
suited to investigating shared and more individualistic understandings. Equally,
different approaches reflect different assumptions about the nature of knowledge

in the social sciences. When we use surveys we are, then, acting on more positivist views of social science knowledge, whereas qualitative methods reflect views that knowledge in the social sciences is provisional, uneven, complex and contexted.

That means that your choice of interview approaches – and the choice of interview, as opposed to other research methods – is more than a matter of common sense. For one thing, it involves you making a deliberate choice of research tactics that are fitted to your research purpose.

We have also argued that different social science perspectives have different implications for research design and for thinking about reliability, validity and generalizability (Chapter 4). They impact on research practice, so that positivists are likely to be uneasy at the idea of the interviewer as a participant in a social situation, and dubious about the value of interviews that take the form of unstructured conversations (Chapter 7). Obviously, different ontological and epistemological theories lead to different understandings of the meaning of data, to different transcription practices and to different analytical approaches (Chapters 10 and 11). Finally, whereas narrative, story, film, biography, auto-biography and pictures are becoming semi-legitimate ways of representing the claims of postmodernist researchers, most research reports follow a traditional format (Chapter 12). In the words of one commentator,

> Some researchers think that an 'open' stance to research implies freedom from traditions, but this is a dubious proposition . . . traditions are important, even when one takes an 'open' stance, because they provide a set of orienting assumptions about what to study . . . researchers need to pay attention to assumptions, foci of study and methodologies. (Jacob, 1987: 40)

The following chapter begins a move from the important and rather grand concerns reviewed here to more particular examination of interviewing as a versatile method to use in your social science enquiry.[6]

## Notes

1  When we refer to questionnaires, we have in mind printed or electronic questionnaires that research subjects read and then complete *in writing or on a keyboard*.

2  There are many ways of describing research methods that are designed to explore people's understandings, perceptions, feelings etc. We have used qualitative, but near similes include 'illuminative', 'interpretative', 'exploratory', 'naturalistic' and 'investigative'. Since ethnography and phenomenology are both concerned with exploring meaning, the terms 'ethnographic' and 'phenomenological' may be used to signify the qualitative intent. Others draw on an older philosophical tradition, and use '*verstehen*', which is the German word for understanding. Sometimes 'qualitative' itself is given the same meaning.

3  We acknowledge Hammersley and Atkinson's point that all interviews are, in a sense, structured and that 'the important distinction to be made is between standardized and reflexive interviewing' (1995: 152). While it is an attractive distinction, we have taken the pragmatic line that discussions about questionnaire and interview design in the literature on research methods are overwhelmingly couched in terms of more and less structured formats. Adopting the standardized–reflexive distinction could have caused problems for readers exploring a range of 'how to do research' books.

4 However, this is not always seen positively. Easterby-Smith, Thorpe and Lowe (1991) argue that:

> the researcher should be warned against assuming that the 'non-directive' interview, where the interviewee talks freely without interruption or intervention, is the way to achieve a clear picture of the interviewee's perspective. It is more likely to produce no clear picture in the mind of the interviewee of what questions or issues the interviewer is interested in, and in the mind of the interviewer of what questions the interviewee is answering! Too many assumptions of this kind lead to poor data which is difficult to interpret' (1991: 75)

5 'Qualitative' is a term covering a multitude of non-positivist research stances. The qualitative river has many currents and pools, such as constructivism, phenomenology, ethnography, oral history, critical theory, and symbolic interactionsim. Each current is distinct from others, forever intermingling with them and yet part of the same river. And, as they flow on, so they change, merge and diverge.

6 Gage has observed that 'the term "social science" is at its root an oxymoron' (1989: 4). Certainly, most social science is not positivist. However, a science can be seen as a mode of thought (positivism) and as a scrupulous process of enquiry. The second characteristic may apply to 'social science', although – disconcertingly, perhaps – it also applies to history.

# 2    Triangulation in Data Collection

As we indicated in the previous chapter, rather than think in terms of 'either/or', in other words of adopting either one method of investigation or another, you may choose to design a study that combines different techniques to explore one set of research questions. This has been described as 'triangulation' (Webb et al., 1966). Triangulation is a technical term used in surveying, military strategy and navigation to describe a technique whereby two known landmarks or reference points are used to define the position of a third. Webb et al. (1966) were among the first to employ the term metaphorically in the social sciences. The basic idea of triangulation is that data are obtained from a wide range of different and multiple sources, using a variety of methods, investigators or theories. So, for instance, you could administer a structured interview schedule, and conduct a set of unstructured interviews, and complement those data with a series of observations. Similarly, rather than just gather data from one particular group with an interest in the study, you could seek out the views of several sets of stakeholders and, in that way, introduce a comparative aspect. In this chapter, we discuss both the conceptual and practical dimensions of triangulation in data collection, with a particular emphasis on the functions of confirmation and completeness.

## Why triangulate?

Triangulation is not an end in itself, and researchers considering whether to adopt this approach need to think carefully about what they hope to achieve. In effect, triangulation serves two main purposes: *confirmation* (Denzin, 1970) and *completeness* (Jick, 1983). Initially, triangulation was regarded as a strategy to overcome problems of validity and bias (these issues are more fully explored in Chapter 4). By collecting diverse sets of data derived by different methods, there was thought to be less chance of making errors, or of drawing inappropriate conclusions, than would be the case if relying upon just one data set. However, triangulation is not just about using as many different methods or sources of data collection as possible. When the approach is used for confirmation purposes, the individual strengths, weaknesses and biases of the various methods must, first, be known and, secondly, applied in such a way that they counterbalance each other. From this point of view, it is important to try to blend and integrate the different methods, and not simply to design a study that comprises distinct, mutually exclusive approaches. Generally, advocates of the quantitative research tradition and positivism (see Chapter 1) will find triangulation an attractive proposition because, for example, it can contribute to the confirmation of hypotheses; to the measurement of discrete variables and concepts; and to the development of sensitive and trustworthy instrument scales and indices.

Debates over the relationship between quantitative and qualitative methods (Bryman, 1988) have led to renewed interest in the use of triangulation, and in recent years this approach has been seen as a way to obtain a greater completeness. For instance, you may be keen to learn about people's reasons for adopting particular behaviours or pursuing certain activities. To this end, you might wish to conduct semi-structured or unstructured interviews. But in order to set the data they yield into some sort of context you may also want to collect data showing the commonness of the set of activities in question. This is where survey work would usefully fit in. The completeness function of triangulation is also relevant to work that adopts an explicitly qualitative stance, where investigators tend to dislike structured approaches and instead welcome any information that adds depth and breadth of understanding.

Approaching research questions from different angles and bringing together a range of views has the potential to generate new and alternative explanations, ones that better capture the social complexity that the fieldwork explores. For example, researchers examining the changing experiences of women might decide to collect accounts from different generations of the same family: great grandmother, grandmother, mother and daughter. These multiple viewpoints may, or may not, be consistent. The convergences are useful: researchers will have more confidence if different kinds of data lead to the same conclusions. And even if the data pull in opposite directions, it is likely that investigating the reasons for the discrepancies will shed light on processes that otherwise might not have been recognized. Given this possibility, divergent results can be equally fertile areas for theory-building, policy and practice (we return to the issue of divergencies later in the chapter).

It is important to bear in mind that triangulation for confirmation and triangulation for completeness are two distinct, though complementary, matters. In report writing, it is often unclear which of the two functions the term is being used to refer to. From the point of view of clarifying and justifying your triangulated approach, we reiterate Knafl and Breitmayer's (1991) advice: explain whether the goal is to confirm or complete the resulting data set, and then situate the following discussion in the appropriate supporting literature.

## Triangulation techniques in data collection

Since the concept of triangulation was first introduced into the social sciences, others who also share concerns about validity and bias have further developed the original notion of multiple methods. Denzin (1970), in particular, has moved beyond the use of multiple methods to study the same phenomenon, and has introduced the notion of 'multiple triangulation' which he implements at the level of the overall research design. Multiple triangulation refers to a typology of strategies which can be combined in one investigation: methodological triangulation; data triangulation; investigator triangulation; and theoretical triangulation.

In the event, Denzin's work has influenced several generations of research methods students. So what are these different types of triangulation that are available to enhance the quality of research enquiries?

- *Methodological triangulation* refers to the use of a research design drawing on a variety of methods to collect and interpret the data. Denzin proposes either 'within-method' triangulation or 'between- (or across-) method' triangulation. Within-method triangulation means using a variety of techniques within the one single method (for example, survey work might employ a package of measures focusing on the same variable). In contrast, between-method triangulation is where two or more distinct methods (say, semi-structured interviews, observation and diary accounts) are employed to measure the same phenomenon, but from different angles. The rationale is that cumulatively the weaknesses of one research method are offset by the strengths of the others.
- *Data triangulation* means the use of a research design involving diverse data sources to explore the same phenomenon. The data sources can be varied, or triangulated, in terms of person, time and space. So, for example, data might be collected from different comparison groups, or at different points in time, or from a range of settings. Moreover, in respect of the 'person' dimension, Denzin suggests sampling across three levels of unit of analysis: aggregate (at the level of the individual); interactive (at the level of interacting individuals, such as families or small groups); and collectivity (at the level of organizations, groups or communities).
- *Investigator triangulation* is where different researchers, interviewers or observers with a shared interest in the focus of study are employed. This strategy is deemed advantageous on various grounds. For instance, team members are likely to have intellectual and methodological backgrounds in different disciplinary areas, and can bring a diversity of expertise to bear on the research problem. At the same time, investigator triangulation can remove any potential bias generated by a single researcher.
- *Theoretical triangulation* alludes to approaching the research with diverse perspectives and hypotheses in mind. The researcher might compile a list of all possible theoretical points of view with respect to a common set of research questions, and from these derive a number of propositions. Empirical data would then be collected on whatever phenomenon the proposition at hand directed attention towards. Finally, the researcher would test each proposition against the data in efforts to assess the relevance, utility and power of each.

## Criticisms and responses

As we have indicated, proponents of triangulation have claimed that this technique is one way to strengthen confidence in the research findings. Initially, few commentators took issue with that argument, but in recent years several critics of Denzin's conception of multiple triangulation have come forward (for his responses, see Denzin, 1989). For example, Fielding and Fielding (1986) have challenged Denzin's views that triangulation strategies do actually function to reduce bias and improve validity:

> theories are generally the product of quite different traditions, so when they are combined one may get a fuller picture, but not a more 'objective' one. Similarly, different methods have emerged as a product of different theoretical traditions, and therefore combining them can add range and depth, but not accuracy. In other words, there is a case for triangulation, but not the one Denzin makes. (Fielding and Fielding, 1986: 33)

In a similar vein, Blaikie (1991) argues that it is inappropriate to combine methods founded on the different epistemological and ontological assumptions associated with various theories and methods. For Blaikie, a mixed-methods study may end up as something of a 'hotch-potch', with no underlying intellectual rationale to justify the choice of methods. A further cause for concern has been that the concept carries too positivist a bias. It is argued (Silverman, 1985; Guba and Lincoln, 1989) that it implies there is only one true social reality, and researchers simply have to decide on the most appropriate methods to measure or describe it. Yet this view stands in opposition to postmodernist thinking, namely that there are different social worlds and it is not the case that one version is 'right' whilst all the others are 'wrong' (see Chapter 1). Finally, Mason (1996) claims that different methods or data sources may well throw light on alternative problems or research questions. In other words, implementing a mixed approach may mean that the results relate to different objects or events rather than different aspects of the same phenomenon. Mason (1994) also points to potential problems when analysing data obtained from multiple sources, suggesting this is a much more complicated exercise than simply adding all the various data sets together.

In spite of these criticisms, a triangulated study still has potential merits, especially if triangulation is conceived less as a strategy for confirmation and more as one for in-depth understanding and completeness. Box 2.1 summarizes some of the advantages and disadvantages of triangulation.

### Using triangulation in social research

What are the practicalities involved when applying triangulation to your research? We will attempt to address this with accounts of three studies that used a triangulated approach. The three we have chosen vary in terms of scale of enterprise. One study on informal carers (Taraborrelli, 1993) had to be completed within a year, had no budget to cover fieldwork expenses, and one person alone was responsible for the data collection and analysis. Data collection lasted just four months, in order to allow sufficient time for analysis and report writing. At the other extreme, the Greenwich Open Space Project (Burgess et al., 1990), which was concerned with understanding environmental meanings and values, was a two-year study. It was funded by the Economic and Social Research Council to the sum of £21,000, with an additional grant of £6,000 from the Countryside Commission for England and Wales. There were four people in the research team. Parry's (1992) work falls in between the two: research for a PhD,

---

**Box 2.1   Advantages and disadvantages of triangulation**

## Advantages

- Can increase confidence in results.
- Can strengthen the completeness of a study.
- Can address different but complementary questions within a single study.
- Enhances interpretability: one set of data gives a handle to understanding another set.
- Divergences can uncover new issues or processes that can result in turn in the development of new theories, or the modification of existing ones.
- The researcher is closer to the research situation, contributing to a more nuanced understanding of the focus of study.

## Disadvantages

- Might be time-consuming; resource implications.
- Undertaking replication and comparative studies can be difficult.
- Researchers may not be technically competent in particular methods.
- Researchers might be tempted to make inconsistent data sets artificially compatible in order to produce a more coherent account.

---

which generally involves three years of full-time study, and with limited funding and support.

There are two reasons for selecting these particular examples. First, to demonstrate that even relatively small-scale work does not need to be confined to a single method or source of data collection. In fact, Jick (1983: 138) makes the point that even if it is not explicitly documented, 'it is probable that the triangulation approach is embedded in many doctoral theses'. Second, as West (1990) common-sensically points out, researchers can apply different models ranging from simple to complex designs of triangulation, according to the time and resources available to them. For West, even where there are constraints, it ought to be possible for the more 'involved' interviewers to obtain some observational data to verify the credibility of participants' accounts. And for those fortunate enough to be lavishly funded, then they will be able to initiate sub-studies designed to probe emerging issues or inconsistent results in greater detail.

In Table 2.1 we classify our selected projects according to three of Denzin's basic types of triangulation: data, investigator and methodological. We are not including references to different theoretical backgrounds because insights into this form of triangulation do not feature strongly in the accounts, with the exception of the Greenwich Open Space Project. Having said that, it is worth pointing out that the other two enquiries used concepts derived from earlier work

TABLE 2.1 *Examples of triangulated studies*

| Type of triangulation | Study | | |
| --- | --- | --- | --- |
| | Taraborrelli, 1993 | Parry, 1992 | Burgess et al., 1990 |
| *Methodological* | Interviews Standard measure of the stresses and difficulties of caring Casual conversations Observation of two support groups Documentary material | Interviews Casual conversations with individuals, and groups of students Participant observation Questionnaire survey Documentary material | Interviews Small, in-depth discussion groups Questionnaire survey |
| *Data sources* Person | Current and ex-carers Organizers Day centre staff | Print and broadcast journalism students Teaching staff | General public: four dissimilar comparison groups of two support groups. (middle class, working class [two groups], Asian women's group) Local authority officers |
| Time | Observed two series of monthly support group meetings over a four-month period | Followed a cohort of students through a one-year diploma course | Each group met four times over a six-week period |
| Space | Two support groups, differentiated in size, organization and membership Family homes | Classrooms, newsroom and coffee bar of university-based | Different neighbourhoods in the London area, each with different qualities and quantities of open space |
| *Investigator* | Single investigator | Single investigator | Multidisciplinary research team |

in their respective fields of study as starting points to sensitize the researchers to relevant ideas and notions embedded in the data they collected.

Table 2.1 demonstrates some key points. For instance, in respect of methodological triangulation, it shows the variety of research methods, both qualitative and quantative, that are available for researchers to draw on. What is significant for the purposes of the present book is that interviews, in one format or another, are an important element of all three research designs. In relation to data sources, another key feature is that the researchers have made efforts to document as many perspectives as possible, and sampled over varying periods of time and space in order to produce a wide-ranging and in-depth analysis. Generally, the studies have followed the advice of Fielding and Fielding (1986: 34), who suggest that there are two concerns to take into account when deciding on a triangulated research design: 'incorporate at least one method of data collection that describes and interprets the context in which the interaction occurs and one that is designed primarily to illuminate the process of interaction itself'. Lastly, Taraborrelli (1993) and Parry (1992) applied the principles of grounded theory (Glaser and Strauss, 1967; Strauss and Corbin, 1990; see also Chapter 11) in the sense that they drew on the raw data to develop concepts and categories throughout the whole of the data collection process.

These examples indicate just how strategies of triangulation can be utilized to good effect. For instance, in her relatively small-scale research Taraborrelli (1993) aimed to chart the careers of the informal carers of people suffering from Alzheimer's disease, a form of dementia. Insofar as data gathering was concerned, Taraborrelli attended support meetings of two different groups established by the Alzheimer's Disease Society, conducted interviews with 23 carers and examined a range of documentary sources. Taraborrelli (p. 185) claims that her study 'benefited greatly from the use of a number of research methods', one implication being that these provided a more comprehensive account, as well as allowing her to follow up unexpected leads. Talking to carers at different stages of their caring career proved particularly fruitful. For instance, by including in the study sample people whose relatives had either died or gone into residential homes, Taraborrelli was able to explore how carers gave up, or exited from, their caring roles, a process overlooked in the original research design but which emerged as important in discussions at meetings held by one of the two support groups.

Parry's (1992) research into the occupational socialization of graduate journalists used participant observation as the main research technique, supplemented by interviews, informal conversations, questionnaires and analysis of candidates' application forms for entry to the journalism school. Not only did the multiple data sets help her acquire a more complete understanding, they also uncovered the complexities and contradictions of the social setting. As an example, towards the end of their year's training many students reported they still held the same idealistic notions about journalism as when they first started on the course. According to Parry, these attitudes were not supported by either her observations of their role-play exercises when presenting news programmes, or by her analysis of the content of the news stories they produced. She writes: 'This [variance] would not have been apparent to me had I not elected to use several research techniques to understand what was happening' (p. 78). Whilst Parry implies that the diversity in findings enhanced, rather than detracted from, the analysis and interpretation, she does not elaborate on which data set she chose to give added weight and value to.

In the Greenwich Open Space Project (Burgess et al., 1990), both the completeness and confirmation functions of triangulation were important. This was because the researchers were keen to develop a new methodology, based on Group Analysis (Pines, 1983), which would be capable of revealing the value that open land held for urban residents. At the same time, the Countryside Commission wanted to use the findings to inform their conservation and recreational policies in general, and questions to be used in a national household survey in particular. As Table 2.1 shows, the study used a mixture of data collection techniques, as well as varying sources of person and setting. The research was further triangulated by the use of multiple investigators. In this regard, members of the research team had different but complementary areas of expertise: geography and ecology. However, it ought to be noted that whilst holding different theoretical positions contributed to the development and implementation of the research design, this also appears to have led to tensions, disagreement and friction amongst team members. In spite of these sorts of difficulties, the work had a successful outcome:

> We were surprised and delighted to find that the Commission . . . accepted fully the value of qualitative field research. . . . As one of our colleagues remarked, it normally takes six or seven years for research to affect policy in any material way. We should be content that we have apparently managed it in two! (Burgess et al., 1990: 163)

## Diversity in findings

We give detailed consideration to data analysis and interpretation later in the book (Chapter 11). However, it is appropriate within our discussion of triangulation to spend a little time looking at the value of data that do not match other data sets. As we pointed out earlier, initial conceptualizations of triangulation placed the emphasis on cross-validation by combining different methods. Not unexpectedly, this meant that researchers made much less of those cases in which different research methods produced different answers to the same set of research questions (Lever, 1981). At the risk of stating the obvious, variation within the data will be less of an issue in studies using triangulation for the purpose of completeness. In these cases, researchers are likely to adopt the premise that social reality is multi-faceted, and their work is an attempt to reveal this complexity. From this perspective, differences in findings can be looked on as additional, useful data. As Parry (1992) found in her study of graduate journalists, such divergences have the potential to enrich the analysis and explanation. And even in those studies that are aiming for convergent results, differences – especially if they can be shown to reflect error or bias in the research instruments – can provide evidence needed to help in the development of more accurate survey procedures (Belson, 1986).

### Learning from diversity

In this section, we draw on two quite different studies to demonstrate that dissonant results about the same empirical domain can be used to advantage, namely to refine data collection techniques or develop intellectual insights. Both studies adopt a multi-method research design, of which interviews are a main data gathering tool. However, one is aiming for confirmation (Belson, 1986), whereas the other is more concerned with completeness (Lever, 1981).

*Study one: Belson (1986)* In view of the generally held belief that findings generated through survey research are accurate, you might think that a good deal of attention would be paid to finding out just how well questions 'perform' in the field. In fact, systematically evaluating a measure's validity is the exception rather than the rule. Belson and other researchers from the Survey Research Centre did attempt this, though, in a triangulated study designed to assess the validity of a survey questionnaire collecting quantitative information. Using an orthodox questionnaire, participants were asked about their purchases of 12 different chocolate confectionery products during the previous seven days. Later the same day, they were questioned for a second time, this time in depth and by a different interviewer. The aim now was to test the accuracy of the statements and claims participants had made in their first interview, and to determine the cause of any difference.

The study was prompted by confectionery manufacturers' concerns of inaccuracies in quantitative estimates of market size derived from survey research. Yet it was important that results were accurate if the market share of their own products, and also of their competitors, was to be calculated. On completion of the analysis, the manufacturers' anxieties appeared justified; Belson found that

> the number of bars, packs, etc. claimed in the first interview was about a fifth larger than the total number finally agreed in the intensive interview (which is interpreted as being nearer the truth). . . . [I]t is clear that there is considerable variability in the degree to which purchases of individual products are overstated or understated. If this is so, then there is a strong possibility that survey-based estimates of brand shares of the market might be distorted. (Belson, 1986: 64–5)

On analysing the possible reasons for discrepancy, Belson suggests that the sources of errors were mainly to do with participants' confusion over the qualifying time period, prompting them to overclaim or underclaim purchases. Other errors resulted from people not fully understanding the questions. Having ascertained the reasons for error, Belson went on to make various recommendations to help develop a more accurate survey procedure to collect this sort of information, thereby endorsing the idea that it is possible to learn from diversity.

*Study two: Lever* (1974)  For her doctoral research, Lever studied the results of children's play activities in respect of socialization into male and female roles. The work embodied a multi-method research design comprising semi-structured interviews, written questionnaires, diary entries recording after-school play activities and observation of school playgrounds. The different methods of data collection produced different results. For instance, the diary entry findings, which involved the children filling in a log describing what they 'actually did', suggested smaller sex differences than the questionnaire responses, where they stated what they 'usually did'.

Lever (1981) proposes that the differences in the two sets of data reflect the children's internalization of cultural stereotyping and expectations, and are associated with the nature of the method or the way in which questions are presented: 'it is possible that some methods elicit role-stereotyped responses while others do not' (p. 204). She goes on to suggest that 'abstract or unconditional inquiries yield responses that more closely correspond to a person's perceptions of social norms than inquiries of a concrete or detailed nature' (p. 205). Lever makes a strong argument in favour of using a multi-method research design that is appropriate to the constraints imposed by the topic, setting and resources available (see Chapter 5). Interestingly, this is *because of,* and not in spite of, the probability that different methods may well yield different results.

### Implications for research

There are lessons about data collection to be learned from these two examples. In their different ways, the studies of both Benson and Lever point to a number of research design problems and technical deficiencies that may contribute to inconsistencies in research results.

Sources of variation can reflect:

- sampling procedures;
- the phrasing of questions (Lever, 1981);
- the misinterpretation of questions;
- whether open or closed questions are used (Farrall et al., 1997);
- using questions that do not actually measure, or relate to, the same pheno-menon (Lever, 1981);
- study participants over- or under-estimating in their replies (Belson, 1986);
- the sensitivity of research instruments;
- the social desirability effect influencing answers (Sudman and Bradburn, 1982; see Chapter 8);
- the format of the interview (for instance, face-to-face or telephone);
- whether interviewees present 'public' or 'private' accounts (Cornwell, 1984).

In later chapters of the book, we address concerns related to some of these issues, including how to make measuring techniques more accurate. Suffice it to say that if there are divergencies in data sets, then it is important for researchers to acknowledge these, look for reasons why this might be so, and, if appropriate, use the resulting data as an aid to further understanding.

### Which findings to believe?

As we noted earlier in relation to Parry's work, it is often the case that researchers who end up with an accumulation of information – interview transcripts, survey data, observational material, documentary evidence – do not address the question of which data set they think provides the more plausible portrayal of the phenomenon being investigated. Bryman (1988) discusses this issue in relation to a small number of studies that combined qualitative and quantitative methods. On the basis of the evidence, he reaches the conclusion that the tendency is for researchers to accord greater weight to qualitative data. Surprisingly, this is the case even where the reasons for incongruent findings are not explored any further. Bryman acknowledges that it is in the spirit of the idea of triangulation that conflicting results may emerge, but he goes on to argue that 'it is not in its spirit that one should simply opt for one set of findings rather than another' (p. 134). Instead, further probing is called for. In asking why qualitative results are believed in preference to quantitative ones, Bryman speculates that researchers are closer to, and more involved with, the study participants. This proximity prompts the researchers to feel more confident about the robustness of the data and about the integrity of their preferred interpretation.

## Conclusion

We have tried to show that the careful and considered use of triangulation can enhance a study. As we said at the start of the chapter, though, triangulation is not an end in itself, and you need to be sure of your purpose when applying this sort of approach: is the goal of triangulation for confirmation, for completeness, or for both? Obviously, you are restricted as to how extensively you apply the principles of triangulation according to the time and resource constraints available (see Chapter 5). Furthermore, whilst it is easy to suggest that incongruent findings ought to be investigated further, the practical issues concerned with doing that may prove formidable for interviewers working on small-scale projects. If feasible, though, the effort involved can pay off: the data might yield an interpretation that offers a new perspective on the research question, one that is far more interesting than you could have envisaged at the outset.

# 3    Why Interviews?

In the first two chapters we have noted a range of social science research methods and seen that there can be a case for using a mix of methods in an enquiry. What we have not yet done is consider what interviews might be good for. This chapter does so. However, we argue that when it comes to choosing research methods, you need to take account of the expectations of both your sponsors and your audiences. A further consideration is that before you interview, you need to assure yourself that you have, or that you can develop, the qualities that are hallmarks of a good interviewer.

## The Power of Interviews

Some of the claims made for interviewing as a social research method are:

- 'The purpose of interviewing is to find out what is in and on a person's mind . . . , to access the perspective of the person being interviewed . . . , to find out from them things that we cannot directly observe' (Patton, 1990: 278).
- Qualitative interviewing is a way of uncovering and exploring the meanings that underpin people's lives, routines, behaviours, feelings etc. (Rubin and Rubin, 1995).
- These interviews focus on the informants' understandings rather than checking the accuracy of the interviewers' account, which is the case with survey interviews and questionnaires; 'it allows *both* parties to explore the meaning of the questions and the answers involved, which is not so central, and not so often present, in other research procedures' (Brenner et al., 1985: 3).
- So, such interviews allow answers to be clarified, which is not the case with self-completion questionnaires.
- Furthermore, interviews, especially qualitative interviews, allow for understanding and meanings to be explored in depth. This is particularly the case with longitudinal research, where each informant is interviewed on several occasions over a period of months or years.
- Qualitative interviews examine the context of thought, feeling and action and can be a way of exploring relationships between different aspects of a situation. Interviewing is a powerful way of helping people to make explicit things that have hitherto been implicit – to articulate their tacit perceptions, feelings and understandings.
- As we shall show, survey interviews can be cheaper, *per response*, than self-completion questionnaires.

- Survey interviews can allow targeting of samples that it would be hard to identify in other ways – intercepting people shopping at a particular store is an example of that.
- Collective interviews can be used to explore the dynamics of intact social groupings, such as a family, work-group, or sports team.
- All interviews have advantages in research involving those who are not fluent readers, or who read reluctantly.
- Oral history interviews allow the reconstruction of aspects of the recent past that are omitted from documentary historical sources.

### Interviews and questionnaires

Here we wish to sharpen an understanding of the strengths of interviews as a research method by comparing them to self-administered questionnaires, their main rival. Table 3.1 is a conventional summary of the main differences between these questionnaires and qualitative interviews. It must be stressed that some interviews, notably surveys, are little more than spoken questionnaires, and that some open-ended questionnaires have the same aim as qualitative interviews. Equally, as telephone interviews are becoming more widely used in social science research, the case for mailing out questionnaires (which are often immediately filed in the waste basket) is weakening. And the development of e-mail questionnaires and internet conferences bring exciting possibilities to research design, although their 'reach' is restricted to those with regular internet access (Selwyn and Robson, 1998). Consequently, Table 3.1 should be taken as a prompt to reflection but the complexity of reality cannot be tabulated so neatly.

Rather than seeing interviews and questionnaires in opposition, it might be better to see them as complementary within a multi-part study. We are not saying that interviews have to be followed by questionnaires. However, questionnaires are a good way of checking the strength and incidence of the story that the interviews seem to contain. In that sense, they can be a good check on an interpretation of interview data, as well as a way of exploring how widely views, feelings and understandings are shared. But questionnaires, like the one in Box 3.1, can also be used as a quick-and-dirty way of getting a sense of issues to be explored in interviews. The permutations of different types of questionnaires and interviews are as unlimited as your imagination and the research problem.

### Not an all-or-nothing decision

We return to a theme of Chapters 1 and 2 in saying that deciding whether to interview is not an all-or-nothing decision. It is not the case that we use interviews *or* other methods. Better to consider interviews *and* other methods. Box 3.2 contains an example of the use of multiple methods, showing how a clinical psychologist whom one of us interviewed had used interviews in the process of developing a numerical rating scale to describe children's levels of pain and breathlessness.

TABLE 3.1 *A comparison of qualitative interviews with self-administered questionnaires*

| Characteristics | Qualitative interviews | Self-administered questionnaires |
| --- | --- | --- |
| Provide information about | As for questionnaires, but far better at exploring these things in depth, learning about the informants' perspectives and about what matters to them. | Attitudes, motivation, accounts of behaviour, opinions, events |
| Best at | Exploring the stories and perspectives of informants (Understanding) | Checking how far the researcher's hypothesis or world view is shared by the sample (Surveys) |
| Can also be useful for | Surveys: closed questions can be asked, as in opinion polls about voting intentions Important when subjects neither read nor write easily and willingly | Open-ended questions allow researcher to ask for informants' stories and perspectives |
| Richness of response | Can be a dialogue between researcher and informant, allowing nuances to be captured (especially where video recording is used) and for questions to be clarified and adapted, and new ones to be improvised. Long interviews quite common | Questions cannot be modified once printed, nor can the nuances of the respondents' voices easily be detected in their writing. Long questionnaires are rarely acceptable – short (and superficial?) is the norm |
| Sensitive to | Informants. Good for finding out about the individual, specific and particular | The research literature and the range of responses amongst groups. (Also true of survey interviews) |
| Anonymity | Can be awkward for some people to say some things in face-to-face settings – danger of only hearing from the confident members of the population | Sensitive questions may be more acceptable in anonymous questionnaires |
| Ethics | Interviewers know whom they have interviewed, although transcripts can be anonymized | Anonymous questionnaire responses easily ensured |
| Sample size | With the exception of phone and intercept interviews, less suitable for wide coverage – better for detailed work with fewer people | Can be very large, and since the aim is often to generalize from the sample to the population, samples often need to be big |
| Time costs | Devising interview guide (checking validity and reliability, see next chapter), piloting (check on usability) – may be less of an issue with qualitative research | Devising questionnaire (checking validity and reliability – see next chapter), piloting (check on usability) |

| Characteristics | Qualitative interviews | Self-administered questionnaires |
| --- | --- | --- |
| Time costs (continued) | Arranging interviews – less of a problem with intercept (or 'clipboarding') and telephone surveys Establishing trust and rapport – less of a problem with surveys Allowing time for diversions during the interview – less of a problem for surveys Travelling, getting lost and hanging around (unanswered calls in phone interviews, refusals in intercept interviews) Limit number of interviews to guard against interviewer fatigue | Distributing questionnaires |
| | Transcription of data (frequently estimated as 7–10 hours transcription time per hour of tape) | Usually swift, especially where optical mark readers are used |
| | Data analysis (time needed for analysis regularly under-estimated, especially where qualitative data are involved) | Usually swift. However, open-ended questions are difficult to analyse, whether they are used in interviews or questionnaires |
| Money costs | Hire of interviewers (perhaps), travel costs, tapes, batteries, transcription of tapes Phone bills and costs of sending respondents an advance letter telling them about the research project and the phone contact to come | Mainly cost of printing, distributing and retrieving questionnaires. Looks cheap per questionnaire distributed but typical low response rates can make it an expensive method per returned response |

## Audience

While research designs should be sensitive to the matters we have discussed here and in the previous chapter, they will also reflect the stances of any sponsors and of the intended audience for the research findings.

For example, much research is done to order, commissioned with deadlines and budgets to meet, which effectively fixes what can and cannot be done. This is as true for undergraduates who have to finance their own dissertation study to be submitted before the end of the year, as it is for us, doing funded research for commissioning agencies. Research sponsors will have their own preconceptions about the best way to do a study, and they will often be positivist preconceptions. Furthermore, some sponsors will want a report that highlights action points and areas of concern but, as we recount in Chapter 5, will not permit any publication that draws on that work.

For students, the audience is likely to be a member of faculty. Quite apart from matters to do with deadlines and resources, it is important to remember that these

---

**Box 3.1   An open-ended, self-administered questionnaire**

(Used by Peter in 1995, early in a study and as one enquiry method)

**Learner autonomy is a key goal of Higher Education. Can you see better ways of fostering it? If so, please outline them here.** [one-third of page left blank for responses]

**What do you think learners need to master if they are to become – and be recognized as – autonomous learners by the end of their course?** [one-third of page left blank for responses]

**The programme that I described overleaf has somewhat limited appeal to undergraduates. Can you suggest any developments that are consistent with current thinking about good practice in teaching and learning that might enhance the programme's appeal to students?** [one-third of page left blank for responses]

---

academic staff will often have their own preferences about research orientations and methods: the wise student is alert to them (Arksey, 1992). Faculty and departments too often have working (and often tacit) notions of what counts as 'proper' research, and may take deviance from those norms as evidence of sloppy research. The 'paradigm wars' may be muted nowadays but their aftermath lingers in some places. We have repeatedly heard North American colleagues tell us that quantitative, positivist research is seen as 'normal' research in social science, especially in psychology, with qualitative and descriptive research being judged to be inherently inferior. So, the choice of methods is best made with the audience in mind.

Nor are professional researchers exempt from such expectations. Many of us have come across referees whose comments on research proposals seem based on assumptions about the properness of certain research designs and who seem to have taken slight account of the problem to be investigated. Journals have their peccadilloes too. Even at the design stage (perhaps, especially at the design stage), the 'streetwise' researcher will have an idea of possible publication outlets for the research findings and be aware of the range of methods that is likely to be acceptable to them.

In choosing methods, think of the outcome in the sense of the relationship between methods and research findings, but also think of social outcomes, in terms of the relationship between the methods and the reactions of the intended audience.

**Box 3.2 The use of serial research methods in the construction of rating scales for child pain and breathlessness**

(This is based on an interview with the clinician who developed the rating scales)

Researchers wanted to create a scale that would allow them to develop a way of estimating the levels of pain felt by children who, because of developmental problems, were not easily able to communicate. Consequently, they were not able to say how much post-surgical pain they felt. Although physicians could estimate a pain level on the basis of the physiological consequences of the surgery, pain thresholds differ from person to person.

Since the children could not report how much pain they felt, the decision was taken to treat parents as key informants about children's manifestations of pain. Earlier attempts to investigate parents' observations of children's pain responses by having them write descriptions had been inhibiting for some parents and had produced rather short accounts. Interviews with parents were seen as a way of getting richer and more extensive data.

Twenty parents were interviewed and asked how they knew when their child was in pain, and what signs of pain the child showed. They were happy to talk, and talked so much that they brought in a lot of material that was not relevant to the interviewer's concern.

The researchers thought it important to capture the nuances of the spoken voice, nuances that might have been lost if the transcripts alone had been analysed. Consequently, the interviews were analysed by two coders, who listened to the tapes while reading the transcripts. When they had reached a high level of agreement about the analysis of the interviews, the basis was laid for piloting a paediatric pain manifestation scale. It is not our purpose to describe the complex and rigorous procedures necessary to develop a reliable scale, but we do want to draw attention to the way in which interviewing was used to explore the territory and to establish the content validity of the scale. (That means whether the scale included the full range of pain symptoms.) Interviews were one part of a multi-method research approach.

A similar study looked at child breathlessness. Formally speaking, the objective breathlessness measures of respirology do not match well sufferers' feelings of breathlessness. If the sense of breathlessness is attended by feelings of panic, or if it is unexpected, then feelings can be stronger than when the child had a greater sense of being in control of similar physiological symptoms. Researchers wished to develop a pictorial scale of breathlessness, which would indicate how breathless child patients felt. The advantage of a pictorial scale is that children, who may not communicate fluently, could identify the picture from the scale that best described their state.

*continued*

Interviews were held with a group of parents of children prone to breathlessness, with a group of 12–16-year-olds and with a group of 8–12-year-olds. This technique of using focus groups can have the advantage that the social interaction can trigger off new ideas, but there is also the risk that dominant individuals can overshadow quieter people (see Chapter 6 for further discussion of this). It is cheaper to run three groups of eight people than to do 24 individual interviews. Since the purposes were qualitative, the limitations of focus group interviews were acceptable.

The discussions were not taped, since this was felt to be intrusive. Instead, a note was kept of the adjectives that respondents used to describe their breathlessness, or that of their children. In addition, the children were asked to draw pictures to represent breathlessness and they then explained what they were trying to convey. In retrospect, it was a mistake to have a respirologist present, who intervened too much in the discussions. It would also have been better to run focus groups containing only a single class of breathless children or parents, since the onset, symptoms and prognosis of asthma and cystic fibrosis are quite different.

However, the results were useful. The researchers had expected children to describe breathlessness in terms of images of physical exercise, such as running. In fact, children used images to do with the throat and its constriction (especially asthma sufferers) and with the lungs and their congestion (especially cystic fibrosis sufferers). On the basis of the children's pictures, which were collected, and of the adjectives they used, the researchers and a graphic artist constructed three provisional, pictorial breathlessness scales. These scales were then piloted and refined by a mixture of further interviews and physiological measures. Statistical techniques were then used to organize the findings on an interval scale (see Table 11.2 for an explanation of this concept).

## Can *you* interview?

While you may be persuaded that interviewing is the method that is best fitted to your research purpose, you need to check that you have the qualities necessary to interview effectively, or to be sure that you can develop them.

Even with survey interviews, potential informants decide to participate partly on the basis of a snap judgement about the interviewer. They wonder 'is this a person whom I wish to spend time with – after all, the only benefit for me is likely to be an interesting encounter? What's the cost? What do they want from me?' The more personable the interviewer and the more intriguing their status, the more likely it is that an interview will be granted.

For example, if we are approached in the street by an intercept interviewer, our thoughts might be:

- Are they trying to sell me anything?
- Am I busy? Is it raining or freezing, or blowing a pestilential gale?
- Do I like the look of them?
- How far am I prepared to say something about myself to a stranger, when I have no idea where the data will end up?

Or, if we are trying to get an interview with someone who thinks they are important (which means they think they are busy), getting the interview may depend upon:

- *Your status*: a student doing a thesis has lower status than someone of similar standing to the respondent. By and large senior people are more likely to get an interview, especially with élite informants, than are junior researchers.
- *The project*: if the project is intriguing, or if the potential respondent can see a possible pay-off, then there is a greater likelihood of getting the interview.
- *Yourself*: if you sound personable, trustworthy and interesting, whether your approach has been in writing, in person, or by phone, agreement to doing an interview is more likely.

In survey interviews, the interviewer usually works from a schedule that must be closely followed and the self comes through only (but very importantly) in appearance, body language and voice.

In qualitative interviews, the interviewer is more like a jazz musician in a jam session. The key may have been set and there is an initial theme: thereafter it is improvisation. Your ability to 'jam' is crucial to the success of these interviews, since there will be times when it will be right to improvise in any of the following ways:

- Vary the question order to fit the flow of the interview.
- Vary the phrasing of the questions to help the conversation to seem natural.
- Probe, or ask follow-up and clarification questions, *ad lib*.
- Let the interview seem to go off track.
- Give a lot of attention to building trust and rapport, which will often involve putting something of the interviewer's self into the interview, perhaps by raising similar or different experiences, by saying 'something that has always puzzled me . . . Can you help me to understand that?', and so on.
- Throw the interview guide away, if necessary (see Box 3.3 for an example).

The following things about us relate to our effectiveness as interviewers.

### Understanding the topic

The investigator who is well versed in the literature now has a set of expectations that the [forthcoming interview] data can deny . . . It is, however, true that preconceptions can be the enemy of qualitative research . . . but the benefits of the 'preconceptions' that spring from the literature review are, perhaps, much greater than their costs . . . a good literature review creates much more distance than it collapses. (McCracken, 1988: 31)

---

**Box 3.3   Throwing away an interview guide in qualitative research**

(This is based on an interview with the researcher whose experience is described here)

A researcher was investigating the attitudes of people with terminal AIDS to experimental drug treatments. Should treatments that might offer relief and remission be permitted, despite the dangers of serious side effects and of hastening death?

Qualitative interviews were used. The interviews were distressing to the researcher who 'sobbed for a year': we return to this theme in Chapter 9. One involved a man whose face was swollen and misshapen beyond recognition by sarcoma. He could no longer see. By his bed was a picture of how he had been, which he asked the interviewer to look at. He wanted to talk about his illness and what it meant, saying virtually nothing about experimental drug treatments. Respecting him and his needs, the researcher did not press the interview guide but instead took on the more therapeutic role of listening and talking with him. To do otherwise would be ethically uneasy in any circumstances, and quite wrong with a dying man. He thanked her for the conversation. Despite having got nothing from the interview that was usable within the research, and despite being very upset by the experience, the researcher now looks back on it as a lesson in the importance of being more sensitive to the informants than to any research agenda: she sees it as a lesson in practical ethics.

---

The better we know or understand an area, whether through sensitive reading or from our own experience, the better we can connect with the interviewee. Sometimes, it is necessary to become an 'insider' in order to make this connection (see Box 1.2, above; Chapters 7 and 8 extend this point). Connecting is not, of course, the same as overwhelming. It means that we have a knowledge that allows us to interpret, understand and respond.

*Understanding people (including ourselves)*

> If what people have to say about their world is generally boring to you, then you will never be a great interviewer. Unless you are fascinated by the rich variation in human experience, qualitative interviewing will become drudgery. (Patton, 1990: 279)

Being interested in others is certainly important in sustaining enthusiasm for the job of interviewing. Being self-aware helps us to do the job well. The more we have recognized the different sides of ourselves and glimpsed the different people we can be, the more we can see them in others. This helps to make our questioning and prompting more sensitive. Self-understanding is also valuable in alerting us to ways in which who we are can skew the interview. For example, if the interviewer knows that he or she has a tendency to try to stamp their presence on a situation, that self-awareness can help them to hold back and try to listen to the informant, hearing the informant's view of the world without overlaying the interview with their own presence.

### Body language

> The person taking me to get the train to get to my interview said that in her research department, she'd not be allowed to do an interview in jeans (and I mentally added 'let alone in blue suede shoes, open neck shirt and earring'). However, the dress seems to me to be okay for the circumstances (a university in the long vacation). (Peter's field notes, July 1997)

The *Guardian* newspaper carried a report on 12 March 1998 claiming that 7 per cent of the impact of any piece of communication is verbal, 37 per cent comes from the tone of voice and 56 per cent derives from body language. Are we aware of what messages are sent by our dress, appearance and body language? We have more to say about dress in Chapter 7.

### Affect

> The researcher's empathy, sensitivity, humour and sincerity are important tools for the research . . . How the researcher asks questions depends on how he or she feels about the topic or the interviewee. And what the researcher hears from the answer may depend on his or her mood and prior experience. (Rubin and Rubin, 1995: 12)

Can you build trust that brings rapport? In other words, how socially skilled are you? And being socially skilled is not the same as being voluble. For example, a quiet and sensitive person may make a far better qualitative interviewer than an egregious party-goer who overwhelms others. If social skill is a minimum requirement for qualitative interviewing, it is not sufficient for interviewing within a research stance that places great importance on building close relationships between the partners in interview research (see also Box 1.3 and Chapter 7). And, as Rubin and Rubin suggest, it is helpful to use self-awareness to monitor and to try to regulate our moods. The fieldnotes in Box 3.4 show something of the emotional, or affective, experience of interviewing.

### Conclusion

The thinking behind the choice – or rejection – of any interview approaches to a research problem has now been set out. In suggesting that it frequently makes sense to use interviews as one of several enquiry methods, we have previewed one aspect of research design, namely triangulation. In the following chapter, we consider more systematically factors that will affect the ways in which you design your interview research project.

---

### Box 3.4  Feelings about an interview

(This is an extract from a researcher's fieldnotes)

I'm a little phased by having been away from home for two days, not sure that this interview will really happen and dogged by low-level anxiety about some personal difficulties. But I've done hundreds of interviews and think I'm skilled at relating to and being easy with people. Spend some time on breathing, relaxation and affirmations . . .

Like all colleagues in this study, he [the informant] is a prolific and engaging talker, with nice, open and engaging body language and a speech style that leaves little room for me to talk. To begin with, I'm happy to put aside my three page interview guide and let him shape the conversation. It is relevant, interesting and, above all, it tells me what he thinks is important. . . . I become increasingly worried about what we're not covering . . . I'm enjoying listening to my colleague and, as with other interviews in this series, I feel an emerging sense of who he is, as well as warming to this person. But I can feel tension – I'm doing it wrong, I'm not getting through the questions on the guide. I start looking for points to interrupt him. I manage to slip in a rather complicated question and, when he simplifies it, I settle for his interpretation at the cost of losing data that would have been interesting for comparative purposes. Eventually, well aware of the time, I rather derail my informant, cover some of the closed questions in the protocol, scan it to see what important areas we've not covered (very few, thank God!) and turn him towards the remaining big area.

Relief. It more-or-less worked. Confidence high and self-esteem groomed.

---

# 4    Designing an Interview-Based Study

This chapter is based on the assumption that you will be doing a project in which interview approaches offer a good prospect of getting answers to your research questions. Most of the points we discuss have to be confronted regardless of whether an enquiry is interview-based or led by other methods. It also sets the scene for Chapters 5 and 6, which also focus on design issues, although the discussion becomes increasingly concerned with design issues that are particularly important for interview research.

We begin this chapter with some thoughts on how you might identify a topic to investigate. Then, you have to choose the enquiry methods, which we assume will include interviews. Here, the guiding principle is that the methods should be fit for the purpose – they should have the power to provide data that you can use to answer your particular research questions: different questions, different research designs. While you are engaged in the twin processes of choosing the topic and the methods, you should also be doing a search of the literature. We suggest that this is the right time for you to begin drafting your report and we make some suggestions for drafting the literature review section of it. Lastly, we address some of the more detailed design considerations that you will have to consider in an interview-based study – sampling issues, the trustworthiness of the design, and the claims that might be made about its generalizability.

## Staking out the territory

What is the topic that you will investigate? This decision causes beginners problems and is not unknown to experts either. The kind of rational thinking about research that pervades much of the writing about social research points to the following strategy for identifying a research topic:

- Your reading on a topic might make you think that there's an aspect, an area, or an application of an idea that hasn't been pursued. You might wonder whether findings would apply to different groups, or to different situations. You might suppose that the conclusions were a result of the research methods used, and that different methods (substituting interviews for questionnaires, for example) or different uses of a method (substituting unstructured for structured interviews) would lead to different conclusions. Or you might reasonably want to do something that is commonplace in natural science, which is to replicate (copy as closely as possible) a study in order to check out the strength of the conclusions.

Our experience is that people find topics by other means as well – sometimes it seems that more topics come from the less publicized sources of inspiration than from those that are commended in the research literature. For example:

- Interest. You've got a feeling for a topic, such as housing issues, single old people, children and the internet, discipline in high schools. Alternatively, a topic may be attracting a lot of media attention and seems to be ripe for a small-scale but systematic enquiry that is sensitive to the relevant academic literature.
- You sensibly believe that an important part of doing research is the relationship that can be created with the supervising tutor. Consequently, you pick a congenial academic and say that you want to work in the area in which she or he is expert.
- It is suggested to you that you might like to work in a certain area.
- You get no real choice. You have to do a piece of action research while on placement, or in your place of work. So, you might be expected to do something about the education of hospitalized children, about post-natal support for opiate-addicted mothers and neonates, or about prison health services. And you have to do it within the situation in which you are working, which may not be a very promising research setting.

## Who cares? From topic to topicality

Social research may be valuable because:

- It gives the researcher a chance to practise and master research techniques – *apprenticeship.*
- The findings add to knowledge about the topic, or call into question existing concepts, assumptions or findings – *substantive value.*
- Research techniques are applied to new areas, or new techniques are developed – *methodological value.*

Research reports should generally have substantive or methodological value, even in the case of reports that come from apprenticeship research. In other words, they will be more than collections of information. It is not enough to have a topic to investigate, nor to collect a lot of information about it. Fair responses to that information would be 'So what?' 'What does the information mean?' 'Why is it significant or topical?' 'Who cares?' The true story in Box 4.1 is an example of a very poor choice of topic while Box 4.2 indicates the difference between information collection and useful research, a distinction that is developed in Box 4.3. The heart of the difference lies in purposefully connecting the information to a conceptual or theoretical base.

Once a topic is identified, it needs to be connected with relevant other work and thinking so as to make the value of the study clear. This is illustrated with reference to 'action research', which could be (uncharitably) described as all action and no research. It is done with the aim of trying to make a difference to a

---

**Box 4.1  A proposed study with no obvious usefulness**

A mature, overseas student, on a course concerned with the assessment of students' learning, insisted that he wanted to study the operation of the educational bureaucracy in his country. He agreed that there was nothing unexpected likely to come out of this study; that the Minister of Education already knew that his ministry was a featherbed for his family and friends (after all, the minister himself had lifted them gently into that bed); and that a research report would make no difference (except that the student, had he completed the study, would have probably been wise to make himself very scarce).

The story, which still puzzles Peter, illustrates the 'so what?' question, describing a study with no topicality and no usefulness. Nor was there any indication that new concepts would have been developed, or old ones applied and extended. It seemed quite pointless, an example of interest without thought.

---

**Box 4.2  A way of answering the 'so what?' question**

A research study, for example, would not be very interesting if the write-up said, 'I used $x$, $y$ and $z$ methods to gather information and the findings appear below.' Rather, it is the theoretical or conceptual base in which particular methods are couched that makes them interesting. Consider the following statement: 'Because I was interested in exploring the conceptual position taken by authors in this area, methods $x$, $y$ and $z$ helped me answer the following questions. The findings are presented below and are compatible with theories and ideas derived from the literature. The methods employed were adequate to answer the questions I had raised' (Grasha, 1996: 95).

---

situation. It typically involves examining practices and trying out ways of improving them. What this means is that the research needs to be purposeful and focused, not just information collecting. In fact, the need to be aware of the literature and other thinking is all the greater here, since other people's research and writing are a fruitful source of ideas about the most promising approaches to making a difference. Where work is purposeful, uses theory and research findings – when it is connected – then it is better, not least because it contains an answer to the 'so what?' question. And the more that answer is emphasized, the more attention is likely to be paid to the findings.

It might be objected that progressive focusing was recommended in Chapter 1, whereas here we are commending clarity and focus from the start. There are two

**Box 4.3   Commentary on a selection of research topics**

| Research topic | Comments |
| --- | --- |
| A study of a day care centre | Topic too big. Focus unclear. No indication of what the value of the study might be, nor of who might be interested by it |
| An action research project in Ward M1 | Too general – what aspects of Ward M1 are going to be studied? Why? Who will be the audience and who will benefit? In what ways? And with action research, it is important to know that you can make changes, see them through and evaluate them |
| How effective is Social Work Team PR5? | More focused than the other questions but the notion of 'effectiveness' is a minefield – it is really too big to tackle in one undergraduate study. The concept of effectiveness also appears in Box 7.4 |
| How effective do clients of Social Work team PR5 believe it to be? | Much better. With the right literature review this could be good, because work on effectiveness tends to be producer-centred, not client-centred. This could question the validity of that tendency |
| A study of teenagers' attitudes to pollution | 'Pollution' is too broad a topic. More seriously, this research is unlikely to tell us anything new – it is unlikely to have any value beyond apprenticeship |
| How do police deal with rowdy youths? An interview study of beat officers in two contrasting areas | Good to see a focus on contrasting areas and on a manageable sample. However, defining 'rowdy' is going to be tricky (but not impossible). The serious mistake is to forget that interviews do not give information about practice: *they tell us what people believe they do* |
| What is the best way of teaching the concept of place value to six-year-olds? | A well-formed question that will not yield to interview methods. A long-term, experimental design will give the most secure results |
| Under what circumstances do 'empty nesters' give to charity? | There is value in knowing why people think they give to charity but it is well known what people actually do is often quite different from what they believe they do: it is an area where the public voice tends to overwhelm the private voice. Unsurprisingly, then, research into |

*continued*

|  | altruism, of which this is an example, is dominated by experimental studies |
| A survey of the needs of recently bereaved unemployed men below retirement age | In many ways a well-defined study. However, is a survey the right way to proceed? Yes, if there has been a good reading of other research and some unstructured or semi-structured pilot work. Otherwise . . . |
| *Your tentative research question* | *Your comment* |

responses to this apparent contradiction. The first is that progressive focusing should be seen as progressively focusing on the best ways to understand and investigate the research question, which will lead to some changes in the initial question and which might lead new questions to be brought into the research. This response is essentially that progressive focusing takes place from the start of research into a question of value. The second response sees progressive focusing coming from the topic. As you read more about the topic, talk to people and, perhaps, do some pilot research, questions arise, which are refined and developed as the project progresses. In this case progressive focusing leads you to the research question, which is then sharpened by further focusing. Often, it is only through progressive focusing that researchers identify the value and significance of their work. The difficulty is that can take up time: and time is always in short supply in research projects.

If research is to be valued, it needs to have a purpose, to be shaped by important substantive or methodological concerns. Making the case that these concerns are important involves relating them to the literature, as well as listening to stakeholders' claims that this is an important issue for them. However, the research community is unlikely to be very interested in a story of significance to one social work team unless it is related to the prevailing research discourse – to the existing literature. The following advice on doing a literature review should be read in conjunction with that in Chapter 12 on writing up the results.

### Reviewing the literature

To illustrate the importance of reviewing the literature, we introduce the action research approach to enquiry. It is usually small-scale research that is intended to help the researcher or practitioners to take actions that are planned to make a difference and whose impact will be evaluated. That evaluation will often set off a further round of research, leading to the analogy that action research is a spiral of activity, a process. Because the problem and situation are immediate, there is a temptation to jump straight in to the research, sometimes without thinking too carefully about the methods, let alone about the instrumentation in any detail. Understandable though that is, there are three major disadvantages:

- Rediscovering the wheel: the investigator has to invent instruments when perfectly good ones already exist. Furthermore, if they were used, the investigator would get data that could be directly compared with the study from which they were drawn, broadening the interest of the study's findings.
- Missing significant findings: the investigator does not realize that some good answers to this problem already exist; or that there are good conceptual frameworks that can profitably guide the research; or that this is an impossible enquiry because it demands large-scale and sophisticated research and analysis.
- If the study is never connected to general thinking, it stands alone. Readers can still draw their own conclusions, but they may remain unaware of some of the possible significances of the results.

The case has been that it is important, even in action research, to examine the relevant literature. How might this be done? Suppose this is to be a study of female washroom attendants. This is manual labour, performed by women, in circumstances that are full of taboos and symbols. It is a service occupation, poorly paid, held in low esteem and sometimes quite unpleasant. The way that female washroom attendants regard this work is related to their sense of self and self-esteem, which means that there is a greater or lesser interplay between their identity and culture as a washroom attendant and their other identities and cultures.

At first sight, it is rather hard to see why washroom attendants would be taken as a subject of intrinsic interest. However, there could be a lot of value if these people were studied in order to test out or develop theories about how women balance work and home lives; self-esteem; occupational motivation; taboos; or women's perceptions of their bodies. Different theoretical concerns imply different research questions, different methods and different ways of making the claim that the research is of value and significance. One aim of the literature review will be to see which methods and questions are normally applied when investigating any one theoretical line.

Another aim will be to see what the big issues and questions are in any theoretical stance. Suppose that the attendants' work is changing. They are now expected to cover two washrooms, not just the one they tended in the past; their pay is not increased annually, overtime is no longer available and job security is threatened as budget pressures grow. There is talk of introducing charges for the use of the facilities and also of having women cover both male and female washrooms, and of male attendants doing the same. These changes could be interpreted within the literature on the intensification of work, as well as within the often-related literature on women's work. Both are quite diverse and extensive fields of study, as a literature review will show. One question for the prospective researcher is which interpretations within the literature appear to be more convincing and more relevant, which implies a critique of the others on grounds such as they are incomplete, their conceptualization is inadequate, or there are problems with the empirical research. In turn, this will help to clarify the directions for the study and set the tone for the report.

This rather assumes that there is little problem in identifying the relevant literature. Nothing could be further from the case. Searches of CD-ROM or on-line data bases can be infuriating. On the one hand, they can throw up too many references (it is a good idea to limit the first search to the past five years, or less). On the other, many references will be impossible to access and many will be trivial or of little interest. And there are all the valuable references that are missed because no human imagination would guess the right keywords to find them. A good technique is, first, to locate a couple of recent and quite comprehensive references and follow up some of their citations. Finally, keep in mind a sense of proportion. Within the time available, there are limits to how much can be read. Usually, the aim is not to produce an exhaustive literature review but one that links an enquiry to wider concerns and issues. In other words, the review is there for a purpose, to provide one answer to the 'so what?' question. It establishes the substantive significance of the investigation and, where the enquiry is methodologically innovative, it shows the reader what there is that is innovative about the methods – how they are an advance on the methods used by earlier researchers.

At some point, the reading will need to be written up and presented as a section of the research report. Table 4.1 is a guide to one way of doing that, but because the way you organize the literature review will have to depend on the research question, it has to be appreciated that other structures are feasible.

Three further points deserve mention:

- Be sparing on historical background (and one of us has had a career as a historian). It is legitimate to survey the history of an issue, but only when it is clear how this affects the proposed research. Where the purpose of a historical overview is unclear, it can damage a review by making the reader suspicious of a writer who appears to be inflating the report with irrelevant material.
- The literature review may be concise.
- Reading the literature on a topic generates research questions (see Box 4.4 for an example). However, research questions develop and new ones can emerge during the research. The implication for the literature review is that whatever is read and written early in the study will be re-written later in the study in the light of new emphases. Research manuals often imply that the review is done, then the fieldwork, and then the findings are found. In fact, the review, and the reading that goes with it, are usually revisited and rewritten after the findings are in.

Much more extensive advice about reading research reports is to be found in Locke, Silverman and Spirduso (1998). Cooper (1998) goes into considerable detail about the processes by which a set of research reports is drawn together into a synthesis, such as the literature review described here.

## Making your research credible

Readers want to know that the research has been carefully done, so that findings can be trusted. Within the positivist tradition, this involves taking care to maximize validity and reliability, while taking steps to ensure that the findings

TABLE 4.1   *A literature review template*

| Focus | Example |
|---|---|
| Preview of the issue | *Throughout the Western world, those in full-time employment have found that they are frequently being expected to work longer, to do more . . . This has often been called intensification* |
| Main literature findings – empirical | *Studies have been conducted in a number of countries, involving both low- and high-status occupations. The findings have generally been that . . .* |
| Are there any notable exceptions to the general trend? | *However, . . . . [You may not need this section]* |
| Are there any explanations that need to be considered? [Be ruthless here: your study may not be much concerned with *why* so much as with *what*, or with the *effects*] | *[There is general agreement that economic factors are the major cause of intensification, although ideological factors also need to be considered]* |
| Are there any problems with the ways in which existing research has been conceptualized? | *A major problem with the notion of intensification is that it assumes that objective changes, such as requiring workers to take more responsibility, are perceived in just one way (as an imposition rather than as, say, empowerment)* |
| Are there any problems with the sampling? | *Attention has been concentrated on professional groups, and not on low status groups, such as women who do manual work. It is not clear, then, whether intensification is a widespread phenomenon, or a concern of the 'chattering classes' alone* |
| So, explain what issues you are going to examine: what are your research questions? Who cares about your findings? | *This study will therefore . . . The findings will help to decide whether . . .* |
| What methods have been used? Are they suitable? Would other methods enrich understanding of the phenomenon? Justify this claim | *Much of the research has taken place on the assumption that demonstrating increases in the demands made on employees is the same as demonstrating the existence of intensification, which has largely been done on the basis of documentary sources and survey research. However, whether changes are seen as intensification is a matter of individual perception. Exploring these perceptions requires the use of interview methods . . .* |

from the sample can be readily generalized to the population. First, we discuss validity and reliability within that tradition, since they are important prompts to thinking well about research design and they are directly applicable to survey research. However, they cannot be straightforwardly applied to qualitative research,

---

**Box 4.4  From research topic to research questions**

(This is based on a study in which Peter was involved)

The researchers became interested in the occupational socialization of new higher education lecturers. The topic is important, since patterns established in the first years in the job persist. They approached the topic with three principles in mind: that it was necessary to consider the 'whole person' when studying academic staff; that socialization should not be seen as a one-way process; and that informal socialization and professional development were likely to be more significant than formal processes (this point came from a major study of schoolteachers in which Peter had been involved). These principles were to be tested against the evidence collected in the research.

The literature review threw up far more research questions than the duo could pursue. The research guide included those that could be fairly pursued through long, loosely structured interviews; which would shed light on the three principles; and which seemed to have the potential to advance thinking about the topic. As the research progressed, the researchers continued to find new literature, which influenced their interviewing, although it was not necessary to revise the interview guide.

Typical interview questions were: Which of four views of academic work (taken from the literature) is closest to yours? Which of four views of the goals of undergraduate teaching (taken from the literature) is closest to yours? How would you describe the relationship between your work and your out-of-work life? (Prompts taken from the literature.) Were there any formal induction arrangements? If so, please describe them and say how good you found them. Have you got a mentor? If so, please describe the mentoring process and evaluate it.

---

so this is followed by a summary of thinking about the credibility of qualitative research. The last section of this chapter concentrates upon the way in which findings can be generalized from surveys, action research and case studies to more general contexts.

## Validity

We take validity to raise the question of whether you are actually investigating what you claim to be investigating. Campbell and Stanley (1963) give the classic account of threats to validity. Many of them we just have to live with, on the principle that flawed information is better than none, and there is sometimes little that can be done about some threats. So, while survey research aims to be reliable and valid, because the survey format itself constrains respondents, it compromises validity. It is a matter for judgement whether the cost to validity is large (and it

where the survey instrument has grown out of piloting that has
litative interviews) and acceptable.

intitative and qualitative approaches, threats to validity are legion,
e qualitative researchers would use alternative terms to 'validity'.
your study may claim to look at the attitudes of young people
towards the police. Research based on interviews with 15-year-olds at school
might have validity problems because those playing truant, whose attitudes
towards the police might be quite distinctive, would be missed. Another threat to
validity is when we fail to create a situation in which the respondent feels easy and
able to talk. One report tells of a researcher who talked to business executives on
train journeys:

> What struck [the researcher] was the extent to which the views and opinions of the
> managers, off-guard and to a person they were unlikely to meet again, contradicted the
> 'reality' contained in much contemporary management literature. Had the interview
> taken place in the manager's office, the results might well have been quite different.
> (Easterby-Smith et al., 1991: 78)

Validity is enhanced by:

- Interviewing techniques that build rapport, trust and openness and which give
  informants scope to express the way they see things.
- Schedules that contain questions drawn from the literature and from pilot work
  with respondents.
- A set of questions that fully covers the issues raised by the research question –
  key aspects are not ignored.
- Not asking questions that are irrelevant to the research topic – a waste of scarce
  interview time.
- Prompts that encourage informants to illustrate, expand and clarify their initial
  responses, talking in detail and about specifics.
- A sample that is fit for the purpose of the research. If the work is preliminary,
  opportunity samples and snowballing (see below) are acceptable. If the aim
  is to make claims about a group, or to give a rounded account of an event,
  sampling needs to ensure that all points of view are appreciated. Big samples,
  preferably selected at random, are needed if you want to claim that your
  findings are very likely to hold good for the population.
- Thinking about the possible effects of interview times and settings. Ideally,
  respondents should be interviewed more than once, with the setting changing.
- Interviews that are long enough. Interviewers often find themselves pressed for
  time (see Box 3.4). However, no matter how long an interview, we have found that
  'one of the most basic rules of interviewing is that the most interesting material
  emerges when the recorder is switched off' (Powney and Watts, 1987: 139).

### Reliability

If it is assumed that there is a stable reality 'out there', which is to be precisely
measured and described, then it is important that the findings are not corrupted by

the research process: the design and tools need to be reliable. Some qualitative researchers would want to talk in terms of the consistency, trustworthiness and authenticity of the research, although they would still find themselves addressing many of the issues covered here. In survey research, reliability is mainly about trying to reduce interviewer bias so that we can trust that the findings are neither the product of the research instruments, nor of the interviewer's quirks and improvisations. It is likely to be important to make sure that all informants are asked exactly the same questions and given similar sorts of clarification. The findings would be unreliable if it turned out that some questions were explained to some respondents who were puzzled by them but not to other puzzled respondents. This is especially important where several interviewers might be involved in a large-scale survey.

Complete reliability is not attainable, although the guidelines for survey researchers (Box 4.5) show how it may be maximized by limiting variations in interviewing practice (see also Brenner et al., 1985). There is also further discussion of reliability in the context of telephone interviewing, which is described in Chapter 6. Reliable data analysis is covered in Chapter 11.

---

**Box 4.5  Typical guidelines for survey interviewers**

- Look interested.
- Stick to the schedule: read the questions exactly as printed, in that order; read all of them.
- If there are pictures, cue cards or other apparatus, use them as scheduled.
- Try not to signal approval or disapproval of any answer.
- Do repeat the question if asked.
- If the respondent refuses to answer a question, that has to be accepted, and without any signal of irritation.
- Make sure that you understand a response.
- If not, probe in a non-directive manner ('Would you tell me more about that, please?'); if need be repeat (*but* do not alter) the question.
- If an answer is not adequate (it is an answer to a different question), thank the respondent for the answer and repeat the original question ('Thank you. And could you tell me . . . ').
- Do not answer for the respondent, explain the question, or give any other new information, unless the schedule allows it.

The schedule should give guidance on the clarification you can give if asked, and that should be based on the experience of piloting the schedule. Practice varies from being allowed to repeat questions but not to clarify, to being able to explain the meaning of words or phrases, to, sometimes, being allowed to re-phrase the question (which compromises reliability).

---

The assumptions that underpin qualitative research mean that classic concepts of reliability do not sit very well with this approach:

> Qualitative research is not looking for principles that are true all the time and in all conditions, like laws of physics; rather the goal is understanding of specific circumstances, how and why things actually happen in a complex world. Knowledge in qualitative interviewing is situational and conditional. (Rubin and Rubin, 1995: 38)

The quest for situational and conditional understanding is quite different from the quest of positivist social science. Consequently, the concepts of reliability and validity cannot be imported from positivist approaches to qualitative ones. 'Reliability', based on assumptions that phenomena are regular and unchanging, is particularly inappropriate in epistemologies that see situated cognition, complexity and change as pervasive and normal features. Therefore, it is important to recognize the futility of imagining that 'if you could strip the interview of all of these [biasing] factors, the "real" or "true" or "unbiased" response would emerge' (Briggs, 1986: 21). Yet, it can be a useful exercise for the qualitative researcher to ask traditional reliability and validity questions as a way of getting a fresh perspective on the research design.

This view of the inappropriateness of traditional notions of reliability and validity in much qualitative research does not imply that qualitative researchers are cast into the pit of relativism:

> The ethnographer is not committed to 'any old story', but wants to provide an account that communicates with the reader the truth about the setting and the situation, as the ethnographer has come to understand it. (Altheide and Johnson, 1994: 496)

By and large, qualitative researchers have responded to the problem of demonstrating the credibility or trustworthiness of non-positivist research in two ways. First, by recognizing the value of continuing to ask, but not to be bound by, the questions raised by classic accounts of validity; and secondly, by developing their own criteria (Lincoln and Guba, 1985), which have a lot of common ground with the rules of historical enquiry. The three most relevant concepts here are:

- *Consistency*: this is akin to 'reliability'. The requirement is that the researcher shows how the research has been done and decisions have been made, so that the reader could conduct an 'audit trail', examining the good sense and plausibility of the researcher's thought and actions. There should be evidence that the inevitable inconsistencies in the data had been considered and there should be some account of how they have been handled. This largely embraces what Rubin and Rubin (1995) call transparency and consistency. It implies that researchers will describe their findings and their analysis, and their own work in detail – 'thick description' as it is sometimes called.
- *Truth value*: this involves providing evidence that what the researcher has captured is recognizable as a fair representation of things as informants see them. It involves triangulation of methods and triangulation by examining

different perspectives on the research topic (see Chapter 2
checking with interviewees that what they said is what they m
interpretations make sense to them. It should come from imn
research and, to some, it implies participant research. Inevitabl
and inconsistencies will be highlighted, and, following the princi
tency, the researcher should show how they have been dealt with.

- *Neutrality*: this is a requirement that the researcher considers their own role in the research. Patton (1990) has remarked that in qualitative research, the research is the instrument. Clearly, the researcher cannot be the objective agent depicted in some positivist views of scientific enquiry. The researcher has an influence, and a different researcher would have a somewhat different influence. The aim is not to try to standardize researchers, but to have them reflect on the ways in which their background (class, gender, race, special concerns), personality (which is critical to achieving rapport and trust), mind set (assumptions and preconceptions), and actions have contributed to their account. The aim is to check the 'rampant subjectivity inherent in more phenomenologically based paradigms that will prove to be the nemesis of new paradigm research' (Lather, 1986: 68): *the aim is to check*, not to obliterate.

## Reliability and validity in qualitative research

In a nutshell, the qualitative response to the issue of reliability and validity is to require researchers to demonstrate that what they do is fit for their research purpose. Invariably, this shades into questions about the characteristics of good research. It is not possible fully to define these in general terms, for good research consists of adequate response, in the research setting, to the questions raised in the checklist at the back of this book (pages 185–191). Nevertheless, a number of features have been identified and should be borne in mind, including:

- The value of the outcomes for action (in action research), for programme development (in evaluation research), for policy and for the research community in general. This implies evidence of a clear answer to the 'so what?' question.
- Consideration of issues of power and of structural inequalities in the research setting (especially in feminist research [Blackmore, 1996] and studies influenced by critical theory [Robinson, 1996]).
- The incorporation of ethical considerations into the work (is it possible for unfair work to be good work?).
- The achievement of a situational equality between interviewer and informant (Benney and Hughes, 1956) or of closeness between interviewer and interviewee (especially in much feminist research – but compare this with the distance that the historian Lummis [1987] advocates). This is important if the researcher is to hear 'private talk', which discloses meanings that are absent from 'public talk', to hear an authentic voice that might tell of things subversive or discreditable, rather than to hear the socially sanitized accounts of the public voice (Cornwell, 1984).
- Sampling adequacy.

- The appropriateness and power of the interview questions.
- Design flexibility: this means that the researcher was responsive to unanticipated meanings and opportunities.
- Transcript quality (see Chapter 10).

## A *postmodern problem*

Questions of the credibility of the research become problematic once it is assumed that informants' accounts are shifting and shaped by the time and circumstances of the interview, and if it is accepted that the interviewer will construct the meanings of the interviews. It is difficult to give advice on judging the credibility of such research. In the literature, the emphasis is on the researcher providing plenty of data on how the research was done so that readers can judge whether this appears to be an honest attempt to explore it systematically. There are no rules for judging, only the requirement that the researcher make the research process transparent, being explicit about what was done and why:

> While the transfer of findings from one case study to another is done by the reader, the researcher has an obligation to provide rich, detailed, thick description about the case. (Firestone, 1993: 18)

When such research is presented in non-conventional forms (Chapter 12), problems multiply, since there is no consensus on judging these research 'reports', although many academics suspect that they – and postmodern research stances – can be licences for the slack exercise of subjectivity and relativism. In such cases it is prudent to establish, in advance, what your sponsor or supervisor would regard as evidence that the research is credible.

## Sampling and generalizing from the study

The question of the ways in which generalizations can be made from interview studies has been touched upon in Chapter 1. Table 4.2 extends that discussion by showing how different interviewing purposes are associated with different sampling strategies and thence with the confidence with which the researcher might make claims about the generalizability of the findings from the sample to the population. (A population is the group from which the sample is drawn: on the basis of samples of trainee midwives, football supporters, or retired men, researchers might make claims about the populations of trainee midwives, football supporters, and retired men.)

Sampling always needs to be done thoughtfully, since the sample of respondents or informants affects the information that will be collected and determines the sort of claims that can be made about the meaning of that information. For example, if the aim is to generalize from a sample to a population, then the sample must be representative of the population and large enough for generalizations to be made with confidence. There is a considerable technical literature on the confidence with which generalizations can be made from a sample to a population

TABLE 4.2 *Interviews, sampling and generalizing from the sample to a population*

| | Interview purpose | Sampling strategy and generalization |
|---|---|---|
| **Researcher makes claims about generalizability** | Survey | Random sample. Size as large as possible. See Oppenheim (1992) for example, for advice on sample size. Researcher makes strong claims about the generalizability of the findings |
| | Survey | Structured sample. Used where there is a danger that random sampling might lead to key groups being unrepresented. The larger the sample, the greater the confidence when generalizing from it, although some consider that structured sampling is not as powerful a basis for generalization as is random sampling |
| | Survey plus qualitative questions | If the survey is the most important element, follow rules above. If the exploration is the most important, see below. Take advice on generalizability from appropriate section of this table |
| | Survey-like | For example, intention is to survey and generalize but not possible to control sampling – use opportunity sample. Researchers are on shaky ground if they try to claim the findings are generalizable |
| | Qualitative – researching an event or time | Assuming no great concern to generalize, use opportunity sampling, look for good informants, increase sample size by snowballing. Keep adding to sample until you are hearing nothing new. But, also take care to hear the story from different perspectives – seek out people who may have a different slant on what happened |
| | Qualitative – cultural interviews (finding out about beliefs, understandings and feelings) | As above, taking care not to concentrate on high-status informants and those who readily come forward to be interviewed – danger of not hearing the private or silent voices |
| | Exploratory – getting into a field | Converse with anyone who might be able to help you get oriented. At best, the researcher can suggest that readers might consider implications of the findings for a population |
| **Reader makes inferences about generalizability** | Exceptions to the rule | A sample of one (for example, Boyle and Woods, 1996) is enough to show that some research generalizations can be too sweeping |

(for example, Oppenheim, 1992). Research undertaken in the 1970s looked at the characteristics of people volunteering for research (quoted in Holden et al., 1993). The authors came to the conclusion that in comparison with non-volunteers, volunteers tended to be: better educated; of higher social class status; more intelligent; in greater need for social approval; more sociable. Although nothing is said relating specifically to volunteers for interview studies, it is important to realize that the act of volunteering to be interviewed is, in itself, a sign that the person may be in a minority in the group in which you are interested.

For qualitative researchers in particular, sampling is an exercise of judgement which balances practical concerns (time, money, access), with the research foci, and with the degree to which *the researcher* wants to generalize from the data. Two important principles to use in making those judgements are:

- Try to get a sample that allows you to see things from all *relevant* perspectives (what is relevant will be closely related to your research foci).
- Keep trying to increase the sample size, or the size of sub-samples that represent different perspectives, until you are not hearing any new points. For intensive interviews designed to explore a topic, a sample of eight is often sufficient, according to McCracken (1988), although survey methods should then be used to check out the findings.

Although most discussions of generalization are about the conditions under which researchers can claim that findings from a sample are likely to hold good for a population, readers also make inferences about the significance of a research report for situations and groups that are of interest to them. It is not possible to prevent readers from generalizing, since that sort of thinking is embedded in the act of reading itself. It is, though, desirable to draw their attention to the generalizations that you regard as secure and – or – significant. In addition, Firestone (1993) argues that it is possible to generalize to theories, as well as to populations; that is to say that your research may give insights into the strength of theoretical positions. For example, the study in Box 4.4 provided data that permitted a re-appraisal of the theory that socialization is a one-way process in which the social environment shapes the new group member.

*Generalizing from cases*   In qualitative research, especially if it involves one case study, or is an action research project, the researcher may be reluctant to suggest that it is wise to generalize to a population. However, that does not mean that no generalization is possible, since the general is always present in the particular. So, a study of a single high school (for example Ball, 1981) can show processes at work that may or may not be present in all high schools but which are likely to be present in many if not all of them. Readers could be prompted to consider whether they recognize these processes as ones that are at work in schools they know, although it is a further research task to explore the extent to which those processes operate in high schools in general. The considerate researcher identifies findings that seem to have implications for other settings, and, as often happens with case studies, suggests that it is for the reader to generalize on the basis of correspondence between the research and the reader's understandings and experiences (Stenhouse, 1980; Walker, 1983).

Similarly, even a single case study can call into question the assumptions of a theory, as Boyle and Woods' study of one primary headteacher shows (1996). Some researchers had suggested that increasing and increasingly complex workloads, the growth of managerialism and an emphasis on bureaucractic tasks had transformed primary headteachers' roles at the expense of the caring and educational priorities that used to characterize the job. The study of a single headteacher showed that these generalizations were too sweeping and was the basis for a critique of theories that say that changes to social structures determine people's behaviour. Boyle and Woods invoked social interactionist theory to argue that people have choices in the ways in which they respond to structural changes. All of this is based on the study of one headteacher.

Furthermore, if it is possible to do several case studies on a topic, then a process of analytical generalization (Firestone, 1993) can be used to test theories more strenuously. For example, the study of educational markets in three areas, which centred on case studies of 12 schools, provided a very powerful test of existing theories about the effects of what the authors called 'public-markets' on educational practices and has generated new theories (Woods et al., 1998).

All research, then, has some generalizability. Problems come when researchers try to make generalizations that go beyond what the research design can support. They also arise when, through failing to answer the 'so what?' question, the researcher gives readers little help in seeing how they, not the researcher, might generalize from the findings.

## Conclusion

Early thinking about the design of the research governs the sorts of claims that can be made on the basis of the evidence collected through interviewing. It is one thing to speculate on the claims that might have been made had the reliability and validity (or their equivalents) been differently framed, or if another sampling strategy had been employed, or if the focus were somewhat altered. That is legitimate and desirable. It is another thing entirely to make claims based on a research design that is not fit for the purpose.

However, research design, especially in qualitative research, is not just an armchair, pre-fieldwork matter. It has to be fitted to the research setting, which frequently curbs the best intentions (as when it is impossible to get a sample with the right characteristics), and sometimes offers fresh opportunities (as when an informant offers access to hitherto unknown sources). A research design that is fit for the purpose will be one that has emerged as the best response to practical considerations. Practicalities whittle away the best research intentions. That is not your failure. It is a fact of research life, as the next chapter argues. Good researchers explain clearly how their project is worthwhile and represents the best response to a problem in particular circumstances which are never, ever, ideal.

# 5 Feasibility and Flexibility

The aim of this chapter is to draw attention to the practicalities that need to be taken into account when designing and carrying out research. Irrespective of its size and funding, the most carefully managed study can be undermined by the smallest thing and go wrong. These sorts of issues are often not discussed in any great detail, possibly on the grounds that bringing them out into the open might serve to deter would-be researchers – especially students, who in many respects work in sub-optimal circumstances, having to deal with constraints such as very short time scales and limited funding. From this perspective, compromises have to be made in the research design between what is desirable and what is feasible. We agree with Blaxter, Hughes and Tight (1996: 145), who state that 'research is the art of the feasible'. Given the fact that you want your work to reach a successful conclusion, we would suggest that when weighing up the advantages and disadvantages of different options you get into the habit of *thinking small*, *thinking focused* and *thinking pragmatically*.

## Feasibility of a study

When first designing a study, it is very easy to become over-ambitious. Almost without knowing it, your ideas have run away with you. For instance, the number of research questions you would like to investigate increases, or you want to follow up unexpected leads. This means gathering a wider range of perspectives across a variety of different settings. Before long, your small-scale enquiry has developed into a study which, to be conducted effectively, would need several thousand pounds, a team of researchers and a time scale of years rather than months. For many of the readers of this book, this level of research is not feasible. The idea that the suggested study is impractical should become obvious during the writing of the research proposal. Rather than run the risk of the research becoming a failure, this is the stage where you should be asking yourself whether the work is 'do-able'. Have you sufficient time and resources actually to complete the work? Are you fairly certain you can access the intended study population(s)? And how safe will you be: are there any physical risks involved in collecting the data? In the following pages we address each of these dimensions of feasibility.

### Time constraints

A research study based around interviewing is generally very time consuming. For a start, there is all the preparatory work. This includes: negotiating access to research settings and recruiting participants to the study; gaining ethical approval from any relevant authorities; arranging and confirming interview appointments; constructing and piloting the interview questions; addressing any data protection considerations.

Then there are the interview sessions themselves. You may plan for them to last about one hour, but just as it is a struggle for some informants to say anything at all, others have been known to talk far too much! Interviews can be prolonged due to distractions such as the presence of children; the interviewee is running late and cannot make a prompt start; interruptions from unexpected visitors, or telephone calls from friends to be answered. Once you take travelling time into account, then it is quite surprising just how lengthy one interview can be. And then, of course, there is the time taken to write up any fieldnotes afterwards, while events are still fresh in the mind.

Analysis and interpretation are equally time-consuming, yet this is not always allowed for. It is a common pattern – even amongst experienced researchers – to spend so long on the data collection that the data analysis has then to be skimped. Depending on how you choose to record the data, the analysis is likely to be based on audio or video tapes, or hand-written notes (see Chapters 7 and 10). In reality, most interviews are audiotaped, and they will need either full or partial transcription; one hour of tape can take seven to ten hours to transcribe fully. Usually, the subsequent analysis involves coding the data into some sort of meaningful categorization scheme (see Chapter 11), possibly using a specialized computer package, in which you may have to acquire proficiency before you can use it.

By now, you will have gathered that your research is likely to involve a substantial amount of time. For a small-scale piece of research, it might make sense to conduct the empirical work fairly close to your 'base': university, college, work, home or wherever. One technique to help develop time management skills, and avoid finding yourself (too) rushed towards the end of the project, is to draw up a timetable or schedule at an early stage. The calendar should contain a list of all the activities involved in the research, and target dates by which they have to be achieved. Psychologically, it is motivating to cross off tasks once they have been completed; at the same time, the schedule acts as a tool for self-discipline in terms of those that have not yet been accomplished. Box 5.1 contains the timetable that Hilary is working to in her current study, which examines the impact on family carers of the Carers (Recognition and Services) Act 1995. This timetable relates to a project that Hilary is employed on full-time, together with a colleague who works half-time. The study involves semi-structured interviews with different population groups: 60 carers at two points in time (six months apart); 16 care managers; and four senior managers. Interviewees are drawn from four different local authority social services departments in the north of England.

More than likely your research comprises just one of many demands on your time. If so, draw up your schedule of research plans based on a realistic estimate of the number of hours per day or week you think you can give to the project in the light of your other responsibilities and commitments. Whilst the timetable shown in Box 5.1 is useful in that it gives a broad brush picture of what needs to be done and when, you may find you need to be more specific than this. To this

**Box 5.1  Timetable for a 24-month research study examining whether carers have benefited from the implementation of the Carers (Recognition and Services) Act 1995**

| | Year 1 | | | | | | | | | | | | Year 2 | | | | | | | | | | | |
|---|---|---|---|---|---|---|---|---|---|---|---|---|---|---|---|---|---|---|---|---|---|---|---|---|
| | 1 | 2 | 3 | 4 | 5 | 6 | 7 | 8 | 9 | 10 | 11 | 12 | 13 | 14 | 15 | 16 | 17 | 18 | 19 | 20 | 21 | 22 | 23 | 24 |
| | Jan | Feb | Mar | Apr | May | June | July | Aug | Sept | Oct | Nov | Dec | Jan | Feb | Mar | Apr | May | June | July | Aug | Sept | Oct | Nov | Dec |
| Draft literature review | | | | | | | | | | | | | | | | | | | | | | | | |
| Recruit research sites, i.e. 4 local authority social services departments | | | | | | | | | | | | | | | | | | | | | | | | |
| Negotiate recruitment mechanisms: 15 carers, 1 senior manager and 4 care managers from each site | | | | | | | | | | | | | | | | | | | | | | | | |
| Begin to generate carer sample | | | | | | | | | | | | | | | | | | | | | | | | |
| Collect and analyse local policy and practice documentation | | | | | | | | | | | | | | | | | | | | | | | | |
| Draw up and pilot interview guides for carer's time 1 interview and professionals | | | | | | | | | | | | | | | | | | | | | | | | |
| Conduct time 1 interviews with carers; start to analyse data | | | | | | | | | | | | | | | | | | | | | | | | |
| Conduct interviews with senior managers and care managers | | | | | | | | | | | | | | | | | | | | | | | | |
| Draw up and pilot guide for carer's time 2 interview | | | | | | | | | | | | | | | | | | | | | | | | |
| Conduct time 2 interviews with carers | | | | | | | | | | | | | | | | | | | | | | | | |
| Data analysis | | | | | | | | | | | | | | | | | | | | | | | | |
| Writing up and dissemination: final report for funders; individual site reports, summary research report for wide distribution; short report for carer participants | | | | | | | | | | | | | | | | | | | | | | | | |

end, you might choose to allocate tasks to much shorter, and more specific, time periods.

A point worth mentioning is that whilst the timetable gives the impression of a research study flowing smoothly, in reality it is often chaotic rather than coherent, proceeding in fits and starts rather than evenly. It also implies a rather linear view, whereas often there is overlap, with tasks taking place simultaneously. Sometimes, especially at the beginning, the work seems to progress slowly. It is wise to take advantage of these 'gaps' by, say, starting to write up the literature review and the methods section, which helps in the formulation of questions for the forthcoming interviews. Once the interviews proper commence, the pace really quickens as time is spent out in the field. However, it often happens that the interviewing phase takes longer than anticipated. Professionals tend to have full diaries, and you can often wait some considerable time before they have any free slots. Arranging interviews with parents during school vacations can be problematic. Children are around, they want entertaining and people have more calls on their time; families are away on holiday. Further, interviews may be cancelled because of sickness or some other unexpected event, only to be rescheduled at a later date. All these 'misfortunes' are generally out of your control, but at the same time you are left with the consequences of the delays: reduced time for the analysis and report writing. To this end, it is useful to include some spare time in the schedule to accommodate hold-ups and unforeseen problems, and just the fact that everything takes longer than you imagine – a rule of thumb guide is 150 per cent (Wilson, 1998).

*Financial constraints*

The project must also be feasible in terms of the financial resources that are available. And unless you have a funder, sponsor or employer who is going to foot some or all of the bill, then you need to be quite sure that you can meet whatever expenses are incurred. Remember that travelling back and forth to interviews can be very costly; if distant locations are concerned, this may mean overnight stays which add to the expenditure. There are other expenses to be taken into account: equipment such as a tape recorder or personal safety devices (see below); consumables like audio cassettes; telephone calls; stationery; photocopying; and postage. Moreover, there is also the question of 'rewards' and 'incentives' for study participants. We discuss this in more detail in Chapter 9; suffice for now to say that whilst inducements in the form of money, gifts or whatever obviously boost the costs, at the same time they are likely to increase the willingness of people to be interviewed.

Putting a price tag on studies involving interviewing seems to be something of a neglected area in the research methods literature. But as a general guide, telephone interviews cost between one-quarter to one-half less than when inter-viewing in person; another low cost approach is focus group research (Andreasen, 1983). Having said that, costs are increased with 'difficult-to-find' groups or when screening criteria are introduced (Krueger, 1994). To give an example, one North American study we are aware of involved either face-to-face or telephone interviews with mothers who received income support, and also their ex-husbands. Because the mothers were 'in the system', they were relatively easy to locate and interview. The fathers, on the other hand, were not, and consequently were more difficult to find. This meant that the response rate for fathers was fairly low; it was reduced even further because it proved difficult to motivate potential participants to talk about money matters on the telephone (see Chapter 8). All-in-all, this was a high cost project. First, it was difficult to locate fathers who would agree to take part in the study; secondly, in the end personal interviews were used as a substitute for telephone ones.

Once again, be as realistic as possible and do not under-estimate the likely expenditure of the research. More to the point, allow some extra to cover un-foreseen circumstances, for instance the interviewee being out at the time you arranged to call, thereby necessitating a return visit.

## Reaching the study population

There are two separate issues involved in locating people to interview. The first is gaining access to the particular research site, which may be a commercial under-taking or agency in either the public or voluntary sector. The second is obtaining the cooperation of the people you actually want to speak with (this discussion is returned to in Chapter 9, where we consider access issues specifically in relation to élite groups). We will look at each of these aspects separately.

*Access to research sites*  Permission to undertake the research must be sought at an early stage. 'Gatekeepers', people with the power to grant or restrict access to research settings, are likely to be at senior manager level, a works manager per-haps, or headteacher, or medical consultant. If the gatekeepers are agreeable to access, more than likely this is because they believe taking part will serve some interest of theirs. From this point of view, it may be worth while trying to gauge how specific that interest may be. However, if the findings (especially of an evaluation study) are potentially critical, and the gatekeepers stand to lose from any negative conclusions, then common sense would suggest that they are more likely to obstruct than render assistance. And if the research is approved in spite of their reluctance for it to proceed, just be aware that wary gatekeepers can still manage to subvert the work through their role as intermediary (for an example, see Parry's [1992] account of how her efforts to gather data from graduate journalists following a one-year, university-based diploma course were blocked by one particular member of the teaching staff). Gatekeepers can implement stalling devices; for example, they may not pass on information about the study to potential interviewees. Alternatively, they may segregate people out rather than in, or not enforce procedures set up to put the researcher in contact with eligible respondents. In these circumstances, gatekeepers are part of the problem rather than the solution. Of course, some concerns, for instance over the amount of work involved, will be legitimate, and these should be treated seriously.

How do you go about persuading an organization to give you access to people or material such as personal case files? The Carers Act project (mentioned on page 61) is taking place within the social services departments of four local authorities; gaining access was one of the first jobs to be tackled. A one-page letter was composed for the directors of five social services departments. The letter started off with general information about the project, including brief details about the funding body, aims, methodology and time scale. The workload implications for staff were also estimated. Particular emphasis was given to the fact that a main intention of the study was to be of use and value to the local authorities taking part, and that findings would be disseminated widely. The letter went on to mention that support for the work was being sought from the Research Group of the Association of Directors of Social Services, and followed up with a couple of sentences about the Social Policy Research Unit's (SPRU; Hilary's place of work) high standing in relation to work on carers. A SPRU brochure was included with the letter to reinforce the general point about the Unit's reputation for excellence in research. The final sentence asked recipients to contact Hilary if they were interested in taking part. Within three weeks, all five of the targeted social services departments had responded positively. Unfortunately, the next task was deciding which one had to go!

Someone undertaking a piece of research as part of an undergraduate or post-graduate course of study might not be able to draw on the same relatively high-powered levels of persuasion. But even so, the model remains the same: a formal letter giving details of the intended work, including the aims, research methods and timetable; an indication of the potential advantages to the organization itself of any collaboration and cooperation; demands on staff time; and something to give additional credibility and integrity to the study – perhaps a covering letter from your supervisor. Such a letter could go straight to the managing director. Alternatively, if the organization has a public relations department or press officer, check with them beforehand who is best placed to deal with it.

Once access is agreed in principle, the next stage is no less important. This is the demanding (and time-consuming) task of negotiating procedures for contacting potential study participants; reaching agreement about matters related to confidentiality and anonymity for both the organization and individual respondents; and determining issues to do with publication of the findings. In many respects, what you are doing now is setting out the ethical steps to be followed during the course of the study (see Chapter 9). In the Carers Act study, a second letter was sent to social services' directors giving assurances about confidentiality. The letter also confirmed that each research site would receive two free copies of the final report. A copy would be sent in draft form, allowing at least two weeks for the correction of any factual errors. This is a key point; under the terms of the agreement, correcting points of fact did not mean sites could claim any rights to control over the interpretation put on the data. It might seem early days to be discussing proposals for writing and publication, but clarifying these at the start is one way to avoid later difficulties. Box 5.2 summarizes some of the problems that can be encountered if no firm agreements are entered into over publication rights.

Hilary's example of how local authorities were convinced that it was in their interests to agree to be research sites makes gaining access seem both quick and

**Box 5.2   Writing and publication issues**

To avoid conflicts over ownership of data and any 'embargo' at a later stage, it is important that researchers obtain written agreement about rights to publish their findings. Although this is more of an issue for funded research, where it is common practice for research contracts to stipulate that material (reports, articles, conference papers) arising out of a study cannot be published unless prior approval has been obtained, undergraduate and postgraduate students can also face problems of control (Punch, 1986). The problem relates to the potential for damage: social, economic and other interests may be jeopardized if findings reflect badly on people or organizations. These issues are closely related to the need to uphold ethical standards (Chapter 9), yet researchers can face conflicts of interests. For instance, constraints on publishing can have significant consequences on their future career prospects.

The following example is instructive. It concerns a postgraduate student whose research involved investigating certain aspects of work at two government agencies. Under the terms of the studentship, gaining access was never an issue. Perhaps reflecting the fact that no negotiations were necessary in the initial stages, the question of publishing did not arise until much later. In retrospect this might seem surprising, but at the time it was not. Future publications tend not to be something aspiring PhD candidates think about. However, on the basis of this case, supervisors should! The student was awarded the degree and the external examiner recommended a book version be produced. And now the problems started: how to publish work covered by the Official Secrets Act? Obviously, permission was required from the agencies. However, whilst one agency did not refuse outright, it initiated a stalling process in the sense that it said the request would have to be considered by particular individuals, as well as go before various committees. When demands for changes were complied with, the agency responded by asking for more changes. The second agency simply did not answer letters. To cut a long story short, authorization was never granted, and consequently the student was unable to publish anything from the thesis, although it is deposited in the library at Lancaster University (Sherlock, 1992).

This is a cautionary tale that demonstrates the weakness of the researcher's position when faced with powerful sponsors and with no formal agreement over rights to publication. And it is worth adding that if researchers have no contract with a university, then the institution is under no obligation to support them in entanglements over rights to publish.

The basic message is not to sign anything without asking advice, and to try to retain as much ownership of the data as possible.

easy, but in reality her experiences are by no means typical. Researchers who have only a limited period in which to complete their work might instead choose to speed up what can generally turn out to be a fairly lengthy negotiation period. One way to do this is to conduct the study in a setting where gaining access is going to be swift and uncomplicated – amongst other students, for example, or colleagues in your own place of work. In other words, where you are already an 'insider' in relation to the organization concerned. The skill then is to choose a focus of enquiry which is relevant to the research site, rather than *vice versa*. Being an insider has associated advantages and disadvantages; some of these are outlined in Boxes 1.2 and 5.3

---

**Box 5.3   Advantages and disadvantages of conducting 'insider' research**

### Advantages

- Insiders can gain access more easily.
- Insiders already have an informed knowledge of the culture, politics, power relationships and issues of the study setting.
- Insiders are familiar with networks for approaching people, especially 'hard-to-find' groups.
- Insiders can draw on shared experiences, interests and language, which can stimulate rapport and interviewer–interviewee interaction.
- Insiders can obtain richer data: interviewees are more likely to be candid and open because they feel confident the interviewer believes them.
- Insiders' familiarity enables them to discern the authenticity of the account.

### Disadvantages

- Insiders may face role conflict: are you a researcher or a colleague or a professional? For instance, if you are a district nurse do you put on your 'nurse's hat' once the interview proper is over and give advice or try to help with any pressing medical problems? (Buckeldee, 1994).
- It can be difficult to interview colleagues, especially if they are higher in status (Platt, 1981).
- Listening to the confidences of colleagues may be detrimental in terms of future working relationships.
- Being too close to the subject matter and the research population can make it difficult to maintain balance, which in turn may compromise the validity of the research.

*Recruiting interviewees* Having cleared official channels, and acquired approval for the investigation, the next challenge is to secure the support of the people you actually want to talk to. In this sense, gaining access is a continual process. As we noted earlier, do not assume that having cleared the 'gate', high recruitment rates will follow automatically. If the level of entry to the site is managerial, organizational power inequalities may come into play (May, 1997). For instance, knowing that the 'boss' has given permission for the study to go ahead, people may feel under pressure – obliged, even – to give consent and be involved. At the same time, they might be suspicious about how the data are going to be used. Their underlying fear is that the information could be fed back to management, and used against the best interests of either the individual employee or the work-force as a whole. Many staff have little power; they do not want to be disloyal to the corporate identity and are anxious about repercussions that might damage their employment record. Hence, it is likely that any information they provide will be a formal and guarded account, bearing little resemblance to the more realistic version of events (Collinson, 1992). Given this barrier to the honest expression of feelings and opinions, it is vital that you stress assurances of confidentiality and anonymity (Chapter 9). This can be done in a research information sheet; Box 5.4 gives some hints and advice about how to go about preparing one. In further efforts to ensure the collaboration of staff, it might be helpful to offer some form of recompense: interim or additional feedback, say, or the opportunity to discuss the findings and in this way retain their interest. If possible, give copies of any reports to lower-level staff, as well as management (Ostrander, 1993).

Once you have finally been accepted into the organization as a *bona fide* researcher, try to use this as leverage to obtain all you can to help you understand the structure of the organization and its way of working. What we have in mind includes organization charts, department guides and accountability charts, the staff handbook and the internal telephone directory. As well as this official material, cultivate informal contacts so that you can find out how the organization 'really' functions in respect of working relationships, say, or how one department interfaces with another. One other suggestion to facilitate managing the project is to establish a liaison contact within the organization, someone senior enough to deal with any problems that may arise, or filter information through to other members of staff.

It may be that the research study does not focus on an outside organization or agency at all, but involves gathering information from a wide range of individuals who are not strongly linked together through any sort of institutional infra-structure. So, how do you go about finding respondents in these circumstances? The best way forward is to try to get into the relevant social network. This is what Hilary did in her RSI study (Arksey, 1994, 1998) when she needed to talk to a miscellany of experts in the field. Having completed a literature review, she noted four names that seemed to recur quite frequently. She then telephoned the individuals concerned, and managed to secure interviews with three of the four. In this, Hilary was helped by having done her background research beforehand (see Chapters 7 and 8). To put this another way, she was questioned during the phone calls about the study, what she saw as important issues in the RSI debate and

**Box 5.4  Research information leaflet**

It is useful to produce a brief information leaflet summarizing basic details about the study. You can give these to potential study participants yourself, or leave them with staff in the research site for them to pass on to potential recruits. Used in this way, the leaflet is an important 'first impression' tool, and can be a factor in someone deciding whether or not to take part. It should be eye-catching, for instance printed on coloured A4 paper, which is then folded into three small pages. Add a project logo, using Clipart software. Short columns, like the ones used in newspapers, are easier to read. Large dark print against a pale background can help people who have poor eyesight.

The information contained in the leaflet should be written clearly, in language that the intended audience will understand easily. A personal approach, using pronouns such as 'I', 'we' and 'you', is more inviting. One way to offer the information is by using a question-and-answer format. Here are a selection of questions which you can then talk to in the leaflet.

- Who are you?
- What's the project about?
- Why are you doing the research?
- Who will benefit from the study's findings?
- Who will be taking part in the project?
- Why should I take part in the study?
- What will be involved if I agree to take part in the study?
- What sort of questions will you be asking me?
- What will happen to the information I give?
- What about confidentiality?
- Who can I talk to about the project?

Depending on your recruitment procedures, you might include with the research information leaflet a card or form for people to complete and return indicating whether or not they agree to take part. As part of this exercise, you need to decide whether you are going to ask people to *opt in* to the study. In this case, you would ask them to contact you if they accept the invitation. Alternatively, you may prefer to use *opt out* methods. This is where you ask people to contact you if they are unwilling to participate. Choosing the latter system can lead to higher response rates, but at the risk of being charged with coercion.

(Adapted from Alderson, 1995)

so on. Thanks to her preparatory work, she passed the test and showed she had a genuine and serious interest, and was not a 'time waster'. Interviews were arranged, and these first contacts provided her with names of others, a method of recruitment (as we noted earlier) known as 'snowballing'.

At the time, this was a wonderful way into a disparate group of very busy people. But on a cautionary note, it is important to realize that following this type of approach may mean the work is biased towards one particular side of the story. To counterbalance any possible accusations along these lines, special efforts should be made to examine the perspectives of those who might not share the same opinions or beliefs.

### Personal safety

There are safety issues involved in research, especially for people interviewing in one-to-one situations, or in dangerous neighbourhoods or at night. So if your study means you may have to spend a good deal of time interviewing in locations where you might feel physically unsafe, then its feasibility is at risk. You may think this rather an extreme proposition, and we would like to think you were right. Even so, we do feel it is important that these sorts of issues are given a higher profile. We examine the whole area of ensuring the well-being of researchers in greater detail in Chapter 9, including suggestions for protecting personal safety (see Box 9.3). Measures include carrying a personal alarm, using a mobile phone and travelling in pairs. Rather than pre-empt our later discussion, the key point for present purposes is that many of the safeguards have funding implications. These need to be taken into consideration in any costing exercises, but are often beyond the reach of students and researchers on tight budgets.

To sum up this section of the chapter. It is essential that when planning your study you pay serious attention to the time and resources that you have available. Your research must be fit for the purpose, including completing it to the set deadline. Initial over-ambitiousness can lead to problems later on; alternatively, you may find gaining access and cooperation more problematic than you expected. These, and other factors, may prompt you to refocus the study. This is reality; it happens to experienced researchers (Bell and Newby, 1977) and novices alike, as you will see in the next section.

## Turning potential failure into success

Even the most well-thought-out study might not develop exactly as planned. Delays in getting on with the work can lead to frustration, and despair that the project will ever reach a successful conclusion. As we said earlier, interviews can be cancelled or postponed by informants. At the same time, you may not be able to travel to an interview because of unexpected rail strikes, for instance, or hazardous weather conditions. Another major setback is if you cannot find anybody to talk to!

*Changing the research design*

Our general message is: do not assume that your study will proceed as you imagined. And if it becomes obvious that the intended plan is not going to deliver the answers to your research questions, then that is the time to reconceptualize the design so that it fits better the general circumstances and constraints within which you are working. This may mean changing recruitment procedures, substituting one group of respondents for another, reducing the scale of the work to make it more manageable, or simplifying the design. *From this point of view, altering the research design is not a sign of failure.* It shows that you have critically evaluated the work accomplished so far and initiated a change of direction in order to turn a potential failure into a success. The possibility of achieving this turn-around in fortunes has been demonstrated in studies.

Lee (1992), in his aptly titled article 'Nobody said it had to be easy', describes his postgraduate research on Catholic–Protestant inter-marriage in Northern Ireland (Lee, 1981). Throughout the whole of the fieldwork period Lee faced problems he had not anticipated. As a result, 'There was little else to do but to abandon, to improvise, to substitute, to take whatever opportunities were presented, and to utilize as fully as possible the material that was available whatever its deficiencies' (Lee, 1992: 126). Just what problems did researching religiously inter-married couples pose? First, Lee found that the Roman Catholic authorities were not prepared to give him any statistical data documenting mixed marriages which had taken place under their auspices. A subsequent approach to the Registrar General of Northern Ireland was more successful, however, and Lee was able to compile a set of figures extrapolated from the 1971 census data. A further difficulty related to a planned survey examining how people used urban space during courtship. Eventually, this element of the data collection had to be abandoned altogether, partly due to lack of resources, but primarily because it became apparent that a survey was not appropriate to gather subject matter of such a sensitive nature.

Although not a complete waste of time, attempts to talk to professionals such as social workers, marriage guidance counsellors and clergymen yielded data limited in both quantity and depth. Sources such as these were constrained by principles of confidentiality, for example, and generally were unwilling or unable to provide the sort of information that Lee wanted to access. The final significant problem that Lee encountered concerned the inter-married couples he interviewed. First, there was a shortfall in numbers and he did not attain his target figure. Secondly, the sample was biased towards a quite specific group: couples who were young, university educated, recently married but without children. As a consequence, the interview accounts were weak in respect of Lee's original research area, namely patterns of marital adaptation and coping strategies. In the light of this, Lee gradually modified his original thesis topic and went on to develop new insights around the set of issues that had now become of central interest, namely inter-married couples' experiences of the dynamics of courtship and the process of getting married.

Changing the interview approach

We have attended to problems that can arise at the 'macro' level, and lead the investigator to make changes to the research design. But what might prompt you to make modifications at the 'micro' level, in other words to meet the demands of the actual interview situation you find yourself in? Later chapters of the book offer guidance about good practice in interviewing, and we do not want to anticipate that discussion. Instead, our aim here is to think about the various options that are available when you arrive to conduct a pre-arranged interview and find that partners or friends are present – individuals who, in spite of your best efforts to emphasize the confidential nature of the impending interview, are unwilling or unable (because of shortage of space, say) to leave the room. And if the 'gatecrashers' are young children, then clearly they must be looked after regardless of any chaos they may cause.

In circumstances of this sort, the only solution is to 'busk it', in other words, improvise and see what happens. For instance, Cotterill (1992) describes how she has interviewed mothers whilst simultaneously entertaining children by building 'Lego' houses, or painting at the kitchen table. With adults, one option is to let the discussion drift into a joint interview where the second person joins in too. However, pursuing this course of action depends very much on the aims of the study in question. We talk about planned joint interviews in greater detail in the following chapter, but an unplanned one is completely different. Certainly, there are examples in the research literature where they have been used to advantage. Drummond and Mason (1990), in their study of the experiences of people with diabetes, intended to interview respondents alone, and generally this was possible. Occasionally, though, the interview was conducted with others present, usually other family members. The researchers were able to realize the full potential of the situation by exploring what it was like to live with someone with diabetes. In this way, Drummond and Mason obtained further valuable insights, which added an extra dimension to the findings.

In other situations, where couples are involved for instance, joint interviews may be completely inappropriate. Then, the best solution is to try to impress on the informant why it is important to be interviewed alone, and arrange a re-appointment. You could point out that joint interviews have the potential to stir up antagonisms and conflicts of interest within couple relationships, and that some things are better said in private. This is even more the case when the subject matter concerns sensitive issues like marital relationships, finance, poverty and unemployment (see Chapter 8). It is not unknown for couples taking part in a joint interview to end up arguing in front of the interviewer, in tears and generally in a distressed state (Radley, 1988). Anticipating this possible danger and in the light of past experience, even seasoned interviewers have been known to take the strategic decision not to proceed with a joint interview (Jordan et al., 1992). The point we are trying to make is that in difficult circumstances the best course of action may well be to abandon or cancel the discussion. This does not leave you open to criticism or mean that you are a bad interviewer. Interviewing calls for flexibility, and extreme cases call for extreme solutions.

## Conclusion

What this chapter has shown is the importance of being as realistic as you can when designing a research enquiry. Skimping on time and resources may mean that you are unable to deliver a satisfactory piece of work by the arranged deadline. You may think that finding people to talk to will be easy, and that may in fact be the case. But once you have located potential interviewees, you have then to be persuasive in tempting them to speak to you. At the risk of stating the obvious, without respondents there are no data; and without data there is no study.

When it comes to writing up the methods section of your report (see Chapter 12), reflect upon the process of the research and in particular what worked and what did not work. Moreover, include suggestions as to what you would do differently if you were starting the study again. It is often the case that we learn more from dealing with problems, for instance gaining access to a 'hard-to-reach' group, than we do when things flow smoothly.

Finally, the Staff Development Office at Loughborough University have produced a set of extremely useful practical guides dealing with different aspects of conducting research. Concise and to the point, titles include 'Managing Your Research Project', 'Time Management' and 'Writing for Publication'. These can be accessed on the World Wide Web using the URL:

http://www.lboro.ac.uk/service/sd/webworkshops.html

# 6    Approaches to Interviewing

It has already been shown that, despite their common features, survey and qualitative interviewing serve different purposes and have different characteristics. This chapter develops those differences as more detailed consideration is given to the different approaches to interviewing. The principal argument is that there are no hard-and-fast rules about which approach to use, nor is any approach a prescription for practice: the choice of approach and the way any approach is worked out in a particular research setting is very much a matter of designing that which is fit for the research purpose. That said, ideas about survey interviewing tend to be more fixed and more prescriptive than with qualitative interviewing, where practices are much more flexible.

In this chapter, we explore some of the ways in which you can vary the standard approach of having one interviewer in a private setting with one informant. It is possible to have more than one interviewer and to interview more than one person at a time; and to interview face-to-face, or over the phone. We conclude this chapter with a fairly detailed description of one interview-based study. This draws together many of the themes that have run through these first six chapters.

## One-to-one interviews and variations on the theme

### More than one interviewer

It can be very useful to have two researchers present during an interview. For example, when interviewing groups of North American students about whether they would choose to do postgraduate study in the UK, Peter found it helpful to have a colleague in the room. Their roles were explained to the interviewees. At any one time, one would chair the discussion while the other would keep notes, referring to the counter on one of the tape recorders that was running, but saying nothing. Advantages included:

- The silent researcher could notice things of interest that were missed by the chairing researcher, whose attention was often held by the management of group dynamics. At the end of the interview each interviewer had a chance to raise points that had struck him while observing.
- The researchers had a good account of the interviews and a guide to where the most interesting quotations were long before the tapes could be transcribed.
- Having two views of what had happened helped to clarify key themes and areas for enquiry and analysis.

- In this case the researchers were 'on the road', going from city to city, hotel to hotel, doing four sets of interviews in four days, and had to give a *preliminary* report to sponsors on the fifth. It was only possible to work to this schedule because two interviewers were used.

### More than one interviewee

*Joint interviews* Joint interviewing involves one researcher speaking with two people simultaneously to gain both perspectives on the same phenomenon. It is an approach that tends to be used in work primarily of a qualitative nature rather than in structured surveys. Family life is one area of enquiry where joint interviews can be used to advantage (Allan, 1980), suggesting that participants will generally be people in marital relationships or living as couples. Quite often, joint interviews are used as part of a triangulated study (see Chapter 2), involving separate conversations with the individuals concerned either before or after the joint interview, and with interviews repeated over a long period of time (Radley, 1988; Backett, 1990).

In Box 6.1, we detail some of the potential advantages and disadvantages of conducting planned joint interviews, which are quite different from unplanned joint interviews (see Chapter 5).

There are various practical difficulties with a joint interview research design. First, this sort of technique is associated with a low response rate. In two studies involving family finance – admittedly a sensitive issue – men were less likely than women to be willing to participate (Pahl, 1989; Jordan et al., 1992). Secondly, organizing joint interviews can be a difficult and drawn-out process, particularly if both partners work. Accommodating two people's schedules may mean that joint interviews are more likely to be arranged for evenings or weekends. Finally, there may be financial implications. The areas where increased expenditure may be expected include the training and time commitments of the interviewer(s), fieldwork activities, transcription and coding, and data analysis and interpretation. Unfortunately, in small-scale studies with limited time and resources available, implementing a joint interview approach may not be appropriate, even if it does appear to be particularly suited to the research questions.

*Interviewing an intact social group* There can be interviews with groups as well as with individuals. Group interviews can show something of the dynamics of social relationships amongst group members – for example, who gets to speak and who does not, what forms of speech characterize different members in the group setting, and whose ideas are listened to. When the group is a naturally occurring social group, then things can be discovered by talking with all members together that could not be gleaned through one-to-one interviews. The researcher may observe the processes of consensus formation and of the rules by which disagreements are played out.

Bruner (1990) describes a method in which family members were individually interviewed about their lives. As is often, but not invariably the case, the informants 'later remarked spontaneously that they had enjoyed the interview

---

**Box 6.1 Advantages and disadvantages of joint interviews**

(Developed from Arksey, 1996)

**Advantages**

- May establish rapport and an atmosphere of confidence more easily.
- Can obtain two versions of events rather than one, which may, or may not, produce a coherent joint account. The distinct forms of information and knowledge are likely to corroborate and supplement each other, but at the same time may contain points of divergence. Inconsistencies between perspectives are likely to be missed if one partner is left out of the study, and his or her views are inferred from the other's data.
- The story that emerges may be more complete as interviewees fill in each other's gaps and memory lapses.
- The information obtained may be more trustworthy as bias in one account may counterbalance that in the other.
- Researchers may gain insights into the interactions and nature of (power) relationships between couples through observation of verbal and non-verbal modes of communication; for example, it may be possible to witness how couples support, negotiate and influence each other, as well as manage disagreements and areas of tension.

**Disadvantages**

- One informant may dominate, to the extent of silencing the partner; the literature (McKee and O'Brien, 1983; Jordan et al., 1992) suggests that men are likely to be the more vocal and overbearing.
- The risk of stirring up antagonisms and conflicts of interest.
- If the research topic is especially sensitive, or there is any likelihood of provoking friction, individuals may not be willing to disclose detailed, honest information in front of their partner and instead provide a more acceptable, 'public' response (Cornwell, 1984).
- Partners may collude to withhold information from the interviewer.
- Interviewees may not concentrate as well when two people are present.

---

and/or that they had found it personally informative. Several said that they had been quite surprised by what came out' (p. 125). These interviews were then followed by a meeting of the whole family where they heard the researchers' account of what it was like to grow up in that family. The subsequent discussion was still going strong after three hours.

This use of a group interview had considerable advantages in terms of the research interest, which had much to do with the interplay of the individual and the family unit. The small size of the family group (six members) and their known and distinctive voices allowed transcripts to be made that identified who had said what. It also helped to validate the individual interviews, as well as highlighting problem areas in them. It is regrettably uncommon for researchers to build on theoretical insights into the interplay between individuals and social units by using *both* individual and group interviews.

*Focus group interviews*  A focus group is a selection of people who are invited to respond to researchers' questions, findings from earlier studies, policy documents, hypotheses, concerns and the like. They may comprise people who are a cross-section of the population, or they may be homogeneous, comprising, say, retired women, 16–18-year-olds, or clients of the probation service.

Focus groups originated in market research. Suppose that a firm wished to advertise a new product: which features should be stressed, how might it be packaged and what price might be charged? Some purchase can be had on these problems by assembling small groups of consumers and asking them, for example, what they looked for in buying a new car. In this case, it is probable that they would be shown mock-ups of different cars, descriptions or drawings, and be asked to say which they preferred and why.

The results of these market research focus groups would *not* prove anything, especially if participants were paid for their views. The number involved would be small and the generalizability would be quite low. There would also be problems because of group dynamics, where dominant individuals might obliterate alternative points of view. Again, perceived status differences may lead some group members to dissemble and conceal views. An example of this from Canada is a focus group that was discussing road safety, specifically related to motorists' behaviour in areas patrolled by pedestrian crossing attendants (who were being injured at an unacceptable rate). As focus group members introduced themselves, it emerged that one man was an officer in the Royal Canadian Mounted Police ('Mountie'). At first, people said that they conformed to speed limits and road signs. Only when the RCMP man said that he regularly drove his private car 10 kph faster than the speed limit, even though he knew he should not, did others begin to talk more openly.

Despite the drawbacks, focus group interviews are very useful for some purposes. For example, researchers need to be sure that their instruments do explore the way people feel, think, and say they act, and not simply test out the researchers' view of how these things ought to be. Focus groups are a low cost way of getting the range of the informants' perspectives and of getting some, tentative purchase on who holds them. As long as the results of these groups are treated as material for thought, reflection and further investigation, they can be very useful and relatively inexpensive. They complement but do not remove the need to pilot and refine research instruments.

One of us has used focus groups to understand the way students choose jobs and postgraduate courses (Hesketh and Knight, 1997). At first sight, this approach is riddled with flaws. Groups can be harder to manage than individuals, so the discussion can loop around on itself and some issues can get quite brief attention.

Groups can be large (unexpectedly, one of ours had 25 people, was not easy to manage, and produced a low quality tape recording). It would be more usual to think of focus groups of about seven people, and even then it is important to have two, good-quality tape recorders with separate stereo microphones carefully placed to ensure usable recordings will be made. Even with good acoustics, good equipment and manageable groups, it can still be impossible to ascribe views to individuals, and some people simply say little. There is no scope to ask for a show of hands to see how many people agree with any particular point, since that would disrupt the flow of conversation and put the researcher in a far more directive role than is consistent with hearing as many ideas as possible. Despite such problems, the Hesketh and Knight study heard a consistent and very important message that people applying for postgraduate courses were not getting the sort of information from higher education institutions that they wanted. That was very helpful to information providers who were able to think better about providing material to potential postgraduate students.

Focus groups are also used to validate research reports. In Chapter 11 we describe some of the problems of analysing interview data. It will be seen that this is not an objective, judgement-free process, which means that the interpretations that come out of the analysis might make sense to the researcher but not to the research subjects. One way of reducing this risk is to validate the findings by giving participants a summary of them. Where this can be followed by focus groups composed of participants, the researchers have a better chance to hear how well the interpretation fits their understandings. It also provides a chance for the researchers to seek explanations of unexpected findings and to clarify details.

Fuller discussion of issues in focus group research is provided by Morgan (1988), Krueger (1994), Greenbaum (1998) and Wilkinson (1998). The set of six books in the *Focus Group Kit* (edited by Krueger and Morgan, 1998) provides a comprehensive treatment in a practical and accessible way.

### One-to-one interviews

Most interviews are conducted one-to-one. To illustrate the range of approaches to one-to-one interviewing, we review here telephone interviewing, as an example of survey interviewing, and oral history interviews to give a sense of less-focused alternatives.

*Telephone interviewing*    Surveys produce data that are far more closely related to the quality of the questions that are asked than is the case with exploratory interviews, where rich data are often defined as those coming from people sharing easily what is foremost in their thinking. There, the exact wording of the questions is less important, given the great flexibility of qualitative approaches.

At first sight, self-administered questionnaires should be the preferred survey method, and it is hard to see why anyone would go to the expense of paying people to read out scripts that could be sent out as questionnaires. Yet, survey interviewing is often the method of choice in market research. We examine telephone interviewing to illustrate the case for survey interviewing.

Once, telephone interviews were treated with distrust, rather as internet-based research is now (Selwyn and Robson, 1998). Those with a phone were better off than others, so telephone surveys provided information about the attitudes and beliefs of more affluent people only. Now, telephone ownership is widespread, although the very poorest are still excluded, more so in the UK than in the USA, and telephone interviewing is now a major method in survey research in marketing, although it is still, in the opinion of Frey (1989), not sufficiently well known as a social science research technique.

In many ways, telephone interviewing does not feel like interviewing. The respondent cannot be seen and the visual cues that are so important in establishing an interviewing relationship are lost. The rapport depends on what is said and on the voice manner of the interviewer. For this reason, careful attention has to be paid to the introductory patter and to the interviewing schedule, and interviewers need to be chosen for the quality of their phone manner. Despite these impediments, Lavrakas (1987) hopes to gain a 90 per cent response rate from those of the target group who can be contacted.

Telephone interviewing has several advantages:

- It is well-suited to random and structured sampling, far more so than clipboarding (which is also known as 'intercept interviewing', where people are stopped in malls, going to football games, leaving churches, and so on. The major problem is that the people at those places are only representative of people who go to such places at such times).
- Telephone interviewing is ahead of its main rival, the questionnaire, because it is quicker.
- Telephone interviewing usually has higher response rates than do questionnaires, especially where people have had a letter saying that they will be called and outlining the purpose of the coming call. (It also means that people can have to hand any files they might need when they are telephoned.)
- The interviewer can help respondents who have difficulties with any question, which is not true of questionnaires.
- Literacy, which is necessary for questionnaire response, is not a limiting factor in telephone interviews.
- The conventions of phone use work for the interviewer, since people feel a pressure to answer the phone (but not to respond to an intercept interviewer), it is customary for the initiator to terminate the call, and there is an expectation that the person answering the phone will then participate actively in the conversation (Frey, 1989).
- It has the advantage over questionnaires that the interviewer can encourage reluctant phone subscribers to participate. Ways of doing that include having a good 'patter', by stressing how helpful it would be to have *their* opinions, by saying that the interviewer will call back at a more convenient time, by saying that the interview will be brief, by pointing out the value of having more information on an important issue, or by saying that cooperation helps the interviewer to earn a living (Lavrakas, 1987). Box 6.2 illustrates some of the things that the interviewer might say in these circumstances.

**Box 6.2   Examples of explanations that phone interviewers give**

(This material relates to the issue of informed consent, covered in Chapter 9)

**The purpose of the survey**
This is a short survey [*give a length of time here*]. The questions are about your attitude towards [*add name of topic*]. We want to know how you feel about this because it will help us to understand what people think. That will help us to get a better idea of [*what to do/how to improve things/what the firm, government etc. could concentrate on in the future*]. I'm doing this as a part of my work at [*name of institution*] and, as well as being useful to [*name the users of the findings*] it is a part of my coursework. Whatever you tell me will be confidential. Your cooperation is voluntary but it would be very helpful if you would answer these questions for me.

**How will the survey be used?**
I shall write up a report for the course tutor. I will not use anyone's names in the report, or say anything that could identify anyone. A summary of the findings will also go to [*add name of user*]. The idea is that these findings should help us to understand [*insert name of the topic*] better so that better decisions can be made/better action can be taken. Your cooperation is voluntary but it would be very helpful if you would answer these questions for me.

**How did you get my number? I'm not in the book**
Your number was chosen by a computer which randomly generates a list of all the numbers that might be in use in this area. I then dial the numbers that the computer comes up with until I find one that is in use, like yours. This method is used because it is the only way we can be sure that I get to talk to a fair sample of people in [*add name of the area*]. If I do not talk to a fair cross-section, then my results will be misleading.

**Why do you want to talk to [*someone of the opposite sex, someone younger or older*] and not me?**
I need to make sure that I get to talk to a good mix of men and women, older and younger people. The computer helps me to do that by telling me who to ask for each time I make a call.

**Hmm. I'm still not sure.**
If you want to check that what I'm saying is accurate, why not call [*name and number of academic supervisor*] and I'll call you back afterwards.

- Interviewer reliability should be high, since a supervisor can monitor calls and spot cases where the interviewer diverges from the script.
- The researcher can quickly see how the work is progressing by reviewing the completed response forms as they are passed on by the interviewers.

The main disadvantages are more or less those common to survey methods:

- Respondents will not be prepared to spend a long time answering questions. There is a consensus (Frey, 1989) that the questions need to be fixed-response ones, since open-ended questions are harder to manage over the phone than face-to-face and answers tend to be less complex and shorter.
- The interviewer has little guarantee that the respondent's mind is really on the questions and not distracted by TV, children, pets, or the dinner that is burning. Phone surveys take more interviewer time than do questionnaires, involve phoning outside of normal work hours, and require repeated attempts to contact the right person at some numbers.
- They demand a lot of concentration and energy to keep to the script and to sound bright.
- Interviewer training is necessary and interviewer supervision is common.
- Each call is more expensive than the cost of sending out each questionnaire. (However, the cost *per response* of the two methods may favour telephone interviews.)
- And, of course, the data produced will be of the quality that comes from all survey methods.

In this balance of opportunities and problems, there is one important aspect of telephone interviewing that commands serious attention, and that is the construction of the sample. As with mailed questionnaires, careful construction of the sample is very important where the intention is to generalize with statistical confidence from the sample to the population. Using telephone interviewing, it is broadly possible to target specific groups of respondents, such as middle-income or low-income groups, by matching residential information (perhaps taken from census summaries) to phone codes, although this is complicated where the codes do not align with the residential districts to be surveyed. Computer-assisted telephone interviewing (CATI) is a powerful way of generating *random* samples. The area codes that are to be surveyed are entered and a computer program randomly generates telephone numbers, within the range of numbers used by the telephone company. This random sampling will select numbers that are unlisted – a substantial proportion of numbers in some areas, especially in the inner city – but telephone subscribers can become quite irritated at being 'cold called' in this way and decline to participate in the survey. There are also manual ways of generating a sample of telephone numbers, although some of the numbers, whether generated manually or by computer, will not be in use, so the size of the sample will always be smaller than that pool of numbers.

If interviewers only speak to the adult who first answers the call, the sample will be systematically biased, since it has been found that older people and women are more likely to be on hand. So, sometimes interviewers are told to ask to speak to the eldest adult male, or to the youngest adult female in the household. However, a request to speak to the youngest male, or to a female wage-earner (strategies designed to get a balanced sample of respondents) will often be met with the response that he or she is not available, so a further call will be needed.

Although the telephone interviewing method has many attractions, it is nevertheless little used in social science research. One reason is because social science researchers are often interested in people who have a characteristic that is not related to their phone number or address. For example, the phone numbers of single parents, widows, recent immigrants and highly educated people cannot be generated by computer or picked out from the phone book. Secondly, where a researcher is interested in people who share an occupation, such as nurses, shop workers, or laboratory technicians, it is not satisfactory to call them at work. Teachers, for example, usually share a staffroom phone, are seldom close to it, and have neither the time nor privacy to deal with a phone interview.

*Oral history interviews* There is no reason why an oral history interview cannot take the form of a survey, although it is quite rare, since the historian is usually preoccupied by understanding the details and meanings of the particular rather than by trying to generalize (which can be a pretty risky business in history, given the effects of forgetfulness and decay, of time colouring the past, and of death carrying off witnesses). Unstructured interviews are avoided since they tend to produce a mass of incompatible data, which can be analysed, but which can leave the researcher wondering whether other informants would have endorsed or rejected points that some had made but which they themselves did not spontaneously volunteer. It is more usual for oral history to use semi-structured interviews that allow informants to depict the past in their own words, following their own sense of what was important. The researcher, guided by the literature, documents and other interviews, will have a loose agenda of questions to ask and themes to explore, but the answers will be open-ended, and the interview will not be dominated by the researcher in the same way as is the case with surveys. Yet, oral historians are often anxious to get a picture that looks as though it might credibly represent the experience of people other than those who were interviewed. For that reason, they may take considerable care to try to get a sample of informants that mirrors the structure of the past in some way, for example, in terms of social class, occupations, geographical area or gender. So, their work may combine careful but non-random sampling with a semi-structured format.

It might be expected that informants' memories of things that happened up to half a century ago might be particularly unreliable (and there are questions about the reliability of our memories of yesterday, let alone of 50 years ago). This has been investigated and the opinion of two authorities (Lummis, 1987; Thompson, 1988) is that informants can speak in detail about things that were salient to them, such as critical incidents and processes they lived day in and day out. In fact, their memory of distant times can, in some respects, be better than their memory of more recent times. However, nothing should be taken on trust, so as much as possible should be checked against other sources. This is a bread-and-butter matter for historians, who were triangulating data long before social scientists had invented a geometrical term for the Renaissance practice of critical document study. Interestingly, oral historians have concluded that the errors they detect can, in themselves be revealing, showing a lot about myths and explanatory frameworks. Arguably, historians have an advantage here over social scientists. The social scientist investigates the contemporary world where informants may feel a need to put up a front. When the subject is something that happened half a century ago, that need is likely to be less strong.

As with social science researchers, oral historians tend to pay a lot of attention to building rapport in interviews so that they get the best quality data, although Lummis reports that he has 'had good open interviews with people with whom I felt little rapport and had no personal liking' (1987: 68). (We develop this theme of rapport in interviews in Chapter 7.) Since they will often interview the same informant repeatedly, there is a fair chance of confidence developing, so that the informant edges from 'public talk' to 'private talk'. A common aim in these interviews is to get as full a description of an event, milieu or time as possible, which means that the interviewer needs to be skilled at listening and probing. The list of probes and prompts is as long as the researcher's imagination. The important thing is to probe for clarification and detail *without* turning the interview into an interrogation and ceasing to listen. Box 6.3 shows some commonly used probes, which might be used by social science researchers as well as by oral historians.

Oral historians, like social science researchers, have considerable problems with data management and data analysis (see Chapter 11). However, the idea that there can be different readings of an archive is again a well-established one in history. The discipline handles this by requiring researchers to substantiate their claims with explicit, footnoted reference to an archive that is publicly available and submits interpretations to the test of the extent to which they are plausible to others in the disciplinary community. Again, there are parallels here with some social science approaches to establishing the credibility of research findings.

Lastly, the results of oral history work may most frequently appear in the form of a conventional academic report, but they also appear as broadcasts and sometimes lead to films, novels or other creative representations of a discovered past. Such practices are becoming more common in some social science departments.

## Designing an interview study: an example

These first six chapters have concentrated on the design of interview research. The following account of a large-scale study in which Peter was involved in 1994–6 draws together a number of themes that have been developed in these chapters. As you read it, you might consider whether the study could have been better designed to address issues identified in the literature; whether a different interviewing approach would have been more productive; whether the research team should have taken seriously a more positivist approach to reliability and validity; and whether they could have done anything to allow them to make

---

**Box 6.3   Some typical probes used in oral history**

(This is inspired by Patton, 1990)

- Detail-oriented probes. For example: 'When did that happen? Who else was involved? What were you doing at the time? What was your involvement in that situation? How did that come about? Where did it happen?' (Patton, 1990: 324). Did other people you knew think/act/feel etc. the same?
- That's interesting. I've heard other people say [*something rather different*]. How do you feel about that? Why? (Disconfirmation probe, to explore security of an answer and the reasoning behind it)
- Can you help me to understand better your position/why you felt that way/why you say that, etc.? (Amplification probe)
- Could you give me an example of that please, or tell me a story about it? (Clarification probe)
- Could you help me to understand better why it happened/what happened/why you felt like that etc.? (Explanatory probe)
- Was that also true for another aspect of life/at another time/all the time? (Category probe, exploring distinctiveness)
- So, was this something you felt strongly/that was important to you/that had big effects/that mattered a lot then etc.? (Significance probe)
- Silent prompt, using a nod of the head, hand movement, silence or eye contact to encourage the informant to keep on talking.

---

stronger claims about the generalizability of the findings. You will notice that we also take the opportunity to explore a distinction between spontaneous and receptive responses to interview questions (see page 87).

*The topic*   Changes in school teaching had led to claims that it was ceasing to be a profession. The same observation could also be made of medicine, law, social work, nursing, or probation work. This seemed to be an important topic in its own right, as well as one that could add to our understanding of professions, which is a significant area of interest in sociology.

*The literature*   We drew on four sets of writing.

First, there was the literature on professions and de-professionalization, which indicated some of the features that were often seen to define a profession *and* warned us that the definition of 'a profession' was much disputed. Consequently, our research could not begin with an off-the-shelf definition: we had to discover whether teachers saw their occupation as a profession and, if so, why.

Secondly, we were interested in the extent to which the concept of a profession was – or was not – embedded in teachers' thinking and practices. This meant examining the literature on culture, which helped us to understand how we might investigate teachers' cultures. Essentially, that directed us to see this as a study of beliefs and values, not of practices and actions.

Thirdly, the literature on teachers' work pointed to some of the pressure points and recent changes, which alerted us to the range of things that might be mentioned by informants.

Lastly, we noticed a body of work which suggested that what teachers taught had an influence on their work, which implied to us that we might think in terms of subject-based sub-cultures of teaching and ask questions accordingly.

We inferred from this literature that investigating these themes would need an approach that was sensitive to the world as teachers perceived it. Observational and experimental methods would be inappropriate for a study of teachers' beliefs. Using focus groups was also problematic. Given teachers' timetable and pressured working lives, it was doubtful whether it would be possible to convene any. Furthermore, they would have been of little help in establishing individuals' cultural understandings. Questionnaires were not seen as appropriate for a study of the depth and complexity of teachers' beliefs. The flexibility, interpersonal nature and interactive style of interviewing was the decisive factor in the choice of method. Telephone interviewing was rejected for some practical reasons, but also because it is recognized as being most appropriate for survey research. Consequently, long, semi-structured interviews were chosen to be the main research method. Fortunately, funds were available for this. An unfunded researcher might have been able to use the same approach (as some of Peter's students have subsequently done, with interesting results) but on a much smaller scale.

*Developing an interview guide*  The interview guide (reproduced in Box 7.5) was the fifth draft, the product of repeated discussion amongst the five researchers and of piloting with ten informants (who were not then used in the main study). It was based on five ideas:

- The guide had to avoid assuming something that was to be investigated, namely whether teaching is a profession.
- There should be few topics of discussion, so as to allow informants to develop their views at length. In the event, the guide contained nine, benchmark questions.
- The information of greatest interest would be that at 'the front of the mind' – that which was spontaneously volunteered by the informants. There would be much about which the teachers could talk, if prompted, but we were interested in the cultural constructs they used, rather than in those they could be prompted to talk about.
- We needed to see whether teachers' cultures were situationally dependent, such that different situations (teaching a subject, pastoral work) called on different qualities that teachers might deem to be professional in nature.
- We wished to know how the work of teaching had changed and whether any changes made teaching more or less of a profession in the teachers' eyes.

The interview guide was designed to allow informants to explain in depth what, if anything, made teaching a profession for them; how their work showed these professional characteristics in action (their professional cultures); and how the professional nature of their work had changed, if at all. Teachers' comments at the end of the interviews frequently showed that they had experienced the interviews as processes of meaning construction, processes that had tapped their practical consciousness. They frequently said that they had appreciated the invitation to use the concepts they constructed to analyse changes in their occupational circumstances. The pay-off to participants in interview studies is dealt with in more detail in Chapter 9.

*Selecting a sample*   Our literature review had suggested that we could talk in terms of 'the culture of teaching', which described cultural features that are common to the majority of teachers in the majority of schools. Yet, we also read that there were sub-cultures nested within the common culture, so we also needed to explore the culture*s* of teaching. For example, there has been growing awareness that teachers are teachers *of* something, which in secondary schools often means, first and foremost, academic subjects, which have different knowledge structures and vary in their range of preferred teaching methods. We also knew that the National Curriculum was affecting school subjects in different ways. In addition, there is some evidence that the subject department is the base organizational unit in teachers' lives and that even in 'effective' schools, departments vary in their effectiveness. Consequently, we decided to sample teachers in three distinct subject areas: mathematics, humanities and technology.

A large sample was needed to give adequate evidence about the culture*s* of teaching. A sample size of 60 from each area was manageable within the time and resources available to the team. Letters were sent to headteachers in schools in North–West England, inviting them to nominate classroom teachers of the three subjects who might be prepared to be interviewed. These teachers were then contacted, with the aim of achieving an equal number of male and female teachers of each subject.

*'Reliable' interviewing*?   The semi-structured, one-to-one interviews took paths that were to a greater or lesser extent unpredictable. So, it was common to find informants mingling discussions of professions in general with their views on the professional nature of teaching; describing changes in their work throughout the interview; and revising their earlier answers when explaining what made one teacher more professional than another. Furthermore, there were differences in the interviewers' natural styles, which were discussed and greater convergence of practice was achieved. Informants also differed. In some cases voluble informants meant that the interviewer said little, and in other cases even the most unobtrusive of the researchers was forced extensively to prompt, reframe and redirect questions.

These interviews were 'reliable' only in the sense that in each case informants were invited to talk at length about what they had in mind in response to nine questions. The team concluded that they were, however, well-suited to the research purpose.

*Generalizability* At first sight, a sample of 178 is sufficient for researchers to make strong claims about the generalizability of their findings. That was not the case.

The first reason depends on a distinction between spontaneous responses, which are unprompted answers to open-ended questions, and receptive responses, which are answers to closed questions. Where a respondent is asked to identify factors that have influenced them and is given a list of ten to choose from, it is a safe bet that their (receptive) answer will contain more factors than would have come from a spontaneous response to the open question 'What influences you?'

In this study the fact that an informant did not say something, did not mean that he or she was unaware of it or unable to talk about it. All that can be said is the way that the interview played out meant that the point was not spontaneously made at that time in that specific setting. At another time, in another interview, the point might have been made. It cannot be said that 33 per cent of informants thought that a defining feature of a profession was that it involved sustained education and knowledge acquisition. The most that can be said is that 33 per cent of informants spontaneously volunteered that point in the interviews. We cannot know whether the other 67 per cent would have agreed, had they been prompted by a closed question that gave them a list of defining features from which to choose. Because the data describe only what these people volunteered, it cannot easily be said that it represents the extent of their understandings: nor can we generalize about the likely responses of a different set of informants or to the population without making it clear that we are only making a generalization about spontaneous responses.

The second bar to the researchers making strong generalizations from their data was that some differences *were* found between teachers of the different subjects. The sample size of each group of subject teachers was no greater than 60. Indeed, if it is decided that 'Technology' is not really a subject but a combination of Home Economics, and Design and Technology, then the sample comprised fewer than 30 teachers of each contributory subject. Generalization from samples of 30 or 60 is more problematic than generalizing from the 178 teachers who actually participated. Furthermore, these were volunteers, and volunteers are not quite the same as non-volunteers (see page 58). It is worth remembering that the Kinsey Reports into human sexual behaviour (1948, 1953) were done with volunteers, which may reassure those intimidated by their accounts of the frequency and scope of human sexual activity.

It was felt that the research findings were consistent and coherent, and that the research could be shown to have been carefully done, which meant that they were securely enough based to have the potential to be generalizable. Participants who saw a report of our findings recognized the picture we painted, which added to the feeling of security in the findings. Then, when our findings were presented at conferences in the UK and overseas, through the international Professional Cultures of Teachers Project, as well as in journals and book chapters, they proved to be plausible to the research community. In other words, readers found the findings generalizable.

*Complementary work*   This series of interviews was complemented by:

- A questionnaire to get demographic and other unproblematic information.
- A series of follow-up interviews with 30 of the informants. This allowed us to check our initial findings, to probe some areas further and to explore new ones.
- A questionnaire focused on informants' experiences of professional development activities.
- A study of documents, newspapers and other materials on the recent history of teaching as a profession.
- A study of the activity of two professional teaching associations.
- Interviews with 13 policy makers and senior education administrators.

This could not really be described as triangulation, since interviews were necessarily the only source of data about teachers' beliefs. However, it was seen as important contextual work. In that sense, the whole study can be described as one using multiple methods and exploring the perspectives of stakeholders other than teachers (McCulloch, Helsby and Knight, forthcoming).

*Problems*

- We had problems conceptualizing 'culture', 'cultures' and 'professional'.
- We spent weeks trying to see how we could explore the professional nature of teachers' work without assuming that this work was professional in the first place.
- We needed a full-time secretary to set up the interviews.
- The volume of transcription was overwhelming. In some cases we had to accept interview notes rather than full transcripts (see Chapter 10).
- The analysis of such a volume of qualitative data was not a pleasant experience, although it did lead us to re-think the concept of reliable analysis of qualitative data (see Chapter 11).

**Conclusion**

With this chapter we come to the end of a long run through design issues. With the next we move into the 'nuts and bolts' of doing interviews. It is possible, of course, to interview without becoming immersed in the issues we have raised. Doing that, though, has a price. The price is that it is hard to know what an answer to the 'so what?' question would be, and without a clear sense of purpose, it is impossible to claim that the methods used are fit for the purpose. And we have consistently argued that the guiding principle in designing interview – or any other research – is not that methods should be chosen out of a belief that one method is intrinsically superior to others, but rather that they should be fit for the research purpose.

# 7    Achieving a Successful Interview

Like fishing, interviewing is an activity requiring careful preparation, much patience, and considerable practice if the eventual reward is to be a worthwhile catch. (Cohen, 1976: 82)

It is more and more the case that social science students undertake some sort of research exercise as part of their first or higher degree course. Very likely the project will involve interviewing, yet, as Cohen implies, eliciting information is not that simple. Even so, students quite often receive little specialized training or supervision in relation to the set of skills that effective interviewing requires. These include language skills (both written and spoken), social skills (for example, the ability to make interviewees feel at ease, tact and patience) and technical skills (handling recording equipment). At the same time, attention has been drawn to the fact that all research situations are contextual and comprise unique elements. Given this, Van Maanen, Manning and Miller (1988: 6) make the claim that 'Increasingly, fieldwork is regarded as a highly and almost hauntingly personal method for which no programmatic guides can be written.'

Against this background, the aim of the chapter is not to present a set of prescriptions but rather to offer guidelines and advice to help achieve a successful interview. The chapter is organized as follows. First, we discuss different ways of gathering data, including question design and developing conversation. This leads into a consideration of interviewer–interviewee relationships and how best to encourage interviewees to answer the questions asked of them. Next, we look at how to record the data generated, before concluding with a few suggestions for critically evaluating interviewing techniques.

## Collecting information

As noted in Chapter 1 (see Table 1.3), there are three major formats of interview, differentiated in terms of degree of structure or formality: structured, semi-structured and unstructured. Below, we take a more detailed look at the ideas and methods which underlie their different approaches to gathering data.

### Structured interviews

Structured interviews, designed to collect information about facts, attitudes, beliefs and behaviours, are generally employed in social surveys. As the researcher, you are responsible for deciding what is important in the study, what set of questions should be asked and who is the study population. It is important to point out that you must be sure you are asking the right questions, namely questions that will reveal information about the specific focus of enquiry. As we have said from the outset, in a structured interview format there is little freedom for respondents to talk about what is important to them, or raise their particular concerns.

Data can be obtained using face-to-face interviews, or alternatively through telephone interviews (see Chapter 6). In both instances, the interviewer uses a standardized interview schedule or scaling instrument to guide the interview. The questions on these documents are either read out or shown to the respondent. Reflecting the positivistic associations of the approach, the point of using such a standardized data collection tool is to demonstrate scientific rigour. To this end, it is important to reduce bias and produce results that can be replicated.

*Interview schedules*  Once you are confident of the precise focus of study and the target population, then you can begin to develop an interview schedule. This lists all the questions that you think need answering in order for you to shed light on the phenomenon being studied. Lofland (1971) is a very good starting point when it comes to designing an interview schedule. Start off by writing down questions which you think might have a direct or indirect bearing on the research. Sort through them all, and discard any that are irrelevant. Scrapping questions can sometimes be difficult, but even if you think they touch on interesting areas you have to be pragmatic – both you and the interviewee have limited time available for your respective tasks. Next, group together the remaining questions that are concerned with the same topic area; amalgamate any that are related. Check that the range of questions you are left with is sufficient to cover the topic area thoroughly – and if so, you have your basic interview schedule. The next step is to formulate individual questions.

The types of questions used in an interview schedule tend to fall into one of two categories: *closed questions* and *open questions*. To recall Box 1.1, closed questions are more restrictive. The interviewer decides in advance on each specific question, and also limits the range of possible response options by asking respondents to choose from a list of predetermined categories. The category 'Other' is often added in order to take account of answers that are appropriate but not listed. If respondents are being offered a range of alternatives to choose from (as in questions 1 and 2 in Box 7.1 below), these could be printed on a prompt card and shown to the respondent as appropriate. There is some possibility of probing responses, or helping people who might not understand the questions; this will be limited, though, given the aim of standardization.

One advantage of using closed questions is that you can incorporate pre-coded answer blocks, and transfer responses into their coded form during the interview itself. Box 7.1 gives an example of what a pre-coded interview schedule looks like. The three questions, or variables, have a variety of possible answers, numbered 1, 2, 3 etc. The coding box associated with each of the variables is in the column on the right-hand side of the page. Coding the interview schedule in advance will save time during the later stages of the research because it is then a simple matter to put (most of) the responses on to a computer (handling data from

---

**Box 7.1  Extract from a pre-coded interview schedule (Arksey, 1998)**

1  **What is your highest educational qualification?**
    CSE . . . . . . . . . . . . . . . . . . . . . . . . . . . . . . . . . . . . . .1  [1]
    GCE 'O' Level . . . . . . . . . . . . . . . . . . . . . . . . . . .2
    GCSE . . . . . . . . . . . . . . . . . . . . . . . . . . . . . . . . . . .3
    GCE 'A' Level . . . . . . . . . . . . . . . . . . . . . . . . . . .4
    Degree . . . . . . . . . . . . . . . . . . . . . . . . . . . . . . . . . . .5
    Other . . . . . . . . . . . . . . . . . . . . . . . . . . . . . . . . . . . .6

 (a) **What is your highest vocational qualification?**
    RSA . . . . . . . . . . . . . . . . . . . . . . . . . . . . . . . . . . . . . .1  [2]
    BTEC . . . . . . . . . . . . . . . . . . . . . . . . . . . . . . . . . . . .2
    NVQ (specify level) . . . . . . . . . . . . . . . . . . . . . . .3
    Other . . . . . . . . . . . . . . . . . . . . . . . . . . . . . . . . . . . .4

2  **Are you currently**:
    employed full-time . . . . . . . . . . . . . . . . . . . . . . . .1  [3]
    employed part-time . . . . . . . . . . . . . . . . . . . . . . . .2
    unemployed . . . . . . . . . . . . . . . . . . . . . . . . . . . . . .3
    retired . . . . . . . . . . . . . . . . . . . . . . . . . . . . . . . . . .4
    long-term sick . . . . . . . . . . . . . . . . . . . . . . . . . . . .5
    self-employed . . . . . . . . . . . . . . . . . . . . . . . . . . . .6

3  **If you are employed, are you a trade union member?**
    Yes . . . . . . . . . . . . . . . . . . . . . . . . . . . . . . . . . . . . .1  [4]
    No . . . . . . . . . . . . . . . . . . . . . . . . . . . . . . . . . . . . . .2

. . .

---

open questions is more complicated, and needs dealing with differently – see Chapter 11). Indeed, it may be that you have the equipment to key answers directly into the analysis software as you talk to the respondent.

Generally, closed questions do not accommodate those situations where the respondents feel that answers such as 'Well, yes and no really', or 'I can't say; it all depends' are more appropriate. The problem is that, even allowing for an 'Other' option in the response block, the predetermined answers are too confining for people to comment on the 'ifs' and 'buts' that apply to everyday life. If the nature of the study is such that exploring such nuances and more detailed personal views are important, then an open question like 'What do you do for recreation?' is better suited to the purpose than asking 'Do you take part in any of the following activities?', followed by a list of six or seven predefined alternatives.

Essentially, open questions are designed more as a trigger to stimulate the informant into talking freely about the particular area under discussion. Whilst this type of question can be fruitfully employed in studies collecting information about people's experiences or opinions, their value is double-edged in the sense that a large amount of material is produced which can prove difficult and time-consuming to analyse. Most interview schedules will include both closed and open questions, but given the drawbacks of the latter, it is preferable to use mainly closed questions.

*Ranking scales*  A ranking scale is one particular form of closed question. This is where the respondent is asked to place items in rank order, which then allows the researcher to determine their respective levels of importance. There is an example of a ranking scale in Box 7.2 (for a variant, see Box 3.2). It is worth remembering that the larger the number of alternatives presented, the more difficult the ranking exercise for the respondent – especially if this is taking place during a telephone interview, where visual aids such as response cards or diagrams cannot be used. Again, use prompts displaying the choices in face-to-face interviews.

---

**Box 7.2   Example of a ranking scale**

What do you think is important to marriage?

Please rank the following in order of importance to you.
Number them from 1 = most important, to 5 = least important

    Fidelity
    Understanding
    Good sex
    Respect
    Common interests

---

*Attitude scales*  Attitude scales can be fruitfully employed in structured interviews. One of the most widely used scaling techniques is the *Likert* scale. This measures people's responses along an attitude continuum. A set of statements or propositions relating to the issue in question is generated. Respondents are then asked to evaluate these in terms of fixed response categories such as 'strongly agree', 'agree', 'disagree' and 'strongly disagree'. In other words, the principle is that of polar opposites: the negative and positive terms are, as near as possible, direct opposites of each other. Sometimes a neutral mid-point will be included ('neither agree nor disagree' or 'undecided'), to accommodate respondents who do not have strong views on the issue in question. But if it is important to the research for interviewees not to sit on the fence, so to speak, then this option should be omitted. Box 7.3 shows two different versions of scale questions.

For a more detailed discussion of measurement scales, see Robson (1993) or de Vaus (1996).

---

**Box 7.3   Examples of scale questions**

**A   The government should make age discrimination at work a criminal offence**

| Strongly agree | Agree | Neither agree nor disagree | Disagree | Strongly disagree |

**B   How satisfactory is the home help provision you receive from social services?**

| Very satisfactory | Fairly satisfactory | Not very satisfactory | Not satisfactory |

---

*Question design*   There are important considerations relating to wording and phrasing that need to be taken into account when designing questions. Unclear, ill-thought-out questions run the risk of producing data that might be inadequate in terms of both quality and quantity. The guidelines below apply to questions used in structured, semi-structured and unstructured interviews. Some of the issues about language and interviewer–interviewee relationships are further developed in the following sections of the chapter.

- *Vocabulary.* The questions must be clearly understandable and appropriate for the particular social or cultural group being interviewed. If words or phrases are complicated, technical or 'jargonized', this can lead to confusion, and the respondent feeling incompetent – affects which are detrimental to the success of the interview.

  Be careful, too, about using questions drawing on concepts. 'Sexual harassment', for instance, may be a commonplace phenomenon for many people these days. However, when Hilary asked women in their late 70s and 80s about any incidents of sexual harassment which they were subjected to during the Second World War (see Summerfield, 1998), it was clear from their blank expressions that this was a concept they had great difficulty in understanding. Rather than assume that there was no such thing as sexual harassment 50 years ago, the question was changed to one which asked whether the interviewees could recall experiencing anything at the hands of men which they perceived as ill-meaning, mischievous, malevolent or unkind. The stories then flowed, and it was clear that sexual harassment had existed; it was just waiting to be named in the 1970s.

- *Prejudicial language.* Try not to use language that can be construed as containing assumptions that may reinforce particular beliefs and prejudices. The British Sociological Association has helpful guidance notes on the use of non-sexist language, non-disablist language and anti-racist language respectively. These are available through the Association's homepage on the World Wide Web (http://dialspace.dial.pipex.com/britsoc/).
- *Ambiguity.* Certain words can be interpreted in different ways, and it is important to make sure that interviewees understand the correct meaning from the point of view of the study. For instance, patients answering the question 'What is your opinion of the treatment you have received from your doctor?' might interpret 'treatment' in terms of medical care or conversely attitude and behaviour.
- *Imprecision.* Terms or phrases such as 'average', 'a great deal' or 'regularly' are vague, and likely to hold different meanings for each of us. Another example is the option 'employed part-time' in the list of possible answers to the question trying to determine the respondent's employment status in Box 7.1. Just what exactly is meant by 'part-time'? How many hours constitute working part-time? In retrospect, it would have been better to have been more specific and offered alternatives, for instance: employed for 10 hours a week or less, 11–18 hours, 19–25 hours, and so on. So, if you are asking for times or numbers, offer specific categories.
- *Leading questions.* Broadly speaking, it is not desirable to use questions that suggest or 'lead' interviewees towards a particular answer. Using emotive language sometimes has this outcome. For instance, there is a tacit suggestion in the question 'Don't you think that after five years living on benefits, it's time that you got a job?' which some people might find difficult to oppose.
- *Double-barrelled questions.* Questions that ask two in one, like 'Do your hobbies include swimming and cycling?', should be avoided for two reasons. First, it would be unclear whether an answer of yes or no applied to the first part, or to both parts; secondly, the answer might be both yes and no, making it difficult for the interviewee to answer. The solution is quite easy: divide the question into two.
- *Assumptive questions.* Try to refrain from using questions that contain assumptions. For instance, the question 'Do you go to work in your car' contains two assumptions: one, that the interviewee works, and two, that he or she drives a car. As it stands, the question overlooks the fact that not everyone engages in these two activities.
- *Hypothetical questions.* According to many methods textbooks, it is best to avoid using hypothetical questions as they are unlikely to generate any useful data. For instance, there is no guarantee that people's responses describing what they would do if they were confronted with a particular event or situation are an accurate guide to their behaviour in reality. Having said this, both of us have found that hypothetical questions can generate insightful data where people do have some direct experience or close knowledge of the issue being discussed (see example A in Box 7.4).

- *Personal or sensitive questions.* We devote the first part of the following chapter to a detailed consideration of techniques for eliciting information that is highly personal or covers sensitive topics. Suffice for now to say that if you feel such questions are necessary, pose them towards the end of the interview when hopefully you will have built up a relationship of trust. This includes asking for details about the respondent's personal characteristics such as marital status, educational achievements and work status. Some people find giving their age very embarrassing. If you do not need to know this exactly, then one possible solution is to show interviewees a prompt card on which you have identified a range of age groups: below 18, 18–29, 30–39, 40–49, 50–59, 60 and over. All people need to do then is indicate whereabouts in the range they fit.

  A number of researchers have made use of the vignette technique (Finch, 1987; Hughes, 1998). Vignettes are short stories generated by the researcher and focusing on hypothetical characters in particular situations. Interviewees are asked what they themselves would do in these circumstances, or alternatively how they think a third party might react. The latter mode of questioning specifically distances the interviewee from the issues being studied, and in this sense is impersonal and so less threatening.
- *Knowledge.* Do not assume any specialist, or even general, knowledge on the part of the interviewee. Whilst they may be willing to answer your questions, you need to make sure that members of the group you are targeting also have the ability to answer them. If the interview topic is complex, for instance attitudes to nuclear waste disposal or biotechnology, then it might be necessary to provide some sort of technical information or description at the outset to help people make a considered response. Of course, such information must be compiled in a way that avoids any particular bias or slant.
- *Memory recall.* Bear in mind that asking people to recall events from the past may not produce totally correct answers – not because people are telling untruths, but simply because they have forgotten. With a little ingenuity, though, you may be able to help overcome memory problems. If, for instance, you wanted to know what interviewees had studied at school, showing them a prompt card listing a whole range of subjects is likely to jog their memory. Conceivably, their responses will be more accurate.

Developing the 'right' questions is a process, and we suggest that first you write out in full the questions you are thinking of using in the interview. Try them on yourself, testing them out against the above recommendations. Once you feel relatively confident about the wording and phrasing of the questions, then consider how best to order or sequence them in the interview. Divide them up so that they follow some sort of logical sequence, and as we mentioned earlier, cluster together those questions on the same subject matter. Having decided on the wording of the questions, and the order in which they are to be placed, show them to friends, colleagues or your supervisor for their comments.

The next stage is to pilot the questions in an initial study; this is important even if time is short, because it is only when they are used in a trial run that you become aware of any shortcomings. Ideally, you ought to test the questions with a sub-sample of the intended study population. The responses and comments you obtain from piloting will help you assess whether the questions are clear, understandable, unambiguous and the like. This is also when you will find out how long it takes to work through the questions, a key factor for people deciding whether or not to take part in a study. It goes without saying that following on from this preliminary groundwork, you need to modify the questions to correct any problems which are highlighted.

Finally, you might want to consider writing an accompanying working paper, setting out the underlying rationale for the questions asked in the schedule. Essentially, this exercise involves brief explanations as to why you asked the questions you did, and in the sequence you chose. There is a sense in which this document is a very focused, mini literature review. This is because the idea is to justify the questions in the light of existing knowledge and your own research concerns. Although this represents yet more work, this is a useful way of formally thinking 'what is the point of asking these particular questions?'. The paper could form an appendix to the design and methods section of the final report.

## Qualitative interviews

Semi-structured and unstructured interviews are both qualitative data gathering techniques, designed to obtain information about people's views, opinions, ideas and experiences. Researchers adopting a feminist approach to interviewing (see Box 1.3) very often use one or other or both of these formats. Each is reminiscent of a detailed conversation, although of the two the unstructured type is far more interviewee-oriented or guided.

*Topic outline or aide-mémoire* Reinharz (1992: 21) reports on a study conducted by two feminist social scientists who used unstructured interviews to investigate the experience of infertility. The interviewers talked to every informant twice. In the first interview, there were no prepared questions beyond 'Tell me about what it's like not to be able to have a baby when you want to'. Quite clearly, in these circumstances very little documentation is needed beyond a topic outline or *aide-mémoire* containing a few brief, very general questions. And if you think that even a short reminder like this is superfluous, in fact it is an interviewing prop that provides useful reassurance – it lets you know that the general areas of the study are being covered, and it lets the interviewee know that you are taking a professional approach to the interview by preparing in advance.

The danger with unstructured interviews is that the freedom to talk has the potential to encourage long, detailed and rambling stories. Irrespective of how interesting these might be, they may not be especially relevant to the subject under discussion. Furthermore, if you are running out of time, then you risk missing some of the issues that are significant to the study. Finally, analysis of a series of very different stories can be problematic. Given these pitfalls, it is important that interviewers develop the skills and expertise needed to facilitate the discussion. In practice, this means redirecting the conversation back to the broad aims of the research, whilst bearing in mind that cutting off the telling of stories has the potential to obstruct people's ways of thinking and telling. Novice researchers might be well advised to attain a reasonable level of competence in semi-structured interviewing before attempting the unstructured format. Semi-structured interviews are likely to be more manageable, given that they are conversations organized, albeit loosely, around an interview guide.

*Interview guide* The interview guide serves as a framework for the main body of a semi-structured interview, and is based on the key questions that the study is addressing. The procedures for designing the guide are essentially the same as those described earlier in relation to interview schedules: start by devising a wide range of questions; eliminate any that are unlikely to contribute towards answering your research questions; pilot to see how well the remaining questions work and revise accordingly. See Box 7.4 for examples of questions that 'failed' in the actual interview situation.

One aspect where an interview guide differs from a schedule is in relation to the type of questions used. While both closed and open questions can be used, open-ended questioning is far more common given that the aim is to encourage communication. Accordingly, in semi-structured interviews researchers are advised to probe and prompt informants' responses in order to seek further elaboration, clarification, specific examples and so on. In many respects, devising the appropriate probes and prompts with which to press the interviewee is at least

---

**Box 7.4 'Failed' questions from a qualitative study examining family carers' experiences of hospital discharge for people with physical disabilities (Arksey et al., 1997)**

**A  What do you think makes for an effective hospital discharge?**

This question generated no worthwhile information; it was too vague, and informants did not understand it. The question was then approached in a different way. Interviewees were asked to identify three changes which, in the light of their recent experiences, they would make if they were in charge of the discharge process. The modified question yielded information which subsequently enabled the researchers to construct a model for good practice.

**B  What impact did hospital discharge have on the family?**

Here, the term 'impact' and the way in which the question was phrased made it difficult for informants to answer. When the original question was substituted with one which asked 'Can you tell me what has changed at home since the patient has been discharged from hospital?', the difficulty then was to stop people talking!

*tant* as developing the core questions (see Box 6.3 in the previous chapter ples of probes used in oral history interviews). They act as reminders to interviewer to check out particular sub-topics, and obtain more detailed or thoughtful information. Likewise, researchers routinely ask follow-up questions in order to pursue new ideas, unanticipated themes or the implications of what has just been said. In contrast to probes, though, follow-up questions cannot be drawn up in advance. Obtaining complete and in-depth answers is important. Data that are insufficiently substantial, precise or clear may not constitute adequate evidence from which to draw conclusions in the analysis stage of the research process.

The questions on the interview guide ought to be coherent and follow an orderly sequence. To help put the informant at ease, begin the interview by posing 'ice breaker' or 'easy-to-answer' questions. These may relate to the more factual aspects of the situation or general background details.

After this early round of questioning has been completed, you are now in a position to progress to the main questions. These should observe a logical order. Depending on what you are studying, following the chronological sequence of events is often a useful organizing principle. As we said earlier in the chapter, leave especially difficult questions – those that cover the more complex, abstract or sensitive interest areas – until the later stages of the interview. By this time, it is likely that enough trust has been built up between you and the interviewee for him or her not to feel threatened about disclosing what may turn out to be quite private information. Once these more demanding topic areas have been discussed, it is important to return to more neutral ground so that the interviewee is not left in a state of personal disquiet. This can be done by gently returning to more general, mundane or descriptive aspects of the study. And by way of concluding the interview, ask the informant whether there is anything they would like to add to what they have said already.

Box 7.5 contains an example of an interview guide; it is the one used in the study examining school teachers and professionalization that was discussed in the previous chapter. Note that in between the main questions are the supporting words and phrases intended to remind the interviewers of the areas they are supposed to probe on.

*Developing conversation and conversational skills*   It is important to remember that qualitative interviews are intended to encourage people to speak. They are guided conversations and the list of questions on your interview guide is just that: a flexible guide and not a rigid framework. We discussed the particulars of question design in the section focusing on structured interviews. Essentially, the same principles apply for questions used in semi-structured and unstructured formats. However, because you are trying to persuade people to speak more openly, some dimensions become more critical. Aspects where you need to be especially adept relate to language and the processes of listening.

*Choice of language*: As we indicated above, the point of qualitative interviews is that people talk about their experiences in their own terms. This means researchers should avoid imposing their customary vocabulary or categories, and

### Box 7.5 Example of an interview guide

What follows is a guide. You will wish to vary the patter, will find that some themes emerge spontaneously and may wish to vary the order of the questions as the interview develops. Probe and ask for elaborations and examples as time permits.

*Preface: Set the interviewee at rest: explain purpose of interviews; anticipated outcomes for us and the pay-back for the informant; rules of confidentiality etc.*

1  What sort of meaning does the word 'professional' have for you?
    *Probe answer for examples, elaboration etc.*

2  Using what you have said in (1), is teaching professional work?

3  Could we turn to your work as a teacher of a school subject? Could you help me to see what is professional about your work as a subject teacher?
    *Probe to see how far categories used in (1) and (2) apply.*

4  Could we turn to another aspect of your work, for example to the pastoral side of your work? Could you help me to see what is professional about it?
    *Probe to see how far categories used in (1) and (2) apply.*

5  Can you call to mind a recent episode or incident that has involved you acting as a professional and tell me about it, please?
    *Probe: What is there about that incident that shows you acting as a professional?*

6  Suppose you were involved in the appointment of a new colleague. You had to choose between two candidates. What criteria would you use in judging which of the two was the more professional?

7  Have there been any changes in the professional standing of teachers over the past ten years?

8  Was there ever a 'golden age' of teaching?

*Close by asking whether there is anything the informant wants to add about the professional nature of teaching. Promise copy of transcript and a summary of overall findings. Ask whether they would be prepared to participate in a follow-up interview (in 6–12 months' time).*

'controlling' the interview through language. Instead, they should take their lead from informants and adopt the words and expressions they use. If interviewees have some sort of local, everyday vocabulary of their own, involving slang or colloquial terminology, ask for the term to be explained since it is likely that there could be a number of feasible translations (Holland and Ramazanoglu, 1994). We have heard of one study examining drug misuse among young people in which it was not until the analysis stage, when problems and inconsistencies began to emerge in the findings, that the interviewer realized that she had misunderstood the diverse slang terms that the informants had used when talking about different drugs.

Similarly, interviewees might use phrases or concepts that are open to a variety of interpretations. In a research enquiry into marital breakdown, for example, someone might say, 'I just didn't know how I was going to manage; of the two of us, I'd always been the dependent one.' To understand the precise meaning behind the word 'dependent', the interviewer should encourage further clarification and elaboration by asking for the term to be explained more fully, together with examples for illustration.

The importance of mutual understanding of meaning cannot be over-emphasized. If meaning is not established, then the subsequent analysis stands to be flawed by unperceived misunderstandings or misinterpretations between the interviewer and the interviewee (see Chapter 11). One way to ascertain the accuracy of your grasp on interviewees' observations is occasionally to paraphrase or summarize what you understand from their answers, and invite feedback.

Researchers adopting a feminist approach to interviewing argue that conventional or standard language can act as a barrier to women fully expressing themselves: the prevailing terminology and concepts simply do not fit women's experiences. Devault (1990), for instance, draws on the terms 'work' and 'leisure' to claim that many of the household activities that women carry out do not sit happily in either classification. In these situations, one strategy is for the researcher and the interviewee to work together to construct a 'shared' language, terms that are either invented or given new meanings, and which seek more perfectly to represent individual experience. A major consequence, however, is that the researcher is actively involved in the production of data (Cunningham-Burley, 1985; Knight and Saunders, 1999).

*Critical listening*: As well as being competent in questioning, the skilled interviewer also needs to be an active listener. This involves attentive listening, not only to the actual words that are being said, but also to how they are being said, for instance emphases, and the emotional tone of the speaker. One way to check on the extent to which you listen rather than talk during an interview is to review a transcript, looking for how often and how much you actually speak yourself.

During the interview itself, you are essentially on the look-out for key words or signals that will help you get a handle on the interviewees' perspectives and experiences relating to the focus of study. The aim is to tease out what for them are significant, special or recurrent themes. By listening carefully, you can introduce new questions as unexpected topic areas are opened up by the informant. In addition, you might spot puzzles or contradictions in the account which you might wish to raise, but taking care not to do this in a manner that could be regarded as confrontational. Highlighting discrepancies in this way and asking for further elaboration has the potential to produce deeper and more insightful answers.

What is left out of a conversation can sometimes be as important as what is included. By drawing on your own background knowledge, you should be able to identify incomplete replies, omissions or gaps in what is being said. Alternatively, if you suspect the informant feels inhibited from expressing themselves fully then, depending on the strength of the relationship that has been built up, you may like to suggest the issue yourself.

Our final point is to remind you that non-verbal signals such as eye contact, a smile, a nod of the head or hand gestures show you are attending to the interviewee. So, too, can brief utterances like 'hmm', 'I see', or 'right'. These messages all serve to indicate that you are listening, understand what is being said and want to hear more. But before you can exploit your communication skills to the full, you have first to persuade interviewees that they really do want to speak with you.

## Building up good relationships

If you believe that the quality of data is dependent on the quality of the relationship built up between the interviewer and the interviewee, then it is crucial to know how best to go about creating and maintaining these ties. There are different aspects to inducing positive feelings; we discuss these under the headings of trust and rapport, background knowledge and personal appearance. The points we make are applicable to all three interview formats, although some are more pertinent to semi-structured and unstructured interviewing.

### Trust and rapport

From the time of the initial meeting, which best takes place in comfortable and familiar surroundings, the researcher must attempt to establish rapport. Rapport refers to the degree of understanding, trust and respect that develops between the interviewer and the interviewee. Fostering trust is a continuous process, but given that many interviews in small-scale research are 'one-offs' and completed within less than two hours, what happens in the opening stage is especially crucial to the success of what follows. Depending on the sensitivity of the topic area, some informants might find the situation quite stressful. We look in detail at how to deal with emotional reactions in the next chapter; for now we would just say be alert to any signs of distress. Closing the interview appropriately is important. As well as saying 'thank you' for taking part, make sure you end on a positive note. In Box 7.6, we have compiled a list of what we see as fruitful ways to develop and maintain a good relationship.

---

**Box 7.6 Some ways of fostering a climate of trust in interviews**

**Opening the interview**

- Be friendly, polite and open. However, this is culturally specific! Elderly people can take poorly to being addressed by their first name, and can see modern casual dress as quite inappropriate.
- Indicate the significance of the study, its potential benefits and that the interviewee's comments will be valuable.
- Refer in positive terms to other interviews you may have conducted during the study.
- Explain how the interview will be conducted, for example how long it should last, and the general areas to be covered.
- Give the interviewee the opportunity to ask questions.
- Confirm your commitment to research ethics (see Chapter 9): make guarantees of confidentiality and anonymity; ask interviewees to sign an informed consent form.
- Ask for permission to audiotape, rather than assume agreement.
- In the case of follow-up interviews, begin those with an appreciation of what was said in earlier ones.

**During the interview**

- Listening, making eye contact, and saying encouraging things all help to make the interview develop in ways that encourage the informant to disclose more.
- Be sensitive to signs of emotional reaction.
- Avoid conveying a sense of urgency or impatience.

**Closing the Interview**

- Leave people with a feeling of success, for instance indicate how valuable and insightful the observations generated have been.
- Confirm what will happen next: how and when the results will be made available; whether interviewees will be offered the chance to check transcripts, or a draft of the research report; if and when people are likely to be contacted for follow-up work.

**After the Interview**

- Write to thank the interviewee for taking part in the study.

Researcher self-disclosure has been proposed as one way to foster trust, although opinion is divided about how much of your own life and interests should be revealed. Some scholars advocating feminist approaches to interviewing argue that interviewers and interviewees should share experiences and points of contact (Oakley, 1981; Finch, 1984). In contrast, others believe that over and above a certain level, self-disclosure can be intimidating and may produce a negative reaction in informants (Measor, 1985; Ribbens, 1989). It is also important to remember a point to be elaborated later, which is that overuse of self-disclosure can be misinterpreted by the interviewee and may risk jeopardizing your personal safety (see Chapter 9). We would suggest that you follow your own intuition, which means you will probably vary the amount you disclose about yourself from one interview to the next. The obvious rule of thumb is to offer information if you think it will encourage trust and openness, but not if you think it may obstruct data collection. Because self-disclosing about your own life has the potential to downplay professional status and diminish power, this tactic may not be especially appropriate when interviewing élites (see Chapter 8).

The notion that informants might be difficult or troublesome does not sit comfortably with efforts to establish good relations, yet as Oakley (1981: 56) notes: 'Interviewees are people with considerable potential for sabotaging the attempt to research them.' Cotterill (1992) is one researcher who, during her examination of maternal relationships between women, found she sometimes had to deal with reluctant and uncooperative informants. Morse (1991) similarly notes that informants may impede the data collection process by resisting the interviewer's agenda, speaking superficially or exaggerating real experiences in efforts to hold the researcher's attention. For people who do insist on pursing their own concerns rather than yours, it is vital to try to drag them back to the business in hand. This is easier said than done, but watching skilled interviewers try to get politicians to answer the questions put to them can sometimes be a useful learning exercise. If the facilities are available, there is much to be gained from observing and reviewing your performance on a video tape.

Maintaining a well-mannered attitude is difficult if the researcher opposes what interviewees say, or feels they are being evasive, deceptive, aggressive or whatever. In the interests of the research, though, this may be the time to adopt an instrumental and calculating attitude (see Chapter 9). Collinson (1992) describes the dilemma he found himself in as interviewees' accounts 'generated in me a mixture of amazement, disagreement, and antagonism' but at the same time he had to acknowledge that 'they were also very "useful" for the project' (p. 104). What should be realized is that negative reactions may have implications for the reliability of the study. This is because the way we react to people influences the questions we ask, what we hear and how we interpret what is said. In other words, the researcher's own responses can distort or bias the analysis. From this point of view, it is useful to keep a log book recording personal feelings and reflections on the interview (Rubin and Rubin, 1995). These written comments can act as pointers, and signal where any bias may enter into the analysis.

*Background knowledge*

Competent interviewing and listening are closely associated with background knowledge (see Chapter 8). Where is this sort of information available? The literature review is an excellent source of background reading. If your study is topical, newspaper and magazine articles can provide insights into popular viewpoints. Alternatively, if it is to do with policy making, find out whether minutes of relevant meetings are public documents, and if so, read them.

Having some prior understanding with regard to individual interviewees, and their own set of circumstances, is also important. For example, when I (Hilary) was interviewing people with physical disabilities, I did not always understand the seriousness and full implications of the disease or condition they were suffering from. Looking back, some of the questions I asked must have seemed inane and meaningless. In a subsequent project involving disabled children, I prepared for each interview by reading about the child's particular medical condition and was then able to ask informed questions.

Demonstrating that you are knowledgeable about the area in which you are interviewing is valuable in two ways. First, you will have more credibility with the interviewee if you can demonstrate in your questions that you are familiar with the context of the study. This is an especially important factor when 'interviewing up', that is interviewing people higher in status than yourself. Secondly, there are implications in terms of the trustworthiness of the study. It is less likely that interviewees will try to be misleading or deceitful because they will fear being detected.

*Personal appearance*

Dress and personal appearance may affect an interview, in the sense that the interviewee may be assessing and making judgements about the (ability of the) interviewer on the basis of what they can see. The literature (Warren, 1988) is full of examples of research projects where investigators have adopted different kinds of dress and hair style in an attempt to establish rapport and gain acceptance.

Collinson (1992) describes how he was concerned to look 'professional' and 'competent' when interviewing managers. Looking 'well dressed' was particularly important, and involved wearing a suit, polished shoes and carrying a leather briefcase. In marked contrast, for his interviews with members of the shopfloor workforce he wore 'relaxed' and 'informal' clothes, joked and swore as the men did, and generally tried to lessen any class or status differentials. Collinson's attire was acceptable to the respective groups, which in turn encouraged people to talk. The strategy worked for him, and there is every reason to think it will work for you. This may well mean you will have to invest in outfits that include the casual and informal, the fashionable and trendy, and also conservative-looking suits that signal you are a professional.

## Recording the data

We have given you some advice about asking questions, and persuading people to answer them. Now it is time to think about how to record responses in an accurate and retrievable form. As the first section indicated, with survey work this is generally a case of ticking boxes, or circling numbers in (pre-coded) answer blocks on the interview schedule. Alternatively, answers can be entered directly on a computer. The options available when qualitative data are involved include hand-written notes, audio- and videotaping.

### Note-taking

Note-taking is cheap; you need only paper and a couple of pens or pencils. On the other hand, it can be slow, is open to charges of selective recording and requires practice and skill. It might be that you take notes as a 'fall-back' measure, as Hilary did when she was interviewing someone whose voice box had been removed because of cancer of the throat. However, if you envisage taking notes on a regular basis then it might be worthwhile devising your own shorthand or other form of customized speedwriting. Another useful aid is a simple form containing sections or headings that reflect the main topic areas to be covered during the interview. Key words, significant terms and the occasional verbatim comment can be written down in the relevant space. As soon as possible after the interview use these 'triggers' to help you expand on what was said. Bear in mind, though, that the longer you wait the more detail you are likely to forget.

The use of hand-written notes, in conjunction with tape recordings, is described in Box 7.7.

### Audiotaping

Audiotaping is probably the most popular method of recording qualitative interviews. There are a number of advantages. The interviewer can concentrate on what is said. There is a permanent record that captures the whole of the conversation verbatim, as well as tone of voice, emphases, pauses and the like (but note that when agreeing to a study taking place, ethics committees sometimes make it a condition that the tapes are destroyed afterwards; see Chapter 9 for further discussion about obtaining ethical approval). Using a tape recorder demonstrates to informants that their responses are being treated seriously. Finally, the costs involved in purchasing a good quality tape recorder, microphone and cassette tapes are not too prohibitive.

There are disadvantages, though. In particular, transcribing the tapes can be a lengthy process; as we have noted before, a one-hour tape can take up to ten hours to transcribe fully. Further, the idea of taping the interview might increase nervousness or dissuade frankness. When I (Hilary) asked a prominent ergonomist whose work involved acting as an expert witness in personal injury litigation cases whether I could tape our interview, he agreed but indicated that his responses would then be 'public' rather than 'private', elaborates the distinction between

---

**Box 7.7   Note-taking while interviewing**

One of us did a series of semi-structured interviews with well over 100 young children. The children were told stories or given a problem and then asked questions. The responses they could give were quite limited in number and could be simply summarized, there and then. They were also asked to explain their thinking, and it was simple to paraphrase the reasons they gave. Analysis of the notes gave a pattern and reference back to the tape recordings of the interviews supplied apposite quotations.

Interviews with 178 schoolteachers were routinely summarized in note form. For example, teachers were asked whether they thought teaching was a profession. Their answers were predictably 'yes', 'yes with reservations', 'not sure', 'no, but . . . ' and 'no'. They were asked to explain their answers and notes were made of the ideas they used in those explanations: for example, one set of notes reads 'Yes: (a) training, (b) level of knowledge, (c) status, (d) ethics.' Again, these points could be fleshed out by reference to the subsequent transcripts and to the tape recordings, as the need arose. For most purposes, the notes were sufficient for data analysis and considerably speeded up the process.

---

'public' and 'private' accounts. (Cornwell, 1984.) In other words, without the tape recorder running he was prepared to disclose 'insider' information about the world of occupational injury claims. My on-the-spot decision was to put the machine away, produce a couple of sheets of paper and write furiously!

We both know of researchers who have 'lost' interviews in the sense that they ended up with either no recording or one which was inaudible. To try to ensure this does not happen to you, Box 7.8 gives hints on audiotaping.

### Videotaping

Recent developments in video technology mean that it is now more widely available. None the less, videotaping is not commonly used to record interviews apart from, perhaps, focus groups. Its current limited role reflects factors such as the expense involved, the specialist training needed to operate the technology effectively, the vast amount of material to be analysed and the possible intrusion it may create in the actual interview setting. Certainly, it is questionable how comfortable interviewees are about video recordings. In one focus group Hilary knows of, the participants refused to take part in the event if it was going to be videoed.

Despite their disadvantages, video recordings produce a wealth of information, both verbal and non-verbal. And if facial and bodily expressions, gestures and the like are as important to the study as is the content of what is said, then this is the medium for you – assuming that you also have the time required to undertake

---

**Box 7.8   Advice on audiotaping**

- Read the operating instructions for the tape recorder.
- Practise using the equipment, trying out features like the pause and record buttons.
- Check the batteries, and change them frequently.
- Always carry spare batteries and spare cassette tapes. We find C90 tapes work best.
- Before each interview, test out the optimum setting for the recording level. A poor quality recording causes problems later on when it comes to transcribing.
- At the start of the interview, position the tape recorder and microphone close to those who will be speaking; there is more scope for this with battery operated machines.
- Try to eliminate background noise, for example ask for windows to be closed if there is heavy traffic outside.
- Turn the microphone on!
- After each interview, write down the informant's name, and the date of the interview, on each tape used. If any tapes are likely to be seen by people not directly involved in the research, use an identifier code in order to preserve anonymity. Other information might be useful, for example the length of the interview.
- If finances allow, make a second copy of the tape, especially if they are being sent away to outside transcribers. The duplicates can always be wiped and reused at a later date.

---

the subsequent analysis. (See Jordan and Henderson [1995] for a more detailed consideration of the use of video technology.)

## Self-evaluation

Interviews, especially in the early days of a research study, can leave a lot to be desired. And regardless of how experienced you are, there is always a need to stand back and assess how the interview went. Accordingly, it is important that at regular intervals throughout the study you take stock to see what worked well, what did not work and where there is scope for improvement. Having diagnosed a particular problem area, see if you can think of how best to overcome or circumvent it. If it helps to talk with someone outside the study, then ask friends, your tutor or supervisor, or an experienced interviewer for assistance.

Some general advice about appraising your interviewing technique is presented in Box 7.9.

---

**Box 7.9   Evaluating interviewing practices**

At regular intervals, review your approach to interviewing in the light of the following questions. In qualitative interviews, check these points against transcripts or audio tapes when available. If possible, ask an experienced interviewer to critically evaluate your interviewing skills.

- How well is the interview schedule or guide working?
- Is the interview taking too long?
- Does the interviewee understand the questions?
- Which questions work? Which questions fail?
- Do you miss places where you could probe for more detailed information or examples?
- Do you miss places where you could ask follow-up questions?
- Do you talk too much instead of listening?
- Do you build up good relationships with the interviewees?
- Is there anything to indicate that you are gaining people's trust and confidence?
- Are you able to encourage interviewees to talk freely and openly with you?
- Do you feel you leave interviewees in a relaxed and untroubled condition?

And possibly the most important question of all:

- Are the data shedding light on the research questions you are trying to answer?

---

## Conclusion

In this chapter we have presented guidelines to help achieve a successful interview. The strategies and techniques we have suggested form the basis of good interviewing practice; the more you try them out, the more you will enhance your skills in this area. In the following chapter, we build on these foundations and consider the special approaches that are needed when conducting research in settings that manifest unique characteristics.

# 8    Interviewing in Specialized Contexts

This chapter addresses the challenge of interviewing in contexts that incorporate special or distinctive characteristics. We start by exploring issues raised when asking questions that cover sensitive subject matter. This is followed by ideas for successfully interviewing particular study populations. We illustrate our position through considering three distinct study populations: children and adolescents, people with learning disabilities and élites. Even though many of the interview practices that apply to these groups are similar to those which we discussed in the last chapter, particular sets of issues arise that are exciting to address and also complex.

Our purpose in this chapter is to attend to the special considerations involved in encouraging people to disclose information that may be personally upsetting or discrediting, and handling any subsequent emotional reactions; exploring ways of eliciting views from children, individuals with limited language skills, or those who communicate in different ways; gaining access to individuals used to VIP treatment; interviewing on complex, technical subjects.

## Asking sensitive questions

Some research areas are more obviously emotive, sensitive or controversial than others, for instance sexual behaviour, child abuse, health and illness, bereavement, domestic violence and unemployment. However, research topics that on the surface appear mundane may none the less manifest sensitive aspects as the work progresses. This is in part because the concept of sensitivity is socially constructed, and what matters in the research situation is what the interviewee finds sensitive (Fielding, 1990). Lee and Renzetti (1990) suggest three factors are common to studies involving sensitive subject matter. First, they are in some way threatening to those being studied. Secondly, they involve 'costs': people might experience feelings of guilt, shame or embarrassment, or face unwelcome consequences. Thirdly, the researchers might be endangering their personal safety, or risking sanctions from friends and colleagues by studying what is perceived to be a tainted subject.

As the researcher, there are two related considerations to take account of when asking questions that are personal and could be conceived as threatening. First, you have to persuade interviewees to answer such questions honestly, yet without losing face. People are concerned about impression management (Goffman, 1959) and want to present themselves in a favourable light, which can mean they are reluctant to admit to improper behaviour. Secondly, it is important not to cause undue upset or distress. Ethically, it is your responsibility to ensure that interviewees are at minimum risk of harm (see Chapter 9).

So, what are the special approaches and procedures to adopt when asking potentially threatening questions? We present guidelines first for structured interviews, and then for qualitative interviews. In practice, some of the suggestions are applicable and useful across the range of interview formats. After a look at how to deal with emotional displays, the section is completed by a discussion about handling requests for help, and the implications this may have for research outcomes.

### Asking sensitive questions in structured interviews

The literature is full of examples of studies where interview schedules have been used to collect factual data such as the incidence and prevalence of a wide range of sensitive behaviours. Recollect, for instance, the pioneering survey work on human sexual behaviour by Kinsey and his colleagues (1948, 1953).

To recall earlier discussions, it is crucial to obtain valid and reliable information (see Chapter 4). But research (Sudman and Bradburn, 1982) shows that in structured interviews people will overstate socially desirable behaviours and activities, such as registering to vote, book reading, going to cultural events like concerts and the theatre, and giving to charity. Conversely, people under-report socially unacceptable behaviours like illegal activities (drug use, say, or benefit fraud), drinking and gambling. Reducing the level of threat in sensitive questions ought to decrease biased and inaccurate responses, and produce data that are more reliable.

An interesting point to note is that there is little evidence to support the generally held view that the more personal the mode of collecting the data, the less interviewees will admit to socially undesirable behaviours, so the more distorted and unreliable the information (Sudman and Bradburn, 1982). In other words, the idea that self-completion questionnaires are better at asking sensitive or threatening questions than telephone interviews, which are themselves better than face-to-face interviews, does not hold water. Broadly speaking, you are just as likely to elicit information about sensitive items using face-to-face techniques as over the telephone; indeed, some research suggests that it is more probable that respondents interviewed in person will answer sensitive questions (Frey, 1989).

Below is a range of strategies for question design that are aimed at encouraging frank and accurate reporting of perceived sensitive or undesirable behaviours. The various techniques have been tried and tested by Sudman and Bradburn (1982) during the course of their empirical work. Some are applicable in 'ordinary' interviews and were mentioned in the previous chapter, but we are repeating them for the sake of convenience. A number of the suggestions appear to flout the conventional wisdom on designing questions for interview schedules; unfortunately it is beyond the scope of the book to undertake a detailed discussion of Sudman and Bradburn's underlying rationale.

- Use open questions rather than closed questions. This is because pre-determined responses are generally ordered from the least frequent to the more frequent (or *vice versa*). There is a tendency for respondents to avoid extreme responses on a list, and some will under-report by choosing a more middling response. Further, the highest response set by the researcher might not capture those respondents very heavily engaged in the activity, again leading to inaccuracies.

- Use long questions rather than short questions. Longer questions can increase the reported frequencies of undesirable behaviours, but – and this is important – the length of questions makes no difference to the respondent's willingness to admit to ever engaging in the activity.
- Use familiar words. Ask the respondent to select their own wording (e.g. 'love making'), and then substitute this for the standard phraseology (e.g. 'sexual intercourse') in the relevant questions. This technique puts people at ease, and has been shown to increase the reported frequencies of undesirable activities.
- Load the question. Suggesting that the particular behaviour is very common lowers the level of threat, so a question could be prefaced with 'Even the calmest of parents get angry at their children some of the time. Did your child(ren) do anything in the past seven days, since [*date*], to make you, yourself, angry?' (p. 75). Using an authority figure to endorse the activity has the same effect: 'Many doctors now think that drinking wine reduces heart attacks and improves digestion. Have you drunk any wine in the past year?' (p. 76). This sort of deliberate loading reduces understatements of undesirable activities.
- Choose appropriate time frames. In principle, questions about events in the past ought to be less threatening than those relating to the present. Pose a question asking whether the informant has 'ever, even once' (p. 77) indulged in the behaviour. If the answer is yes, follow up by asking about the behaviour during, say, the previous 12 months.
- Embed the question. Questions can appear more or less sensitive depending on where they fit in terms of the overall interview schedule. They should not be asked at the start because this might induce feelings of unease and reduce cooperation. Asking a series of more threatening questions first may mean those that are highly salient to the study will then appear less intimidating. Alternatively, you could gradually lead up to the key questions via other, less threatening, ones. A further suggestion involves 'disguising' the main focus of study. For instance, questions about drinking patterns are more likely to be answered if they are part of a set asking about general consumer behaviour rather than alcoholism *per se*.

To some extent, the point mentioned earlier about not causing harm to study participants is less applicable to structured interviews (but see Kitson et al., 1996). This is because the questions asked tend to deal with sensitive issues at a superficial level rather than in depth; moreover, the interview does not usually last very long. Even so, you still need to be alert to possible emotional responses, and part of the next section discusses how to handle reactions of this kind.

*Asking sensitive questions in qualitative interviews*

In our discussion about unstructured interviews in the previous chapter, we gave the example of an enquiry that started off with just one request: 'Tell me about what it's like not to be able to have a baby when you want to' (quoted in Reinharz, 1992). Cannon (1989) used a semi-structured approach in her study examining the experiences of women living with breast cancer. Her opening question was, 'Would you tell me the story, in any way you choose, of what happened when you first noticed something wrong with your breast.' It is stating the obvious to say that the subsequent discussions were emotionally (and in Cannon's case, physically) distressing for both the interviewer and the interviewee. The subject matter being talked about was both highly intimate and emotive; moreover – initially at any rate – the individuals concerned were not well known to each other.

Surprisingly, a trawl of the research methodology texts suggests there is little specific guidance on how best to handle these sorts of situations (there are some exceptions such as Brannen [1988] and Lee [1993]). This means that researchers can be left having to get by on common sense, level-headedness and improvisation. This is not difficult for those aspects of non-sensitive and sensitive interviews that are in essence the same: establishing rapport and trust; facilitating conversation; probing ambiguities and contradictions; following up new ideas; and confirming meaning and understanding by checking out the informant's observations and views. But what about other dimensions? Table 8.1 identifies the issues that do need special attention, together with procedures to help deal with them. Unlike in survey work, the primary concern is to protect the informant; the data are regarded as trustworthy because of the depth of detail and the collaborative way in which they are produced.

*Dealing with displays of emotion*   It is apparent from Table 8.1 that interviewers may need to be able to cope with displays of crying, grief, distress and the like. The situation can be discomforting for both parties: the interviewee is embarrassed and may feel she has lost control, whilst the interviewer is uncertain about how to respond. However, it does not help the situation if you over-react. One way to keep things in proportion is to think of handling any emotional response as a further development of the trust and rapport building that went on in the opening stages of the interview. Kitson et al. (1996) document the training given to interviewers involved in studies of violent death and divorce:

- Acknowledge and accept any tears by maintaining eye contact; offer paper tissues (an action that legitimates the distress).
- Say something along the lines of 'These are hard things to discuss, but perhaps it will help to talk about them' (p. 186). In other words, try to talk through the issues rather than abruptly changing the subject.
- Keep the emotional charge down by sitting quietly until the informant has calmed down and feels ready to carry on. We would add here, do not assume the informant will wish to continue. If in doubt, raise this question and make a joint decision about how best to proceed.

TABLE 8.1  *Good practice when asking sensitive questions in qualitative interviews*

| Issues needing special attention | Procedures to follow |
| --- | --- |
| Informed consent: when first agreeing to be interviewed, informants might not appreciate where the discussions might eventually lead, and the extent of what they might reveal | Provide full information about what being involved in the study is likely to mean. Assert the right not to answer specific questions. Renegotiate consent as the research progresses, for instance at the start of each interview in longitudinal work (see Chapter 9) |
| Disclosures will be very personal, intimate and possibly threatening; they may be discrediting or stigmatizing. Divulging information of this nature increases the informant's vulnerability (not to mention the interviewer's power) | Take appropriate measures to ensure confidentiality and anonymity, including the removal of identifying features from fieldnotes, transcripts, computerized data and cassette tapes. Remember that once results are in the public domain, it is difficult to control how the work is used (see Chapter 9) |
| Interviews will be emotionally demanding, and might encourage outbursts of grief, distress, tears, anger. Pauses and silences will follow as informants regain their composure. These intentions are likely to be lengthy events, occasionally developing into more of a monologue than an interactive conversation. Overall, it is likely that the experience for both parties will be stressful | Be sensitive to the needs of informants. Let them take the lead in choosing whether to introduce especially distressing issues, or when to draw back. Listen, be supportive and encouraging, and empathize. End individual discussions (and the series as a whole if the work is longitudinal) on a positive note (see below) |
| Extent of involvement: the relationship will shift from one of stranger to trusted confidante and intimate, and possibly develop into personal friendship | Strike a balance between (over-) identification with informants and their situation and professional integrity, which might mean maintaining a degree of distance. In any event, involvement is a two-way process and will depend on how individual informants view the role of the interviewer (and the study) in their lives |
| Interviewees might request, or expect, some form of help, advice or information | State at the outset that there are no resources to provide on-going help or support. If appropriate, pass on information and contact details of local agencies to approach for help and advice. Note that interventions can lead to changes in the behaviours and views of informants, which can in turn affect study outcomes (see below) |
| Interviewers may feel: guilty about intrusions into privacy; distressed as informants relate their experiences and become upset themselves; powerless to change the informant's situation | Develop adaptive mechanisms, and maintain a degree of social and emotional detachment. Seek support from other researchers, colleagues or friends (see Chapter 9). Remember that many informants do find the interview process cathartic (see Chapter 9) |

You might find the 'sitting quietly' more difficult than you imagine. Cannon (1989, 1992) notes how she had to learn to sit through pauses for tears without becoming embarrassed or making small talk. A useful strategy for her was to make tea; alternatively, physical contact like holding hands was comforting. Finally, it goes without saying that at the end of the interview you do not make a quick dash for the door, and certainly ought never to leave anyone in a state of distress.

Given the above, it might come as a surprise to learn that there is now substantial evidence to suggest that interviews can be cathartic, even if they give rise to deep emotional reactions. This is because the process of telling the story – perhaps for the first time – has the potential to lead to greater insight and understanding of both oneself and the problem to be confronted, which can in turn be a step towards solving the difficulties. According to Kitson et al. (1996: 184), 'it may be that in giving individuals an opportunity to talk about their experiences, [researchers] perform a welcome service rather than subject them to an ordeal'. Hilary can vividly recall Molly, unexpectedly thrust into the demanding role of full-time carer, telling her that she was the first person Molly had talked with since her husband had suffered a stroke. Although he had been a hospital in-patient for six months, no member of staff from either the hospital or the local social services department had shown any interest in how she was managing. In fact, Molly's greatest source of comfort throughout this whole period was Flossie, the pet rabbit. According to Molly, Flossie was 'the friend who listens all the time'.

## Providing help for interviewees

There can be occasions when people taking part in research studies ask you for practical assistance. These sorts of situations may lead to ethical dilemmas, and it is important to know where to draw the line (Polsky, 1967). As a social science researcher you are doubtless keen to gather as much data as possible, but as Polsky (1967) found out, it is possible that the people you are studying – in his case, New York criminals – may try to capitalize on your researcher role and manoeuvre you into taking part in deviant or illegal activities. Whilst this is a somewhat extreme example, it is nevertheless not uncommon in research studies – especially those involving emotionally sensitive areas – for interviewers to be approached for advice and help. This can pose problems for the researcher, who should not take on the role of amateur counsellor (Owens, 1996). A useful compromise is to act as a point of access and give interviewees a pack containing practical information about appropriate services and/or benefits, as well as contact details of sources of assistance. These might include local citizen's advice bureaux, relevant support groups, telephone helplines or freephone numbers, and lists of voluntary organizations. In one study Hilary was involved in, a support mechanism was set up. A nursing professional from each hospital taking part in the project was identified; her name and telephone number were then passed on to any informant seeking help.

Providing help has implications for research using multiple interviews. Owens (1996), studying male infertility 'careers', describes how some informants asked him for advice and information about technical issues. He points out that explaining terms such as 'sperm motility', and the processes of testing and treatment, has the potential to affect the research outcomes in unknown ways. This is because people might, on the basis of their enhanced understanding, alter their behaviour. These changes are then attributable to the researcher's intervention rather than people's own experiences. Although Owens does not mention it, another point is that not everyone will have been treated in the same way, which is important in longitudinal surveys.

The problem is not easily resolvable because, as Owens notes, turning down requests for help might lead to resentment, which could in turn affect the informant's attitude to the study. Likewise, claiming ignorance and suggesting he did not know the answer could have undermined his credibility. In the event, Owens' solution – reflecting pressures of reciprocity – was to acquiesce to requests for information and explanations.

## Interviewing different research populations

Different interview populations have special features that require particular approaches. In what follows we look at these aspects in relation to a sample of these groups: children and adolescents, people with learning disabilities and élites. We realize the list is not exhaustive, but it is sufficiently wide-ranging to show how research methods have to be sensitive to the specific characteristics of the group being interviewed.

### Interviewing children and adolescents

The literature (Fine and Sandstrom, 1988; Beresford, 1997) shows that children and adults exist in distinctive social and cultural worlds. Consequently, children's views of reality can diverge from those of adults. Nevertheless, the opinions of children and adolescents have been neglected in some streams of social research, on the grounds that children are not competent to understand and describe their world due to cognitive and linguistic immaturity. For example, a common interpretation of Piaget's developmental theory is that children have a limited competence to understand, formulate or express ideas and thoughts. (That said, Piaget's theories were heavily dependent on his extended, 'clinical' conversations with infants and older children – Piaget, 1929.) However, there is now a greater awareness that children are capable of providing worthwhile data from a young age (Amato and Ochiltree, 1987; Fine and Sandstrom, 1988). This revised thinking has been accompanied by legislation giving children the right to be heard. Article 12 of the United Nations Convention on the Rights of the Child, 1989, and the (UK's) Children Act, 1989, both advocate actively involving children in issues that affect them. Together, these developments have resulted in increasing attention being given to eliciting children's views and experiences directly.

Both structured and non-structured interview formats have been used in studies of children and adolescents. However, even if children do have greater cognitive abilities than was once envisaged, researchers still have to bridge the social

---

**Box 8.1  Differences between children and adults that may affect an interview**

- Cognitive development (more concrete, less abstract).
- Language development.
- Attention span.
- Life experiences.
- What is meaningful, and hence what is remembered.
- Status and power.

---

worlds gap. Box 8.1 sets out the main differences between children and adults, distinctions that have methodological or ethical implications when conducting interviews with the former.

Our emphasis here is on obtaining information from children; we deal with ethical matters in the next chapter. It is sufficient to note that power and status differentials between children and adults mean that it is difficult for children to refuse to consent to take part in a study. Likewise, they have less control over the nature of their involvement in an interview. Unfortunately, guidance from professional bodies on protecting children from harm is limited. For instance, the Statement of Ethical Practice of the British Sociological Association (1997) contains no explicit reference to ethical considerations in respect of children and adolescents.

How do you go about collecting the data? What interviewing tools are there to facilitate children and adolescents expressing their views? Our suggestions are presented under three separate headings: building and maintaining trust; communication; and techniques to generate conversation. Before proceeding, it is worth pointing out that children of around the same age vary greatly in terms of their verbal ability and understanding, as well as maturity and experiences. Furthermore, common sense suggests that what is suitable for a 6-year-old is not suitable for someone ten years older. In sum, the onus is on the researcher to tailor the mode of interviewing to the individual.

*Building and maintaining trust*

- From the outset, set the child at ease and in control of the situation. Point out that he need not answer individual questions, and that the interview can be stopped at any time if he wishes. Suggest that you are there to learn from him, and that there are no right or wrong answers.
- If the interview is being audiotaped, let the child 'play' with the recorder by inserting the tape, speaking into it for a few moments and then listening to the 'dummy run'.
- One way to make the child feel confident that she can contribute successfully is to start off with easy 'ice breaker' questions that you know she will have the answer to.

- Depending upon drawing ability, asking the child to draw a picture relevant to the focus of study and then to talk about it can be a useful way to open an interview, especially with the more reticent children.
- Be on the alert for children showing emotional responses. Some are more imperceptible than others, and can cover a wide spectrum: fidgeting, crawling under or behind the furniture; affecting to spot something outside the room and running away; evasiveness or reluctance when answering questions; crying. A natural instinct when dealing with distressed children is to respond by giving them a cuddle; however, for interviewers physical comfort is not appropriate. Rather than touching, one possibility is a change of voice. Depending on age, you might want to take along a teddy bear or other soft toy. You could then hand this over, saying something like: 'You look like you need a cuddle; here's someone else who does too.' And unless you had the foresight to include funding for a team of teddies in the research budget, try to impress that this particular teddy returns home with you!

## Communication

- Use plain language that children understand: 'kid's language' (Amato and Ochiltree, 1987: 670), rather than standard grammatical English. Language problems are less acute when open questions are used and you can establish the appropriate terminology at the start of the interview. However, if you intend to use closed questions you must ensure at a very early stage that both the questions and the predetermined answers reflect the children's perceptions and knowledge about a topic, rather than your assumptions. Pilot testing should solve this problem.
- Employ age-appropriate questions. It is commonly assumed that pre-school children are able to talk about the 'here-and-now'; 5- to 6-year-olds can answer 'why', 'when' or 'how' questions; children aged 8 and over can talk about some abstract concepts such as health or safety; children of 12 or so can deal with the more difficult abstract concepts such as time and frequency. However, these are no more than rules of thumb – Peter's work with 4–14-year-olds found some sophisticated reasoning amongst the youngest and some laconic simplicity amongst the eldest.
- Some children will respond more quickly than others, so allow time to think.

## Techniques to generate conversation

- *Write and draw*. Oakley et al. (1995), in their study of children's beliefs about cancer, used an interview schedule asking children 'to write or draw anything you know about cancer'. The pictures were scanned into a computer database, for later retrieval and analysis.
- *Drawing*. Hilary used this technique in a study looking at the housing needs of disabled children (Oldman and Beresford, 1998). The opening question was, 'Would you draw me a picture of your house?' As the child drew the picture (or directed the interviewer, if she did not possess sufficient skills), she

simultaneously described her experiences and feelings about how the house 'worked' for a youngster with mobility problems. Gold stars and black spots were applied to those features of the house which the child identified as 'good' and 'bad' respectively. See Figure 8.1 for an example of the picture drawn by a 9-year-old girl who only used a wheelchair; the stars and spots are included also.

- *Pictures and photographs*. These provide useful visual cues of the issues being discussed, and are a 'coathanger' for conversations exploring behaviour and viewpoints.
- *Exercises or 'games'*. In a study of health beliefs of children (Backett and Alexander, 1991), the children were asked to post pictures of foods into one of two posting boxes labelled 'healthy' and 'unhealthy' respectively. Older children (over 8) also undertook a card sorting exercise which involved ranking seven cards describing health-related behaviours from the most important for keeping healthy to the least important. They were then asked to explain this choice.
- *Apparatus*. Piaget's work frequently used simple apparatus and tasks to focus discussion.
- *Sentence completion*. Giving children partially completed sentences and asking them to complete the rest can be a useful technique if the topic is a difficult one to talk about. Large print size is easier to read and understand.
- *Popular culture*. News stories, popular music and television can all be used to good effect. Hazel (1995) suggests that one way to broach key issues in interviewees' lives is to mention the problems faced by characters in soap operas and other popular television programmes. However, this strategy is more likely to be successful with females. In his empirical work, Hazel found that girls tended to focus on fictional culture – and especially soaps. Boys, on the other hand, inclined towards factual accounts and hard news.

## Interviewing people with learning disabilities

Like everyone else, people with learning disabilities have views of their own and a right to express them. One outcome of the change of emphasis from institutional to community-based living, as well as the disability rights movement and processes of 'normalization' (Brown and Smith, 1992), is that now people are being encouraged to air these views. However, this group is another marginalized community in social research. A major barrier has been the lack of suitable research methods. For instance, conventional interviewing procedures, with their stress on verbal fluency, are not especially effective with people who communicate in different ways and perhaps with difficulty.

It is important to grasp at the outset that people with learning disabilities are a highly heterogeneous group. They include people who are both able and keen to offer their accounts and others who struggle to respond to questions in a meaningful way. But what are the specific issues to be addressed when conducting interviews with people who have learning disabilities? The following summarizes points made by Booth and Booth (1996) in an article discussing narrative research with such informants. First, they tend to have restricted language skills and under-standing; some use little or no speech whatsoever. The ability to respond to

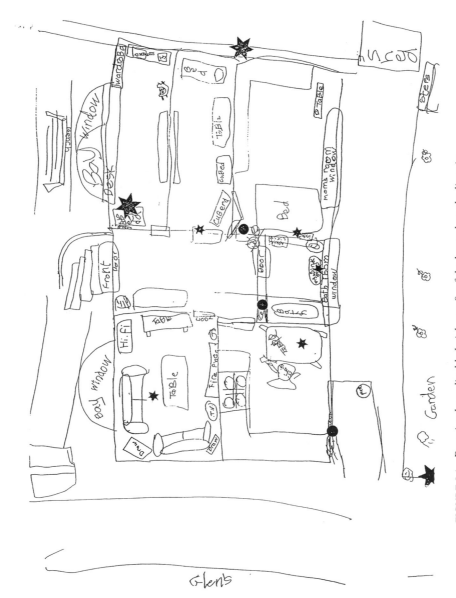

FIGURE 8.1  *Drawing by a disabled girl, age 9, of the bungalow she lives in*

questions can be further inhibited by socialization practices that serve to foster deference, and discourage criticism. It can also be influenced by question format; to take just one example, open questions can be hard for people to answer and so yield low levels of response (Sigelman et al., 1981a,b, 1982). Further, many people who have learning difficulties use a concrete frame of reference. This means that whilst they can relate to the here-and-now, they are less able to look back and generalize from, or evaluate the significance of, past events in their lives. Finally, as well as tending to live in the present, people may have difficulty with dates and numbers. Consequently, they have a more limited sense of temporal sequences.

The challenge for researchers is to develop methods that will enable people with learning disabilities to freely express their own points of view. However, because people are so heterogeneous, the implication is that one particular mode of interviewing will not necessarily work well for everyone. From this point of view, interviewers need to adopt a flexible approach so that they can adapt to the capacities and experiences of each individual. In the remainder of this section we present different ways to collect information; a trawl of the literature suggests that some modes of questioning are more effective than others.

*Types of question to ask*

- Use open questions that are relatively direct and specific, simply phrased and that concentrate on one point at a time. Rephrase the question if the informant is unable to answer.
- Try to use questions that require brief responses – a short phrase rather than a lengthy sentence. For instance, in a study (Minkes et al., 1994) where young people (10–19-year-olds) with learning disabilities evaluated the services they used, informants were asked: 'What do you like best about . . . ?' and 'What do you not like about . . . ?'.
- Cross-check for consistency by asking the same question in different ways, or by posing the opposite as a question. For instance, if someone says she enjoyed her work placement, this could be followed up by 'You don't feel unhappy coming here?'. Attempts should be made to probe any inconsistent answers; exploring ambivalence can often be illuminating.

*Types of question to avoid*

- Avoid open questions that are long and complicated, or too abstract.
- Do not use questions that ask about time and frequency (Flynn, 1986), such as 'When did you . . . ?' or 'How often do you . . . ?'
- Closed questions are best avoided. The evidence (Sigelman et al., 1981a,b, 1982) suggests that with yes/no questions people with learning disabilities tend to acquiesce and answer 'yes' regardless of the content of the question. Furthermore, they are likely to choose the second option in either/or questions, and the last option in multiple choice questions, a tendency known as 'recency'. However, other studies (Conroy and Bradley, 1985) found lower levels of acquiescence and recency, which fell even further as people moved

out of institutional settings and relocated. This suggests that response biases may be a feature of the context in which the interview takes place as much as the question format.

*Aids to communication*  Given the complexities of relying solely on verbal methods, other techniques or question styles offer potential. Visual cues such as photographs, pictures or symbols can be used to advantage with people who might not have good speech skills, but can understand and respond to simple questions. For instance, in one study (Booth et al., 1990) people with learning disabilities pointed to, or picked up, photographs in answer to direct questions such as 'Who do you like?' or 'Who don't you like?'

Facial drawings are another tool to increase the potential for communication. The 'smiley faces' shown in Figure 8.2 are a visual version of a Likert scale with five stylized facial drawings ranging from 'very happy' to 'very sad'. People do not need to make a verbal response, but can just point to the face that shows best how they feel about a particular activity. The advantage of a research tool like this is that, irrespective of fluency in speech or reading, people have the opportunity to make evaluations. For instance, they can express feelings of satisfaction or dissatisfaction regarding their social lives, say, or contact with service providers. This is a big step forward from yes/no and either/or questions.

FIGURE 8.2  *The five 'smiley faces'*

Booth, Simons and Booth (1990) used a three-faced scale of happy/sad faces. These pictures were used in conjunction with photographs of the current residential placement of people with learning disabilities, and also their old homes. Informants were shown each photograph and asked 'What sort of face would you have if you lived here – a happy one, a sad one or sort of in-between?' They were then prompted to choose a face showing how they felt, and place it on top of the photograph.

*Joint interviews*  For people whose use of speech is particularly idiosyncratic, it might be worth involving someone closely connected to them who can understand this 'private' language. The third party – a friend, relative or advocate – can then take on the role of 'translator' or 'interpreter' and assist in a number of ways. First, by expressing questions in a way that the person will grasp; secondly, by helping you to understand better the informant's use of speech and style of communication; and thirdly, by giving prompts over specific dates, events or people. There are drawbacks, though. The person acting as translator may also filter the forthcoming information, so in effect you are hearing her interpretation and perspective rather than that of the person with learning disabilities. Moreover, it is not impossible that their presence will serve to inhibit responses. In their joint interviews, Booth and Booth (1994) found that sometimes the translator would try to take over the conversation.

Generally, try to ensure that the interview follows an informal, conversational format and does not drift into anything resembling an interrogation. If time permits, supplement the information obtained with observation in the places where people live, work or go to school. Use any pre-visits to try to get to know those you will be interviewing. This sort of informal contact makes you less of a stranger, and is part of the process of building up good relationships. It will also help in understanding the individual's particular style of communication, which contributes to increasing the chances of achieving a successful interview.

The theme emerging from these two brief reviews is that the more flexible and creative your approach, the more responsive and informative the individual you are speaking with – and this applies to children, adolescents and people with learning disabilities.

### Interviewing élites

Our third interview population, the élite sector, is another minority community in social science research. Yet whether in the role of leaders or experts, élite individuals – people used to exercising power and influence – are important. This is all the more reason why their belief systems, activities, roles in decision-making processes and relationships with the rank and file ought to be subject to empirical examination. By neglecting élites, social scientists, who typically study the 'underdogs' on the grounds that this is one way to tackle social equity issues and empower subordinates, are in fact limiting the purchase of their enquiries. Having said that, interviewing prominent people does raise particular methodological issues. In particular, obtaining access can be difficult.

*Negotiating access*   Generally, leading figures in political, social or business circles are influential, held in high esteem and used to having others defer to them. Add to this the fact that they have little time to spare, do not usually put talking to academic researchers high on their list of priorities, and are protected by lower level personnel, and you can understand why gaining access can be problematic. Getting through the (closed) doors of the boardroom took nearly two years in one case (Thomas, 1993), but persistence did pay off in the end. Other researchers have found making contact with élites expensive in terms of phone calls, facsimiles, travelling to pre-arranged appointments only to find they have been cancelled at the last minute, and because of an expectation of 'alcoholic and gastronomic bribery' (Winkler, 1987: 136). The underlying implication is that if the proposed study is limited in terms of either time or money, then part of the initial planning stage must involve calculating whether you can negotiate access and carry out the fieldwork within the resource constraints. It is also important to be confident that you can report the work without individual participants being identifiable (see next chapter).

Once you are clear that, in principle, the study is feasible, then you need to think about the practicalities. Here is a compilation of techniques that should increase your chances of success in setting up interviews with prospective interviewees:

- Write a letter of introduction setting out the purpose of the study; the methodology; your credentials for doing the work; and how the outcome of the research might be of benefit to the individual concerned. Explain the purpose of the proposed interview, and suggest that conducting the same exercise with someone lower down the ranks would not serve as a substitute. Depending on confidentiality agreements, you may want to mention the names of other people who have agreed to speak with you. Follow up the letter with a telephone call to try to arrange a meeting. Let the interviewee choose the time and place; some people may want to talk outside of the organization, in a café or restaurant for instance. As we indicated earlier, élites have a full time schedule so be prepared to fit in with them instead of the other way round.
- If the work is being conducted within an organization, start at the top and work down the hierarchy. For instance, if you want to study company directors, try to gain entry to the boardroom through the chairman or managing director. Having won the cooperation of the chief executive, use this to obtain the agreement of other senior staff. This might involve making some sort of presentation to all the board members. Although this exercise could prove rather intimidating, it would also be a good opportunity to show that you have a fair grasp of the subject area; people are far more likely to say yes if they can see you have done your 'homework'.
- Draw on pre-existing personal contacts who are members of the élite in question.
- Ask friends, relatives and colleagues if they can provide a point of entry. For instance, if you want to talk to business executives, you may know someone who either teaches on a Masters in Business Administration (MBA) course, or is studying for the degree, and can arrange an introduction. This approach is more likely to succeed if you are connected to an organization or institution which the élite will recognize.

*Background knowledge* As we have implied both here and in the previous chapter, demonstrating you have a sound knowledge of the area under discussion is important. It helps you to gain access, and is also a way to win the respect of people who are higher in status. In other words, drawing on your cultural capital can create greater symmetry in the interviewer–interviewee relationship. Further, background knowledge is a factor in establishing trust and rapport. For instance, it is not impossible that your own knowledge base might be checked out by the élite at the beginning of the interview. If you appear to be unfamiliar with the issues involved, and unable to hold a relatively informed conversation, then you stand to lose first credibility and secondly the flow of information. This would be unfortunate, especially as it could be prevented by more adequate preparation.

However, élites are used to being asked what they think; all things being equal, they are likely to converse freely and at length (even to the point of being indiscreet) if they are well-briefed themselves. This is one reason why élites are often resistant to structured interviews, especially any who may be bombastic or bullying. They do not want to be pigeon-holed into particular categories, or become part of some statistical aggregates. In any case, from the point of view of question design there can be wide differences between élites, and even amongst members of an organization. More often than not, asking people the same set of questions would be inappropriate.

Setting that last point aside, what are the areas that you might need to be conversant with? Basically, it is important to demonstrate expertise at three levels: that of the individual, the institution and the issues of concern. A more detailed breakdown of useful knowledge areas in contrasting élite sectors is given in Boxes 8.2 and 8.3. As you can see, the underlying principles are quite similar and can be extended to accommodate other élite sectors.

Some of the information mentioned in Boxes 8.2 and 8.3 will be easier to acquire than other aspects. Primary sources for this sort of material include written books and articles by the individuals themselves. These may be the more scholarly publications, or alternatively memoirs, autobiographies and personal

---

**Box 8.2   Background information for interviews with political élites**

- Biographical data of interviewee, including education, previous career, home constituency, position in party.
- Interviewee's position and concerns on issues in which historically and currently involved.
- The party system, party strategy and internal party divisions.
- Governmental structures, and the policy process.
- Specific policy areas relating to the study.
- Technical language.

---

**Box 8.3   Background information for interviews with business élites**

- Biographical data of interviewee, including education and occupational history.
- Interviewee's role, status and authority.
- Management structure and organizational roles of the institution the interviewee is associated with.
- Economic, social and political links with wider business environment.
- Specific areas of interest to study.
- Technical language.

diaries. Speeches, published letters and verbatim reports provide a further stock of information. Secondary materials comprise government documentation, public records such as committee reports or reports of annual general meetings, specialized publications and journals, archival material and newspaper reports. Staff from libraries or museums, and members of local historical societies, may well have details of the histories of community leaders and their families. Collecting the relevant information might seem daunting, but the strategic use of just a few elements can serve the purpose of suggesting that you are 'in the know' and thus increase responsiveness. At the same time, the interview data can be checked against the background material for the purpose of methodological triangulation (see Chapter 2).

## Conclusion

In this chapter we have looked at issues that are distinctive to the study of sensitive issues and particular interview populations. It is clear that similar difficulties and dilemmas can arise in otherwise quite different settings. In many ways, the suggestions we have made in relation to the different approaches needed for specialized contexts correspond to good interviewing practice generally. The challenge for interviewers is to incorporate these further techniques into their core skills repertoire.

# 9   Protecting Rights and Welfare

A major issue within contemporary social science concerns whether the contribution to the stock of knowledge provided by research findings justifies any negative effects on the people taking part. In recent years the ethical climate has shifted; for instance, nowadays Milgram's (1963) study of obedience to the authority of the researcher is viewed as indefensible; the general consensus is that as social researchers we have responsibilities to fulfil (Holden, 1979). Consequently, respect for the rights and welfare of all the various social groups being interviewed for the study must be demonstrated throughout the conduct of the research, including its dissemination. Equally, it is important to uphold the interests of other parties involved in the work, for instance funders, sponsors, employers, your supervisor and colleagues. What all this means in practice is conducting *ethical research*. However, it is naive to assume that the concerns of the different groups will inevitably coincide; on the contrary, you may well find yourself having to deal with competing obligations and conflicts of interest. In these circumstances, it is a likely prospect that you will not be able to fulfil the diverse responsibilities simultaneously, and will have to make difficult judgements to resolve the issue in question.

The first part of this chapter considers practical ways of applying ethical standards to social research. We are concentrating on protecting the interests of study participants rather than funders, the research community and wider society. This is because we think that any wider application is likely to be of marginal interest to readers. For a critical discussion of ethical issues, see Bulmer (1982), Homan (1991) and Alderson's (1995) *Listening to Children*, which provides a comprehensive and insightful guide on how to uphold children's rights and welfare. In fact, many of the issues she raises are also pertinent to members of other vulnerable groups.

The remainder of the chapter takes a contrasting slant, and focuses on how best to safeguard interviewers themselves from the risks attached to undertaking research activities. This is an area which is often neglected in the literature, yet as Dunn (1991: 388) warns interviewers: 'research may be hazardous to your health'. Given this, we examine the emotional and physical demands that interviews can impose on researchers, and also address issues related to personal safety.

## Safeguarding the interests of interviewees

Decisions about protecting rights and welfare need to be carefully thought through in advance of the fieldwork stage. This process is more or less forced upon you if the proposed study has to undergo prior review and approval from a research ethics committee or review board, as is routinely the case in North America (and often the UK, if the work takes place in a medical setting). These committees often ask to see the interview schedule or guide to be used. They might want to know about procedures for the acquisition and documentation of informed consent (see below), and what provisions are being made for safeguarding participants' privacy. As noted previously, they may demand that any tape recordings of interviews are destroyed once the study has been completed. Whilst the preparatory work is time-consuming, it helps concentrate the mind. For instance, having to identify questions to be used in an interview can reveal where you may be touching on sensitive issues that might leave the interviewee feeling distressed or anxious. So just where may potentially harmful effects arise?

### Potential harms

Possible harms that people may incur during the actual interview itself include undue intrusion into private and personal spheres, embarrassment, distress, nervous strain, a sense of failure or coercion. In addition, there may be costs in terms of the time spent in taking part in the interview(s); the expense of travelling, say, to a focus group, or having to take any time off paid work. At the end of the study, the results may attract the attention of the media. If this happens, you have very little control over how the material is used, and there have been examples of social science research being used against the (individual and collective) interests of those researched (Morgan, 1972). Not surprisingly, informants may be upset or angry to read about the work in terms that they consider to be uncomplimentary or discreditable. From this point of view, it is important to have a written agreement setting out your rights in relation to writing and publication (see Chapter 5). Overall, people may be left feeling they have been treated as objects rather than collaborators.

This is quite a long list of possible negative outcomes, and before proceeding further it is important to stress that there can also be benefits. In other words, the effects of taking part in a study are not as unbalanced as they might seem.

### Potential benefits

Whilst it is necessary to remember that the primary purpose of an interview is to collect data, there are nevertheless a number of ways in which people taking part may benefit or be personally empowered. Knowing they are contributing to a worthwhile endeavour can be gratifying; it may increase confidence. The experience may be interesting, fun even. People's own knowledge levels may increase if follow-up or support mechanisms are incorporated into the study. A colleague of ours was involved in a study investigating genetic testing and screening. Interviewing people raised questions in the informants' minds that they had not thought of before, questions which the researcher did not have the expertise to answer. Her solution was to leave contact details of a genetic counsellor who was willing to offer advice and assistance. As noted above, for some individuals interviews can be cathartic: the chance to talk at length, primarily about yourself and your opinions, on a one-to-one basis, is rare and to be welcomed – a chance to collect your thoughts and develop new ways of seeing yourself. And even if some of the questions could be seen as prying, people may feel flattered: here is subtle confirmation that what they are saying is important.

In terms of tangible benefits, you may wish to think about paying or giving a small reward in return for help with the research (Social and Community Planning Research, 1998; Hughes, 1999). In the past, financial reimbursement has been frowned upon on the grounds that people would then be taking part in research for the wrong reasons – not out of altruism or the general good, but just for the money. Against that can be set the argument that payment is one way of demonstrating to research participants – who in social research are often the disadvantaged and poor – that their time is as valuable as other people's and that the study wishes to acknowledge this (Kitson et al., 1996). In a sense, this notion has been legitimized by funding bodies. For instance, the UK's Economic and Social Research Council (1997: 35) in its *Guide for Postgraduate Award Holders* states that the support grant can be used to cover costs such as 'gifts for local informants'. However, if this sort of reimbursement is not feasible, a low-cost alternative (although not necessarily 'low-effort') is to mail participants a short report of the main findings that is clearly and simply written. As well as being a nice gesture, this also shows people that the study reached a concrete conclusion and that the research was valuable.

Having set out some of the consequences that can arise from an interview study, the next part of the chapter considers procedures to be followed in order to respect rights and welfare.

### Professional codes and guidelines

Many research councils and professional associations involved in social research have formulated codes of practice setting out how researchers should behave ethically. Whilst the principal purpose of these codes is to protect the subjects of research from harm, Homan (1991) suggests there is also a measure of professional self-interest. For instance, it is claimed that unethical treatment of study participants may yield poorer results; likewise, it may tarnish the reputation and image of the research community.

Codes of ethics are very general; they do not even pretend to provide unambiguous guidance concerning particular situations or definitive answers to specific activities. Nevertheless, they are useful and provide a practical model to apply throughout the various stages of the research. Even if you are not a member of any professional association, you would be well advised to acquire a copy of the most recent version of the appropriate code. The British Sociological Association's (1997) *Statement of Ethical Practice* is available through its homepage on the World Wide Web (http://dialspace.dial.pipex.com/britsoc/). So too is the American Sociological Association's *Code of Ethics* (http://www.asanet.org/default.htm), and the American Psychological Association's *Ethical Principles of Psychologists and Code of Conduct* (http://www.apa.org/). Study what the relevant guidelines have to say carefully, particularly points in relation to obtaining informed consent and maintaining confidentiality. These are issues that you must take into account when designing your study.

There is often no perfect solution, but codes of ethics can help you develop personal judgements about the rights and wrongs of social research. If time permits, it is always advisable to discuss potential problems with ethical dimensions with your supervisor or more seasoned researchers, and so learn from the experiences of others. In the field, though, you may have to resolve research dilemmas on the spot. There can be a tension between ethical ideals and practical difficulties. In these circumstances, compromises have to be found, otherwise the research role can become untenable (Homan, 1991). This sort of principled decision making is in some senses idiosyncratic. For instance, we may not all come up to the same set of ethical standards – what one researcher might regard as a satisfactory outcome, another might feel is less than ideal.

## Informed consent

We have mentioned the concept of informed consent earlier in the book. Its purpose is to safeguard participants' privacy and welfare, and to give them a choice about whether or not to take part in a study. The modern concept of informed consent developed from the atrocities carried out on prisoners in Nazi concentration camps in the name of 'medical science'. This research involved dangerous, often lethal experiments, and a number of doctors went on trial at Nuremberg accused of mistreating prisoners. Subsequently, the Nuremberg Code of 1947 on research practice was devised. This was a ten-point code designed to regulate biomedical research. The first principle focuses on informed consent. Later, the concept was imported into social research.

When obtaining consent, one balance that has to be struck is between over- and under-informing people. Basically, it is important not to make the whole process too complicated by going into great detail. For instance, if the research format is a relatively innocuous structured questionnaire, then it is sufficient to present a short description of the research and what is involved, making it clear that respondents are free to refuse to answer any questions they consider private, embarrassing or whatever. Here, the emphasis is on accuracy rather than comprehensiveness. However, we should stress that local practice varies, and in North America, for example, written consent may be required, even when the research takes the form of structured, closed-question interviewing.

People taking part in qualitative interviews, which are more likely to touch on sensitive issues, ought to be given fuller particulars about the study they are being asked to take part in. So whilst a core of basic information should be included in a research information leaflet (see Chapter 5), further explanation of the research would help individuals to make an informed decision, having assessed the hoped-for benefits against any possible risks or costs. Essentially, you should ensure that informants are aware of:

- The purpose and nature of the study, including the research methods and timing.
- The anticipated benefits, risks or costs (for those taking part in the study, and also the wider society).
- Contact details of the researcher, and the research base.

- The names of any funders or sponsors.
- The sorts of questions being asked, and how long the interview should take.
- Their right not to answer specific questions, or to change their mind and withdraw from the research altogether.
- The degree of anonymity and confidentiality: what information will be disclosed, for what purposes and to whom; the use of quotations.
- Arrangements to safeguard confidentiality.
- Plans regarding dissemination (see Chapter 12). Graduate students undertaking research ought to let informants know that the resulting dissertation is a public document which can be obtained from libraries. If the eventual aim is to produce a book version of the thesis, then this should also be stated.

Reflecting points made in our earlier discussion about the study of sensitive issues (see Chapter 8), it is quite often the case that informants do not realize at the start of a project – particularly one that involves a series of interviews – how much personal material they are likely to disclose. As the research progresses, encroaching deeper and deeper into their private lives, you may choose to renegotiate consent and the basis on which people remain in the study. This might avoid situations whereby interviewees later come to regret the amount of information they have actually revealed – far more than they ever anticipated.

*Informed consent forms*  On the basis of full information, potential interviewees are in a position to make a rational decision regarding participating in the research. Generally speaking, it is preferable to have written agreement that someone has volunteered to participate in a study. In any case, obtaining the person's signature on a written consent form is mandatory in many studies that take place in a medical context. Box 9.1 offers an example of the informed consent form that was used in the Carers Act study first mentioned in Chapter 5.

The consent form should be printed on letter-headed paper from your research base or institution, and at the same time clearly display your own contact details. Leave space at the foot of the form for people to sign their name. As the interviewer, you keep the signed copy of the consent form; however, it is good practice to leave a copy with the participant so they have a written reminder of what they agreed to.

If it is a likely prospect that you will include extracts from interviews in any report writing, you should ask people to agree to that explicitly. This is because copyright of the words, whether they are taken down verbatim or recorded, is owned by the informant and, strictly speaking, permission is needed before any quotes can be used.

Whilst informed consent is a mechanism to show respect for the rights and welfare of research participants, it also shifts some of the responsibility for harm from the researcher to the participant, assuming you have discharged your responsibilities properly and explained about any possible harm or discomfort. At the same time, the process can transform people from passive objects into active subjects (Alderson, 1995).

**Box 9.1   Example of an informed consent form**

(For the purposes of this book, details of the institution and contact information have been removed)

### HELPING CARERS TO CARE

*This consent form is to check that you are happy with the information you have received about the study, that you are aware of your rights as a participant and to confirm that you wish to take part in the study.*

*Please tick as appropriate*

|  | YES | NO |
|---|---|---|
| 1  Have you read the research information leaflet? | | |
| 2  Have you had the opportunity to discuss further questions with a member of the research team? | | |
| 3  Have you received enough information about the study to decide whether you want to take part? | | |
| 4  Do you understand that you are free to refuse to answer any questions? | | |
| 5  Do you understand that you may withdraw from the study at any time without giving your reasons, and that this will not affect future service provision in any way? | | |
| 6  Do you understand that members of the research team will treat all information as confidential? | | |
| 7  Do you agree to take part in the study? | | |

Signature  ———————————————  Date  ———————————

Name in block letters, please  ————————————————————

I confirm that quotations from the interview can be used in the final research report and other publications. I understand that these will be used anonymously.

Signature  ———————————————  Date  ———————————

Name in block letters, please  ————————————————————

*ns* Underlying the principle of 'consent' are two notions. First,
s are competent to make rational and mature judgements; and sec-
r agreement to participate in a study is given voluntarily (Homan,
ties are raised in respect of social research involving those who
s not competent to make personal decisions. As noted above, children comprise one social group who traditionally have been attributed far less
rationality and intellect than adults. Other groups whose ability to make rational
decisions may be questioned include people with learning disabilities or mental
health problems, the very old and the very ill. The question for social researchers
in these cases is: who has the authority to give or withhold consent? The situation is not clear-cut, but we can give you some basic guidelines.

So far as children are concerned, as a general rule parents or guardians of
children under the age of 16 should give written consent to the child's participation in research. Good practice suggests that children who can understand
should also be asked, regardless of parental agreement. If the parents say 'no' and
the child says 'yes', then the parents' view prevails. If the parents say 'yes' and
the child says 'no', in fact there is no real point in continuing as it is unlikely you
will get any active cooperation in terms of answering questions. If the research is
taking place on school premises, best practice is for the school to notify parents
and allow them the opportunity to ask for more information about the study, the
researchers and other related aspects. This measure will help allay any anxieties
parents may have. In some instances, it is possible that the head teacher or class
teacher will act *in loco parentis* and grant consent on behalf of pupils.

Research involving people who are deemed too mentally or physically ill
to be wholly rational and able to make informed decisions is similar to that
with children, in the sense that others must give proxy consent on their behalf.
Appropriate people to ask include relatives – next of kin, for example – carers, or
professionals such as doctors.

### Confidentiality and anonymity

Confidentiality is about not disclosing the identity of study participants, and not
attributing comments to individuals in ways that can permit the individuals or
institutions with which they are associated to be recognized, unless they have
expressly consented to being identified. Assurances that personal information will
be kept confidential can influence whether or not someone will actually take part
in a study. A second 'bonus' is that responses to questions may well be more frank.
The most common procedure to safeguard confidentiality in records and reports is
to anonymize people by the use of code numbers or by assigning them different
names. We describe these techniques in a moment, but as a preliminary we would
like to suggest that treating interviews confidentially is not as straightforward as
might appear at first sight.

There are underlying issues to do with empowerment: some people would
rather be named and acknowledged. Skeggs (1994: 86), on the basis of her study
of the lives of young, working-class women, reports that 'they were especially
upset by pseudonyms, wanting to see their names with their comments in print . . .

they say it makes them feel important'. Similarly, a colleague of Hilary's who took part in a study of the experiences of mothers of girl children reported that one interviewee was given her transcript – which by then contained pseudonyms rather than real names – to comment on. And yes, these were her words in black and white, but at the same time they were not because by now all the names had been changed. As the interviewee later commented to Hilary: 'This wasn't my story any more. My mother and brothers, my two girls – they all had different names. And I found the whole thing almost emotionally upsetting.'

There is some debate concerning the issue of confidentiality as it relates to élites (see Chapter 8). The question is: to what extent should researchers try to conceal the identity of those already in the public eye? Opinion is divided, but generally it is thought that some degree of exposure is to be expected – it goes with job, as it were. Interestingly, Spector (1980) found that many people in power did not even expect the option of anonymity. On the contrary, they were accustomed to speaking on the record and often welcomed publicity, and having their views reported and attributed. In any case, in research involving small, well-defined groups, members may be so well known to each other that with a little reading between the lines, so to speak, they can identify non-attributed quotations. Medhurst and Moyser (1987) go so far as to say that even well-informed general readers might be able to name correctly some of the participants in their study of Church of England bishops.

Confidentiality in research implies that the identity of participants, and everything they say, will remain private or secret. But are promises of confidentiality absolute or are there some circumstances where a breach of confidence is justified? For instance, it may be that you are told stories about child or elder abuse, illegal activities or thoughts of suicide. Your work might point to some kind of business malpractice or fraud. Is this the point where your civic responsibilities prevail over your role of researcher and you report the confidences? And if so, to whom? There is no cook-book answer we can give regarding any possible intervention on your part, except to say that you need to give careful consideration to all the factors with a bearing on the issue. If you then come to the conclusion that someone is at serious risk of harm, or that it is in the public interest if you share the information, then the case could be made that the principles of confidence no longer obtain (see, for example, Dunn, 1991).

*Procedures for implementing confidentiality: structured interviews*  Concealing the identity of research participants is a relatively easy task for data obtained through structured interviews. Indeed, the problem might not even arise. Quite often, intercept interviewers do not even ask for names and addresses of respondents. Where identities are known, though, it is necessary to replace names with corresponding index numbers. This exercise can be carried out as part of the data processing and analysis (see Chapter 11). In this way, the identity of respondents and the information they provided are split up; actual identifying details such as names and addresses should be stored in a different place from the data, so they cannot be matched. The larger the survey population, the less likely it is that anything will be recognizable about individual respondents; once people's answers are translated into codes, they disappear into a mass of anonymous statistical data indicating patterns and trends.

*Procedures for implementing confidentiality: qualitative interviews* Upholding confidentiality is more difficult in semi- or unstructured interviews. This is because information that could be used to identify informants tends to be more dispersed – in letters, research records, fieldnotes, transcripts, audio or video tapes – and so is more complicated to change or hide. It is stating the obvious to say that generally names and other personal details must be disguised. You may also find it necessary to change people's gender, race, age or occupation, as well as information pertaining to family relationships. The location of the study, whether that be a place of work, hospital site, a local community or whatever, might also need to be hidden by giving it a fictitious name.

You will find it easier to disguise people, and in this way protect them from harm, the more you characterize them as general and ordinary, rather than focus on any exceptional or special attributes. The problem with adopting this approach is that, whilst it does not distort the data, it does diminish the specificity and the detail of the analysis (Barnes, 1979). One of us was involved in a study where key practitioners of different professional background and status were interviewed (Arksey et al., 1997). In the final report, these individuals were referred to only as either a 'health care practitioner' or a 'social services practitioner'. On odd occasions, the word 'senior' was added. It could be argued that some of the potential value of the report was lost in this process. For example, a comment made by a consultant responsible for managing a specialist unit, whose philosophy is likely to influence most aspects of the establishment, carries far more weight than if the same comment was made by a junior nurse. This sort of differentiation is lost if efforts at concealment result in a flattening of the organizational hierarchy. Similarly, the same point made by a physiotherapist, a hospital nurse or a district nurse based in the community reads differently, yet distinctions in meaning and implications disappear if the specific professional orientation is not given. As Homan (1991) notes, this generalized level of analysis might prejudice the implementation of improvements in social policy and practice.

*Storage arrangements* As well as protecting data by disguising names, personal details and other possible identifiers, you need to take care that as few people as possible have access to research records and other material. To this end, it is important to have secure storage space. This may mean asking for a lockable filing cabinet and/or cupboard, items which were not available to one doctoral student we are aware of who was working on a study of men with AIDS. This researcher had to leave data unsecured in an office shared with others, a situation that should not have been permitted.

*Data protection and privacy legislation* Most countries, including North America and all European Union member states, now have data protection laws. For instance, in the UK the majority of data users who hold personal information (and this could be as little as a name and address) about living individuals on computer have to register under the Data Protection Act 1984, and comply with its eight principles. Whilst this Act is designed to protect individuals' privacy, it does not apply to information, however personal or private, that is held and processed manually, for example in card indexes or paper files. However, this situation will change with the implementation of the Data Protection Directive (95/46/EC), which is to be implemented in the form of a new Data Protection Act. Whilst key elements will continue, some types of personal data that are processed manually will now no longer be exempt. Transitional arrangements, though, will exclude manual filing systems from compliance with most of the law until 2007. To keep up to date with what is happening, use the Data Protection Registrar's homepage: http://www.open.gov.uk/dpr/dprhome.htm

Copies of the current Guidelines are available from the Data Protection Registrar (1997); there is also a series of accompanying guidance notes, which are shorter and deal with specific issues in more detail. One of these, *Student Information*, is aimed at people carrying out project work. If it is at all likely that in your research you could be defined as a 'data user' under the terms of the Data Protection Act, we suggest you get hold of a copy of this publication and, if necessary, register through your institution.

Those working outside the UK need to check what effects any equivalent legislation might have on their information processing activities.

Finally, and by way of completing our discussion of how best to safeguard the interests of interviewees, it is worth pointing out that not enough investigation has yet been done to speak with any confidence about the effects of being interviewed for research purposes. Benefits are often presumed on the basis of taking precautions against potentially harmful consequences, rather than on the basis of evidence (Kelly et al., 1994). Where attempts have been made (Acker et al., 1983; Procter and Padfield, 1998), this has generally been along the lines of the interviewer asking the informant to describe his experiences of the research process. Common sense suggests that informants may find it too intimidating to report to the interviewer that they did not like her approach, found her questions too intrusive or too complicated to understand. There is a strong case for using independent researchers if we really want to discover what impact taking part in a research interview has on people; this would be a separate study in its own right.

## Protecting the interests of interviewers

Quite often, the methodological textbooks leave readers with the general impression that potentially injurious effects from the research process are restricted to the study participants. Any personal consequences for the researcher tend to be somewhere in the background, if mentioned at all. Yet these can be difficult to imagine, especially as research is a far cry from following the set structure of an undergraduate course. There, you are engaged in similar activities to others in your study group, and usually have regular feedback on progress. Research activities, on the other hand, can be quite solitary. In some respects you are dependent on your own resources, and need to be self-motivated and self-disciplined in creating and carrying out the work. So, whilst it is certainly true to say that a good deal of research is pleasurable and satisfying, at the same time it can be quite emotionally stressful. There may also be risks in terms of personal safety. This is the subject matter to which we now attend. After all, it is only reasonable that interviewers, like interviewees, are well informed about potential harms.

### Emotional and physical demands on interviewers

The reality is that some interviews go really well; you walk away on a real high, excited and proud with the data you have just obtained (see Box 3.4). In complete contrast, others will be more problematic and stressful. With the best will in the world, some interviewees simply do not have a lot to say. That does not help you though; as the interviewer, it is only too easy to blame yourself, and feel inadequate, frustrated or stupid. Furthermore, depending on the sensitivity of the subject matter, some interviews can be more demanding and emotionally draining than others. The format of the interview can also make a difference. For instance, semi- and unstructured interviews are advocated as empowering to participants; they are the ones in control. If this is the case, then the assumption must be that the researcher is less powerful. From that perspective, the interview is possibly even more of an emotional experience. On the other hand, levels of tension are generally decreased in a structured interview (Ramsay, 1996).

Figure 9.1 sets out the relationship between the type of interview and the levels of demand placed on the interviewer. The increasing depth of the shading shows how the potential for stressful reactions increases as the interview becomes more open, and deals with more sensitive topics. What must be borne in mind, however, is that the same interview will not be uniformly hard on everyone. Different people will be affected in different ways and to different degrees. This is because it is not the event itself that is stressful, but your perception of it.

| Interview content | Interview format | | |
| | Structured | Semi-structured | Unstructured |
|---|---|---|---|
| Innocuous | | | |
| Sensitive | | | |

*The progression from light to dark shading illustrates the range of possible effects of an interview on an interviwer. Depending on the interview format, and the sensitivity of the topic area, the impact can range along the continuum of not at all stressful to very stressful.*

FIGURE 9.1 *Relationship between type of interview and potential for stressful reaction*

Being exposed to the anguish of intimate and personal disclosures can be painful. Dunn (1991) conducted extensive interviews with women who had been battered. The impact of the research on her physical and emotional health was severe. She suffered sleeplessness, stomach disorders, neck and shoulder pain, and severe headaches. At the same time, Dunn was affected by the emotional state of the women she was speaking with: 'I would often become choked with emotions during the tearful interviews. These same emotional responses were repeated numerous times in the course of reviewing and transcribing the tapes and analysing the data' (p. 390).

In another case, this time arising out of a study of young people and sexuality (Holland and Ramazanoglu, 1994), one interviewer was diverted away from the research objectives by the interviewee; he wanted to discuss his own agenda, namely the death of his mother. Eventually, the interviewer accepted his need to talk about his mother. However, she found the experience particularly distressing as she had herself suffered the unexpected bereavement of a close relative only very recently. In fact, this point is elaborated by Kitson et al. (1996): researchers who have undergone similar 'losses' to the interviewee in relation to, say, divorce, death, rape or violence may have special difficulties in coping with the issues, to the point that the work may become intolerable. In some situations, being an 'insider' can serve to make the research untenable, rather than give you any advantage.

As well as difficulties in relation to personal disclosures and (over) exposure to disturbing material, another source of strain can be the study participants themselves. As we noted in Chapter 7, some interviewees can be unkind, deceitful or calculating. In extreme cases, it is the interviewer who is exploited by the study participants, rather than the other way round. Adler and Adler (1991) report how the drug dealers they were studying expected gifts and favours in exchange for providing information. This included 'borrowing' money when times were hard; 'loans' which were often not repaid.

You might find yourself at the receiving end of remarks or behaviour that you find offensive. Women interviewers working in male dominated organizational environments are especially vulnerable to sexist treatment (Gurney, 1985; Ramsay, 1996); feminist researchers who are exposed to male understandings about women, sexuality and power are likely to find their values severely tested (Ramsay, 1996). What strategy should be adopted? Challenging the sexist observations, and presenting an alternative view, carries the risk of bringing the interview to an abrupt end. Alternatively, keeping silent, or not openly objecting, is potentially oppressive and contradicts feminist principles. In order to achieve a successful conclusion to her study, Gurney's (1985: 56) solution – and she is not alone in the stance taken – was to endure much and say little: 'At the time the risks of confrontation seemed to outweigh the benefits. I therefore tolerated things which made me uncomfortable, but convinced myself they were part of the sacrifices a researcher must make.'

Clearly, it is best to try to avert these sorts of situations arising in the first place. To this end, it is important to project a 'professional' image and manner. This can be conveyed by outward appearances (clothes and make-up, where appropriate); by 'props' (briefcase, identity card, tape recording equipment and interview

---

**Box 9.2   Reducing stressful reactions to interviews**

- Assess your normal coping mechanisms, and decide what activities (for instance, running, cycling, sketching, cooking) you find stress-reducing; take part in each at least three times a week; save some 'special time' for yourself every day.
- If possible, conduct only one interview per day.
- Monitor your own responses; keep a daily diary listing your physical and emotional reactions to each interview.
- Initiate a social support system; discuss any reactions with family, friends, colleagues, or health care professionals.
- Share experiences and problems with others; exchange ideas for staying healthy.

Adapted from Dunn (1991)

---

schedule); and by the authority of research skills and knowledge of the subject matter.

In the light of the above, it is only sensible to take steps to reduce the strains of interviewing. On the basis of her research experiences, Dunn (1991) offers some practical guidance to help deal with emotional and physical responses to interviews. These are detailed in Box 9.2. Speaking for ourselves, we would emphasize the importance of debriefing with colleagues or friends as soon as possible after each interview. Confidentiality can still be upheld as long as data are discussed anonymously.

### Personal safety

Many interviews take place in relatively public locations that are neither fearsome nor frightening – the classroom, for instance, or the workplace. However, the more private settings, for instance someone's home, can be less safe. We do not intend to be alarmist about the potential risks involved in interviewing people who, initially at any rate, are strangers. Clearly, it is important to strike a balance between sensible caution and paranoia, and we now present a number of strategies that you might like to think about adopting in order to reduce potential risks. What follows is developed from the guidelines for research staff produced by the Social Policy Research Unit, where Hilary works. Other possible sources of information include the Suzy Lamplugh Trust (The [UK] National Charity for Personal Safety) and trade unions.

Planning ahead is important in reducing risks. For instance, as much as possible arrange interviews during the daytime and on weekdays. Further, try to find out beforehand all you can about the neighbourhood in which you are interviewing. Should you discover the area is at all difficult or unsafe, and if finances allow, use either a private car or a reputable taxi firm to travel to and from the exact location of the interview. If there is no option but to walk, get hold of an up-to-date street map and make notes of where you are going so there is no need to ask for directions. Avoid danger spots such as badly lit subways, car parks, derelict ground or alleyways; do not be tempted to take short cuts, even if you are running a bit behind schedule. Carry a personal alarm and/or a small torch as precautionary measures. If you feel really uncertain, ask a friend to accompany you.

As you enter the property where the interview is to take place be aware of your surroundings, and assess possible risks. Take note of the layout, including escape routes. Try to sit near the door, and without anyone between you and the exit. If the presence of a dog makes you feel anxious, ask for the animal to be put in another room until you leave. In the opening stages of the interview, drop hints that other people know where you are and when you expect to return. An alternative safeguard is to say that you have arranged to be collected at a specified time. Maintain a professional image by wearing clothes that 'look the part', and by showing your proof of identity. At the same time, take a balanced approach towards establishing the necessary degree of trust or rapport (see Chapter 7). As we stressed earlier, a good relationship between interviewer and interviewee is essential to gain accurate data. However, the behaviour you are showing as a technique to secure confidence – informality and disclosure, for example – can give off the wrong signals and be misinterpreted by the respondent as (over) friendliness. When the situation involves cross-gender interviewing, there is always the possibility, however remote, that the interviewee can mistake efforts to build rapport for sexual advances. All the time, listen for 'funny feelings' from yourself and trust your instincts; if you feel at all uneasy make an excuse, abandon the interview and leave. Remember the adage, 'it's better to be safe than sorry'.

Maintaining contact is crucial. Always carry spare change and a phonecard in case of emergencies. Although not cheap, mobile phones are useful: knowing

---

**Box 9.3  Guidelines for personal safety when interviewing**

- Cost personal safety measures into the research budget.
- Plan for safety: take a colleague or friend; use transport effectively.
- Carry and show interviewer identification.
- Leave an itinerary of your movements with a colleague or friend.
- Arrange to check in with a colleague or friend.
- Carry appropriate personal safety equipment: mobile phone, personal alarm, torch.
- Let the interviewee know you have a travel plan.
- Assess the layout of the interview location.
- Be aware of how rapport may be misinterpreted.
- Dogs – befriend them, or ask for them to be removed.
- Actively take decisions about the situation.

that you do not have to rely on inconvenient public telephones can be very reassuring. Before you set off for the interview, give a friend or colleague written details of your movements, including who you have arranged to interview (whilst emphasizing the need for confidentiality), where you are going, your route and when you expect to be back. If you are staying away overnight, leave the address and telephone number of your accommodation. You might choose to arrange to check in on your return from the interview. And if your plans change, then let someone know.

We have summarized the main points to bear in mind regarding personal safety in Box 9.3.

## Conclusion

In this chapter, we have considered the risks of harm to both research participants and researchers, as well as presenting techniques aimed at reducing any negative effects. It could be argued that we accentuated the negative aspects of interviewing, and downplayed the positive. This was deliberate, in the sense that we wanted to concentrate minds on the issues that we think are important, and in this way encourage best practice. However, we now want to redress the balance by making one last key point: keep things in perspective. Do not dramatize the issues so that they assume a level of risk far higher than interviews – even those concerned with sensitive topics – typically entail (Hammersley and Atkinson, 1995).

# 10 Transcribing the Data

> ... committing verbal exchanges to paper seems to result in their immediate deterioration: context, empathy, and other emotional dynamics are often lost or diminished, and the language seems impoverished, incoherent, and ultimately embarrassing for those who have cause to read back over their contributions (including the interviewer/researcher!). (Poland, 1995: 299)

Transcription is a part of the organization and management of the data. It is the production of a written record of the interview. However, recalling the discussions in Chapter 1, we observe that many social scientists would deny that there is one, real version of reality to be captured. Accordingly, a transcript is one interpretation of the interview, and no more than one interpretation. Furthermore, most transcripts only capture the spoken aspects of the interview, missing the setting, context, body language and 'feel'. In many, but not in all transcripts pauses and hesitations are edited out. Decisions are made about the ways in which speech is represented, there are invariably guesses about what was said, and there is the issue of how to turn speech into written prose, all of which extend the distance between a transcript and the interview event. Mishler (1991) draws a helpful parallel between a transcript and a photograph. Just as a photograph is one, frozen, contexted, printed and edited version of reality, so too with transcripts. So, in a sense, the question is not so much whether a transcript is accurate as whether it constitutes one, careful attempt to represent some aspects of the interview.

The transcription of data can be done at many levels of detail. The level of transcription will depend on the research purposes. With survey research, transcription is scarcely needed, and it is better to talk of data capture. With more qualitative interviews, notes summarizing the key points are sufficient for some purposes, although in other cases it is important to have transcriptions that include grunts, 'er', 'well . . . ' and 'mmm', as well as timed estimates of the length of pauses. Mercifully, this level of transcription is not normally needed in many studies, where the researcher is interested only in the meanings and not in the hesitations, false starts and throat clearing that accompany them. However, these features are important to linguistics researchers and those interested in discourse analysis.

Consequently, transcription is neither neutral nor value-free. What passes from tape to paper is the result of decisions about what ought to go on to paper. Sometimes, 'bad' language gets edited out. Sometimes, a typist decides to type only words, not pauses and 'er', 'mmm' and 'huh!'. Similarly, there is the notorious problem of how to punctuate speech: where should full stops, semi-colons and commas go? What about paragraph marks? These decisions are the more acute the further one moves from closed questions to open questions, from concise respondents to voluble informants. Transcriptions are, quite unequivocally, inter-pretations. For that reason, if for no other, it is wise to keep interview tapes as an archive to which reference can be made if transcriptions prove to be inadequate for the level of analysis that becomes necessary.

## Data capture

With survey interviews, data are normally transcribed by the interviewer completing a schedule as the respondent answers. This is only possible because the schedule and interview have both been designed so that this transcription involves the inter-viewer in making few inferences about the meaning of what the respondent says. Interviewer training will also have provided training in interpreting responses and, where computer-assisted telephone interviewing is used (CATI), the reliability of the interviewer is monitored. So, transcription is relatively simple, although Dijkstra, van der Veen and van der Zouwen (1985) have shown that survey inter-viewers do vary in the way they ask questions and code (transcribe) responses.

There is another possible source of error in transcribing survey data. It has to be moved from the interviewer's schedule to a computer database. It is common to pay clerks to type the information on the schedules into a computer program, which is a potential source of error, the extent of which will be greater or lesser depending on the motivation and accuracy of the typist. There is a faster, cheaper and more accurate method available. It involves designing the schedule so that respondents' answers can be read by an optical mark reader (OMR). These machines are fast, as accurate as is the marking up of the schedule, put the data straight into a database and cost less to operate than a team of typists, although their capital cost needs to be taken into account.

## Transcribing qualitative data

The commonest procedure is to make audio tapes of interviews and then produce a typed version of the words on tape. Video tapes are an alternative method of data capture and have their own additional transcription problems, discussed below.

### The transcriber's work

Undergraduate and postgraduate students may not have the funds to pay for trans-cription and have to do it themselves. Transcribing the tapes yourself has undoubted advantages: you become familiar with the data; you are reminded of the tone of the interview; and you should get a transcript that is acceptable to you, whereas when someone else does the transcription it is always necessary to hunt out the mistakes and mistranscriptions. But, if you try to transcribe the tapes yourself, you need to be a skilled typist. 'Peck and hunt' typing, applied to transcription work, is a recipe for misery. Box 10.1 presents a further option that is becoming more attractive with the development of technology (see also Anderson, 1998).

---

**Box 10.1 Computer-assisted transcription**

For some years Peter has been transcribing tapes by means of a voice dictation programme. He uses IBM's *Simply Speaking Gold* which has been superceded (and super-superceded) by more robust and powerful software. Affordable, entry-level programmes can be efficiently handled by all new multimedia PCs, although software affordability is at the price of sophistication. With these cheaper, older programmes each word has to be sounded out separately and distinctly whereas more sophisticated software does a reasonable job of recognising continuous speech. Then again, older PCs may falter with top-end software.

The process is to listen to a tape through the headphones and then, phrase by phrase, to dictate a 'clean' version directly into the word processor. This is cheaper than using audio typists, keeps the researcher in control of the transcription process and brings about greater familiarity with the data. However, some people find it hard to persuade the software to recognize their words accurately and feel that typing is faster. That has not, however, been Peter's experience.

The main snags are that the program makes mistakes, which have to be corrected manually, and that it still takes about four or five hours to transcribe an hour of tape. On the other hand, the researcher becomes more familiar with the data, which speeds analysis, and the programme produces a properly laid-out, correctly spelled transcript. As the sophistication of these programs increases, this is likely to become a preferred way of transcribing interview data.

---

Traditional means of transcription are mechanical, repetitive, fatiguing and can be stressful, especially when the recording quality is poor. As we said in Chapter 7, it is advisable to use the best recording equipment that funds can be stretched to. Even so, there are many reasons why parts of some tapes will be barely audible. Sooner or later, the interviewer will forget to switch a microphone on, the interviewing site will have poor acoustic qualities, or low battery power will produce a faint recording. Transcribers seldom have machines sufficiently sophisticated to overcome these problems, and not everyone can use a computer in conjunction with a hi-fi system so that the graphic equalizers lift the conversation from the background noise. Some parts will not be transcribable, and this should be noted in the transcript. Elsewhere, guesses will be made, and a good transcriber will be trained to alert the researcher to the fact that a section is a best guess.

Unsurprisingly, there are problems when there are hundreds of tapes to be transcribed. Very few people can work full time at audio transcription, and a 50:50 ratio of transcription to other activities is necessary if the audio typist is not to quit and if productivity and accuracy are not to plummet. Clearly, this sort of transcription can produce a serious bottleneck in the research process, something of which both authors have experience. Transcription agencies offer an alternative solution for research teams with sufficient funds.

There are a number of transcription conventions, each designed to capture greater or lesser detail about different features of the interview – Mishler (1991), Silverman (1993) and Poland (1995) give examples of different conventions. To illustrate that transcription can be more than simply typing out the words, we reproduce a sliver of a transcript produced for discourse analysis (Potter, 1996: 137).

> Counsellor: Wha_ ( ). what <u>happened</u> at <u>that</u> point.
> Woman: At <u>that</u> point, (0.6) Jimmy ha_ ().
> My_ <u>Jim</u>my is ex<u>treme</u>ly jealous.
> Ex_ ex<u>treme</u>ly *jeal*ous <u>per</u>:son.
> Has <u>a:l</u>ways ¯ been, from the da:y we <u>met</u>.

Transcribers need to be trained in using the convention that is most appropriate to your research purpose. They must be stopped from tidying up the tape in unhelpful ways. Patton (1990) tells of a student whose transcripts had all been put into good, transactional prose by a 'helpful' transcriber. The result was data that were unfit for the research purpose.

Box 10.2 provides some rules of practice that can mitigate some of the problems mentioned in this section – but nothing mitigates them like money does.

### Partial transcripts

A partial transcript is where the researcher keeps full interview notes and has only key sections of the tape transcribed. If the purpose is to use the interviews to get understanding of the range of ideas used, then this may be acceptable, particularly if there were two researchers in the room. One of us has used this technique with focus groups, where the second researcher made notes and identified portions of the tape recording that were especially worth transcribing. However, in order to do this, the focus group's discussions had to be quite tightly managed: fortunately, informants' comments tended to be quite short and free of the complex, wandering and looping structure that is common with one-to-one, in-depth interviews. Since the purpose was to get a sense of the things that mattered to people, not to probe those things in depth, notes-and-partial-transcripts were fit for the purpose. It was also a relatively cheap approach and quick to do, both of which were important in this project.

The underlying assumption, in the context of the research purpose, is that the data are fairly unproblematic.

### Full transcripts: the director's cut?

Full transcription is expensive. Estimates of the time it takes to transcribe an hour of tape vary between seven and ten hours, and poor sound quality will mean that even longer may be needed. Someone working on piecework rates is unlikely to charge less than £50 per hour of tape for this. Operating on tight budgets, researchers often have full transcripts made of the first ten or so interviews and of a sample thereafter. Notes and partial transcriptions are used for the rest. While this can be

**Box 10.2   Some hints on transcription practices**

**If you are to transcribe your own tapes**

- Use C60 or C90 tapes – C120 tapes are more likely to break.
- Knock out the tabs on the cassette so that you cannot inadvertently record over your interview (you can always use sticky tape to cover them later).
- When typing, don't be mean with space. Leave at least a line between each paragraph. If you will be using software for the data analysis, check the format your transcript needs to be in. For example, with the NUD*IST software package (see Chapter 11), it is a good idea to begin each sentence on a new line (or type it normally and save as 'Text with line breaks'). If you will be using software for analysis, don't waste time with **Bold**, Underline, *Italic*, or any other effects.
- When the interviewer speaks, begin the paragraph in capitals, in a standard and consistent way, with letters that show it is the interviewer speaking: 'INT: How did you feel about that, then?' for example. Do the same for the interviewee(s).

**If someone else is doing the transcription for you, also**

- Make it clear that they are not to tidy up the prose. Tell them how you want pauses, repetitions, laughs, hesitations and the like handled.
- Get them to use a standard, non-usual symbol to show where they've not been able to hear what was said, or they're unsure that they transcribed correctly. Peter uses ** or zx, which can rapidly be located using the 'Find' function of a word processor.
- Try to give them one interview to do at a time and set a deadline for its return (on disk and in hard copy).
- Make sure you check the first couple of transcripts quickly, so that you can act if the transcriber is unsatisfactory.
- Insist that the transcriber makes at least two disk copies of the files.
- Impress upon the transcriber that the transcripts are confidential.

One way of getting transcriptions done is to send the tapes to an agency. As long as the tape doesn't contain an identification of the informant, confidentiality is secured. It can be more difficult to be as confidential when the transcriber is a person who lives or works more locally. It is your responsibility to see that transcribers are not given anything that would identify informants or those connected with informants *and* to insist that transcribers do not discuss their work with other people.

pragmatically justified, the price is that many meanings are reduced to the neatness of note summaries, disguising the complexity and subtlety of the interview.

The transcripts then need to be checked for accuracy and suitability. Both have to be done by the person who did the interview, and this can be time-consuming. There are two main approaches to checking for accuracy. One, the faster, is to read the transcript and if it makes sense, leave it at that, correcting only the obvious errors. Up to an hour of checking for an hour of taping is needed for this method, depending on the quality of the tape and of the work. Alternatively, read the transcript while playing the tape. This is more scrupulous and more time consuming. Probably, the decision about which checking method to use rests on a decision about how much it matters if the faster method misses points that the slower method would pick up. In other words, is 95 per cent accurate transcription acceptable, or does it have to be 99.5 per cent? Notice that 'accuracy' is necessarily a relative concept. Even where the aim is faithfully to put words into print, decisions about punctuation mean that more than one 'accurate' transcription could be produced.

However, a bigger question is whether the transcription is a suitable representation of the interview, in terms of the research purposes. Conversation has features that seldom make it into print. For example:

- Abbreviations (isn't, aren't, weren't) – *sometimes* transcribed as 'is not' etc.
- Verbal tics, like 'er' and 'um' – usually ignored.
- Pauses – either cut or shown simply by three dots ( . . . ).
- Repetitions (for example, 'What I mean . . . I mean . . . what I want to say is . . . I mean that it is a real problem') – this might simply be rendered as 'It is a real problem'.

There is a good case for weeding these features out during transcription. For example, a senior education official gave an excellent and stimulating interview. When transcribed literally, it was full of 'er'. This tic broke the flow of the prose and made the person seem dumb. He was embarrassed when he saw the transcript. What did we gain by retaining the 'er'? In this case, nothing. Where other people silently pause for a moment's thought, he kept his voice going with the 'er' sound. We understood it as a sign of thought, not of uncertainty. Unless the level of intended analysis needs transcriptions that retain tics, pauses and the like, they can be excised. Does that matter?

For most social science purposes, where it is the ideas, logic, beliefs and understandings that are wanted, this editing is acceptable. It may be that a straight prose transcription is unsuitable, and that pauses, hesitations and tones of uncertainty, weeded out of the transcript, need to be restored. There are some areas of research, notably linguistics, where it is vital that transcripts are literal records of the sounds on the tape, or as nearly as possible, and that pauses are exactly timed and recorded. Unfortunately, the tone of voice – enthusiastic, bored, confrontational, mocking – easily and routinely does not make it into the transcript. So too with body language. There is no reliable way of conveying either in transcripts, although it is usual to put, for example, [*he/she/interviewer laughs*], if that can be heard. The question is whether it is more suitable to try for richer descriptions of the interview, or whether it is acceptable to settle for an 'accurate' rendering of the spoken words.

*Transcribing video tapes* Video tapes are used because interviewers recognize that an enormous amount of interaction takes place in non-verbal ways, and this channel of information is completely lost on audio tape. Here, video recordings give a better record of the interview. This is especially true of focus groups where the researcher wants to know who said what, and cannot infer it from an audio recording.

Needless to say, there are problems, the most frequently mentioned of which is the obtrusiveness of the camera. It can also be hard to site a camera in a focus group so that everyone is in frame. But, if there are problems with making a video record, the problems of transcribing it are greater.

Since video recording has been done to capture information that gets missed by audio recording, it follows that the transcript must be designed to capture that information. It might then be in two columns, one for the words and the other for non-verbal material taken from the video. But how is that non-verbal material to be reliably captured? Should there simply be a description of behaviours that need little inference, such as sitting upright, looking at the interviewer, or gesticulating? Or should there be more subtle readings of body language and inferences about mood and attitude? The problem is that it is hard to make these inferences and they are disputable. How are they to be made reliably? The classic answer is that two researchers watch the tape and code the behaviour, discussing disagreements until agreement is reached. Leaving aside the point that all this shows is that two people can come to an agreement (but not that a third, fourth or *nth* person would reach the same conclusion), the main objection is the cost of doing this. It can only be justified, we suggest, under three conditions:

*   Where the techniques exist to describe non-verbal information accurately and then to analyse it in ways that offer purchase on the research problem.
*   Where the research demands that such extensive data are collected (that is rarely the case).
*   Where the aim is to produce excerpts that can be used for training or illustrative purposes, or that look as though they will have exceptional significance in the findings.

Here, we are in essence repeating the message that the decision to use video tape and thinking about how to transcribe it depend upon what would count as the best way of discharging the research purpose.

## Conclusion

The way that transcription is done reflects the research purpose and design and is also effectively a part of data analysis. The form of transcription affects the ways in which the data can be analysed. The case of transcribing video tapes has been used to highlight the way in which transcription is an act of interpretation. This can even hold good for surveys, where the interviewer may need to use judgement in order to decide which pre-specified category best captures a respondent's words.

It is to full-blown data analysis that we now turn.

# 11 Meanings and Data Analysis

Literary structuralists have concentrated on the formal stylistic filters in communication between people, to the extent that some seem trapped in an impossibilism . . . too often these theories are phrased in deliberate obscurity, self-referring in their complexity . . . it is easy to forget the important messages that do get across . . . to forget that the informant had something to say; in short, to stop listening. (Thompson, 1988: 246/7)

If I were to try and put my finger on the single most serious shortcoming relating to the use of interviews in the social sciences, it would certainly be the commonsensical, unreflexive manner in which most analyses of interview data are conducted. (Briggs, 1986: 102)

In qualitative research, little is ever usually written about the process of analysis at all . . . little is said about who the analysts are, . . . which particular perspectives they adopt . . . how are disagreements resolved . . . whether full transcripts are used, how much is reported, what level of uncodable or unsortable data is tolerable, what basis is used for filtering data . . . (Powney and Watts, 1987: 174)

The analysis of data is perhaps the most demanding and least examined aspect of the qualitative research process. (McCracken, 1988: 41)

The analysis of the data gathered in a naturalistic inquiry begins the first day the researcher arrives at the setting. The collection and analysis of the data obtained go hand-in-hand as theories and themes emerge during the study. (Erlandson et al., 1993: 109)

The message of the quotations with which this chapter starts is one that most qualitative researchers have learned the hard way: data analysis is difficult and can take the novice – and the more experienced researcher as well – longer than expected. That is an unwelcome discovery when analysis has been planned to fit a short space of time before the report is finalized and presented. To a lesser extent, it is also true of the analysis of survey data as well.

We begin this chapter from the position that one reason why data analysis can be so complex is because there are embedded difficulties with knowing what it is that the data could plausibly be said to mean. From there, we proceed to look at the analysis of data from closed questions, including the use of statistics, to indicate meanings that we see in the data. This is followed by an extended discussion of procedures involved in analysing data from open-ended questions, focusing on the analysis of interview transcripts. We review the use of computer software to support this process.

We have chosen to organize the material on data analysis around the analysis of question types rather than to base it on the survey/qualitative interview distinction. This is because many interviews make use of both types of question and analytical approaches vary according to the type of question rather than the interview framework in which the questions are set. Answers to closed questions are usually tallied, summarized in the form of frequencies and percentages, and subjected to statistical investigation and manipulation. Open-ended questions are usually analysed qualitatively, with the emphasis upon a search for meaning and understanding.

## Meanings

In Chapter 1 we developed the claim that texts (which include responses to interview questions) contain a variety of meanings. We illustrate this by a discussion of answers to closed, or fixed-response, questions, which many treat as if they were self-explanatory and uncontentious. Uncertainty about the meanings of responses to closed questions is compounded with open questions, as Table 11.1 shows.

### Meaning and responses to closed questions

Figure 11.1 is a view of the main factors that interact to shape the meanings we make of social research data. At first sight, interviewees' responses, which are the *text*, seem to be quite straightforward. We illustrate some of the problems by returning to the notion of effectiveness (see Box 4.3). If respondents say they think their social work team is an effective one (or that it is not, or that it is

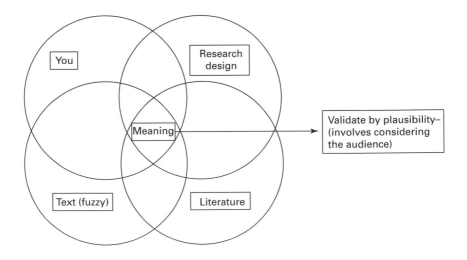

FIGURE 11.1 *Meaning as the intersection of four fields*

TABLE 11.1 *The problematic nature of meaning in responses to closed and open questions*

| Issue | Responses to closed questions | Responses to open questions |
|---|---|---|
| Interviewees' judgements hidden from you | Responses are the result of informants making judgements, which are not known to us, about the best fit between their experience and the response categories | Respondents' thinking should be clear, and good interviewers will have explored it |
| Forgetfulness | Applies to all interview data | |
| 'Halo' effect (putting things in the best light) | Applies to all interview data | |
| Type of understanding | Receptive understanding | Spontaneous understanding |
| Context effects | All data are affected by when they were collected and by the circumstances of collection | |
| Your preconceptions | Closed questions show people's responses to your agenda only | Much more scope for collecting data that go beyond your preconceived notion of how things are likely to be |
| Your judgements | Judgement mainly limited to setting cut-off points | Your judgement pervades the research, which is why it is important to check your judgement with others (inter-observer reliability is one example of this) |
| Literature influences the meanings you see | In the way it affects the research design it limits what you can see, and it may lead you to put more emphasis on some data than on other data | Influences the meanings you find and may lead you routinely to discard large amounts of data |
| The audience | Audience expectations and requirements have affected the design of the study and the meanings that are particularly valued in data analysis | |
| Research design imposes limits on possible meanings | Significance, in the sense of generalizability, affected by sampling design | In qualitative research, it is often the reader who infers generalizability, not the researcher who proclaims it (see also Chapter 4) |
| Statistical significance | Danger of confusing statistical significance with the real-life importance of results | This concept can be used *with great care* to highlight patterns in responses to open questions. Use non-parametric techniques! |
| Cause and effect | It is easy to misinterpret the association of two factors, which is frequently found in the analysis of survey data, as evidence of a causal relationship | Connections may be discerned, but without the formal support of statistical analysis. Again, it is an error to do more than *speculate* on possible causal relationships |

neither effective nor ineffective), then that appears to be that. There is, however, no assurance that they all mean the same when they make a judgement of effectiveness. Nor are matters eased if they have rated the effectiveness of the team on a five-point Likert scale, since a person in a team that most would rate as 'very effective' may have limited experience of other teams, have high standards or be sparing in praise, and only rate it as 'effective'. This is one version of a common experience when trying to answer closed questions: the categories from which we have to choose often do not quite match the subtlety of our experience, beliefs and feelings, so we end up trying to compress that complexity into one simple, ill-fitting category. In other words, even data from closed questions are saturated with interpretation, but not the interpretations of interviewers, who have been rigorously trained to maximize their reliability, but the interpretations of the respondents, who have to judge how best they fit the pre-set responses available to them. Answers may also be contaminated by forgetfulness, or by 'public speech', where we tend to present ourselves in the best, most helpful, light. Lastly, we return to the distinction between spontaneous responses and receptive responses (see Chapter 6). Spontaneous responses are given unprompted, receptive responses are prompted. Open-ended questions prompt the informant to the extent that they direct attention to questions and issues that might not have been much considered. The informants then tell what is at the front of their minds, referring to things that are most likely to be salient in daily life at that point. There is a far wider range of things that we might say with more prompting, which is what closed questions do. However, points that we recognize and agree with are not necessarily things that have much prominence in our normal thinking. For example, the pattern of answers to the two questions in Box 11.1 is likely to be very different.

When reading data from closed questions, it is helpful to wonder whether the pattern of responses to open-ended questioning would have been the same. Our experience is that closed questions often produce responses indicating that people have a more extensive range of opinions than we find when asking open-ended questions. We suggest that the ideas that come from open questioning are likely to be a better fit with informants' actions, since those ideas are the ones that are salient enough to be reported. Ideas that respondents recognize and with which they may agree may have a more 'intellectual' status and relate less closely to action. This is an extension of the distinction between receptive and spontaneous responses that was described in Chapter 6.

In survey interviews, considerable care is taken to ensure that information is collected reliably. However, even if respondents are not deliberately mis-leading the interviewer (a game that some people play on intercept and phone interviewers), there is still a problem with the text. We know what the text *says*, but because of the circumstances and inferences that have led people to give these answers, we cannot be sure about what it *means*. In practice, we treat the data as though this problem did not exist, although there are many analyses of responses to closed questions that can be disturbed by thinking carefully about what the respondents might have meant in answering the way that they did.

---

**Box 11.1  Same issue, different question formats**

**1  Do you have a lot of say about how you do your work?**

[If the answer is 'yes' or 'in some ways', ask informants to explain in what ways they have a say in how they do their work.]

---

**1  Do you have a lot of say about how you do your work?**

[If the answer is 'yes' or 'in some ways', go to question 2: if not, go to question 3 (not shown in this example).]

**2  Do you have a lot of say in:**

(a) How long you work
(b) When you work
(c) Who you work with
(d) The order in which you will do different tasks
(e) How long you will take over different tasks
(f) How you do different tasks
(g) When you take breaks
(h) Is there anything else in your work about which you have a lot of say?

---

*You*, as the researcher, also affect the meanings that are read into the data, although this is far more pronounced with the interpretation of open questions than with closed ones. The design of the study, which has determined the data that you have collected, and which shapes the way in which you will interpret them, reflects your understandings, preconceptions, beliefs, prejudices and feelings. A sound literature review and good piloting should have checked that the research is more than an exercise in investigating your preconceptions, but it cannot take you out of the equation. A quick look at the literature on any social research theme shows how greatly researchers differ in the perspectives they bring to a study, as well as in the methods that they choose to use (which are often the methods with which they feel most at home).

Your judgements also affect the interpretation of the data. For example, Peter asked children questions about a set of stories. The answers were scored, which involved some judgement, which was shown to match well with the judgement of others who used the same scoring system. There were two ways in which the interviewer directly affected the search for meaning. The first was in the choice of a scoring system. There were several possible ways of scoring the answers, and it is arguable that those that were not used would have been as useful, and that they would have produced a different picture. The second involved making a decision about the cut-off point at which it would be said that children had shown mastery at a certain level. A score of 100 per cent would certainly have shown mastery at that level and a score of 0 per cent would have shown none. But what about the other scores? Was 66 per cent to be regarded as mastery, or should the cut-off come at 80 per cent? The decision had a profound effect upon the claims that were made on the basis of responses to these closed questions.

We have noted that *the literature* is one of the sources of preconceptions that we bring to the design of a study and to the analysis of the data. Clearly, the literature offers a range of frameworks that affect the way we see data. For example, people who study motivation and who are well-versed in the literature on locus of control (which means whether people believe that they have a lot of influence over their lives or not), will tend to construct meanings in the light of that literature. Other documents and evidence that we gather during the study will also affect the way we look at the data, even where they are in the form of responses to closed questions. That might take the form of paying much more attention to one set of answers than to another: for example, finding that one group of workers believed that there had been an increase in managerial control of their work, Peter looked much more closely at answers to questions about autonomy at work than to other responses to closed interview questions. This is much more of a problem with data from qualitative interviews, where it is not always obvious that everything in the transcript is relevant. Effectively, much data is discarded in the search for meaning and in the face of a need to simplify massive texts. What gets discarded, or gets less attention from the researcher, is often a reflection of the influence of the literature on the researcher's sense of what is important.

A similar role is played by the *audience* of the research report. In the next chapter we say it is important that research reports are written for a specific audience, and that different audiences (academic staff, practitioners, journals) have different expectations. Here, we suggest that those expectations can influence which aspects of the data get the most serious attention: they can affect the meanings that researchers find in the data.

Lastly, the *research design* influences the meanings that can be seen in the data. We have already referred to the different meanings that are implied by exploring receptive and spontaneous understanding. The design also affects the way the data analysis is carried out. Answers to closed questions are typically tallied up, so that it is reported that 35 per cent of respondents agreed with a statement, 35 per cent neither agreed nor disagreed and 30 per cent disagreed. As we shall see in the next section (Box 11.3), statistical techniques can be used to help us discover whether the difference between the proportions of those agreeing and those disagreeing is likely to be anything more than a chance occurrence in this sample, or whether it is likely to reflect a genuine difference. Yet, even if the difference turns out not to be a chance variation (that is to say, that it is statistically significant), there remains the question of whether the size of the difference is of any great interest from a theoretical or practical perspective. That is for the researcher to judge, and then to try to convince others.

Statistical techniques also allow us to show how far one trait (for example, a high sense of control over one's life) is related to another (for example, career success). It may be that there is a 60 per cent correlation (so the two features are strongly associated, and this is statistically significant). There is a temptation, under the influence of some of the literature, to read this as evidence that those with a high sense of control over their lives have more success at work. In other words, there is a temptation to bring to the figures the meaning that high levels of control are a cause of success. That is not legitimate. It could be that those who succeed are likely to attribute their success to their own characteristics (such as a sense of being in control of their lives), rather than to luck, or to other factors. This is an error that often goes with research designs that use closed questions and quantitative analysis. Computer-based statistical analysis packages, such as SPSS, can reveal large numbers of correlations and show statistically significant patterns throughout the data. The temptation is to assume that because something is statistically significant (that is to say that it is unlikely to be a chance occurrence), then it is important, and to try to make statements about causes and effects on the basis of statistics which show a correlation between two things.

There are two points we want to bring out of this discussion of the use of statistics in social research. One is that clever and complex statistical techniques are no substitute for good design. A typical survey allows you to make statements about correlation but does not permit statements about causation. Nor does statistical significance say much about what the differences in patterns of response mean. Secondly, the design of the study limits the range of meanings that it is legitimate to infer from the data. This can be further illustrated by returning to the matter of generalizability. The question is the extent to which the researcher can claim that what is found in the sample applies to a bigger group. Suppose the study were of the way people cope with negative affect (bad feelings) in their lives. The responses to closed questions may, with luck, give a very clear answer. However, if this were a study of 100 people, it would not be safe to assert that the findings held true for all people in that culture (the research design used too small a sample for that). If it were a sample of 100 students in one university, then it would be fair to suggest that the findings probably held good for other students at the university, although the sample is still too small to make that a strong claim.

*Summary: meaning and quantitative data*  The meanings we attribute to responses to closed questions are *our* attributions, nothing more. In practice, it is often acceptable to put aside the problematic nature of the process of making meanings from data. However, putting aside the problems is not the same as saying that those problems do not exist.

## Analysis

The way data are analysed is largely determined by the research design. In turn, the design ought to be guided by thought about data analysis. There are those who decide to ask open-ended questions with little thought about how the data will be analysed and who are dismayed when they find out how time-consuming and difficult this analysis is. Others choose to use closed questions without having any grasp of descriptive statistics, let alone of the procedures used to test for statistical significance, to detect associations and to uncover clusters of linked elements (see Box 11.3 for a further explanation of statistical analysis).

Broadly speaking, there are two approaches to data analysis: quantitative approaches to the analysis of data from closed questions and qualitative analysis of data from open questions. The distinction is not a rigid one. Respondents may be asked whether they regard social work as a profession, and why. It would be possible to note the reasons they give and to tally them across the sample, so as to claim that 35 per cent of respondents mentioned training and education as something crucial to professional status, 29 per cent mentioned autonomy, and so on.

## Quantitative analysis

Box 11.2 contains an example of the sort of data that are collected in survey research. With small samples and short interview schedules, it is feasible to count up the responses and to tabulate them manually. There are enormous advantages to using a computer to do this. It speeds up the analysis and saves and eliminates a good deal of tedious, routine work. Once data are entered, the computer is unlikely to make mistakes when carrying out the long calculations that are involved in statistical analysis. Most important of all, it is then simple to use a range of statistical tests on the data and to explore similarities and differences amongst subsets of the data: for example, do males and females respond similarly or differently to the questions?

A variety of statistical analysis packages is commercially available, both in mainframe and personal computer versions. A widely used package is SPSS,

---

**Box 11.2  Coding data in quantitative analysis**

In her study of people with Repetitive Strain Injury (RSI), Hilary used a questionnaire that was completed by 308 people (Arksey, 1998). It was a very long questionnaire, which provided data under 91 headings. The coding grid, then, contained 308 cases and 91 variables, categories, or fields. The data were largely nominal (see Table 11.2) and were converted into numbers. Interval data, on age, for example, were grouped, so that those aged under 20 were coded as '1', those 20–29 were coded as '2', and so on. The codes were then entered into the grid under SPSS for Windows.

Three types of answer needed particular care. 'Do not know' was coded with a number mid-way between the most positive and most negative answers. 'Not applicable' was coded as '0', and the cell was left empty where there was no response.

The task was complicated, and because it is easy to lose track of how the data were being coded, Hilary kept a coding file that recorded the rules she was using for coding up the answers. This will not always be needed for the analysis of closed questions, where it is usually plain how answers are to be coded. It may not be important where there are many fewer than 91 fields. It may be prudent, however, to get into the practice of keeping a list of rules and it is vital, as we shall show, in the analysis of qualitative data.

although Minitab and Genstat have their followers, and a spreadsheet such as Microsoft Excel is sufficient for many purposes. With complex designs it is advisable to get advice, at the design stage, about the package that will be the most useful. There is little point in designing a study that produces data that cannot be analysed in the ways you need with the software that you have. For example, Excel is the software that Peter prefers to use when only simple, descriptive statistics are needed. If complex, multivariate analysis were needed, SPSS would be used. The cost of designing a study that involved multivariate analysis would have to be taken into account early in the day, since a user familiar only with Excel would have to learn SPSS and how to do multivariate analysis. Two books that introduce software packages and are helpful about the uses of statistics are by Bryman and Cramer on SPSS for Windows (1997), and Cramer (1997) on Minitab.

An important reservation about the software packages is that the range of statistical tests that they support is often not quite as wide as you might need. To explain this rather puzzling point (puzzling because the software seems to be crammed with tests), we need to distinguish between four types of data. Table 11.2 sets out this distinction.

The significance of this distinction is that different qualities of data need different types of statistical test. Strictly speaking, parametric statistics, which dominate software programs, should only be used with interval or ratio data. Non-parametric statistics, which should be the most widely used in social research, should be used with nominal and ordinal data. Unfortunately, most programs contain too few non-parametric routines, so researchers tend, wrongly, to use parametric tests on non-parametric data. In practice, this misuse of parametric

TABLE 11.2 *Four types of data*

| Data quality | Example |
| --- | --- |
| Nominal | An answer of 'Yes' or 'No' is an example of nominal data. We might code 'Yes' as '1' and 'No' as '2'. We can then see whether there are overall differences in the patterns of response by those coded '1' and those coded '2' |
| Ordinal | Ordinal data are generated when people express preferences from a set of options, or when they rate or rank options. For example, we might ask people to rate the effectiveness of their work organization on a five-point scale from 'very effective' (coded '5') to 'very ineffective' (coded '1'). Notice that we cannot say how big the interval is between 'effective' and 'very effective', nor can we say that the interval is as big as that between 'effective' and 'neither effective nor ineffective'. Similarly, most examination scores are ordinal, although they are usually (mis)treated as though they were interval data |
| Interval | The interval between each unit of measurement is equal, as with temperature, where the difference between 33° and 34°; 47° and 48°; 81° and 82° is the same, 1°. However, we cannot say that 60° is twice as hot as 30° |
| Ratio | Intervals are equal and we can make ratio statements of the sort that 10 cm is twice as long as 5 cm. Most social science data are not ratio data |

tests does not usually matter too much. However, the scrupulous researcher will be aware of the quality of data that has been collected and look for software that supports the non-parametric tests that will frequently be needed.

Box 11.2 contained an example of how data from closed questions are coded up for analysis. Although that example refers to data from a questionnaire, the principles for organizing interview survey data are the same. In that case, data entry was done manually and Hilary typed in the codes for the age, sex, employment status, and so on, for each of the 308 people in the sample. In another study, Peter used massive sheets of squared paper to code interview responses from 100 children. He reasoned that the number of variables was manageable and that it would take longer to get punch-cards made for entering the data and to run what was, in those days, a remarkably unfriendly and cumbersome SPSS program than it would to use paper and pencil and do statistical tests with a scientific calculator. Today, Optical Mark Readers are widely used for scanning data directly from interview records and questionnaires into the software. Some commercial organizations also record interview data on hand-held computers, which download the responses directly into the main research results file. Telephone interviewers often code responses on the spot and enter them directly into the main results file.

The first level of analysis involves only descriptive statistics. Normally, that amounts to tallying the responses under each variable. So, numbers of males and females would be reported, as would the proportions of people of different ages in the sample and the breakdown of responses to each option for each question. Where possible, it is helpful to show these numerical summaries of the table in graph or chart form, although no one will be interested in seeing 91 charts for Hilary's 91 variables, nor will the researcher have the space to do anything more than summarize the data that best answer the research questions. Tables can also be used as an alternative to trying to describe the main features of the data in running prose.

The data are then subjected to statistical analysis. Box 11.3 explains why statistical analysis is used. The results of the first analysis will often provoke further analysis, which will itself often involve examining the impact of a set of variables or exploring the responses of sub-groups within a sample. For example, in one study, it appeared that the answers varied with the length of respondents' careers. Unfortunately, this had not been anticipated in the sampling and there were too few new entrants to the profession in the sample for it to be pursued. None the less, the observation influenced the design of subsequent studies. In general, because closed questions are usually framed by researchers who have a fairly good idea of what it is they are looking for, interpreting the results is not such a problem as it can be with qualitative data.

A notable exception is where closed and open questions are both asked of the sample. As we suggested in Chapters 2 and 3, ideally, the two sets of answers reinforce each other. However, we noted that different research methods can also produce different results, even when it appears to the researcher that the same questions are being asked, albeit in rather different ways. There are no rules for resolving such conflicts. Two strategies are widely used. One is to comb through the questions and the data, looking for clues as to what is happening. The other is

**Box 11.3  Statistics and data analysis**

*Q*:  What do you call someone who doesn't understand statistics?
*A*:  A qualitative researcher.

Statistics, like many science topics, seems to many people to be complex and counter-intuitive. We offer some thoughts to try to explain the logic of statistics but feel that it is only through practice that the complexity issue is resolved.

**Bivariate analysis** is about exploring the relationship between two sets of variables. Hilary looked at the socio-demographic characteristics of her 308 respondents in the Repetitive Strain Injury study to see whether there were any strong relationships between their patterns of response and their age, sex, education levels, and membership of an RSI support group. Three common approaches to bivariate analysis are:

*1  Comparison of average scores (means)*  The mean score of women on a five-point scale of levels of satisfaction with their university experience may be 3.65 and that of men 3.60. The question is whether this difference (which is hardly a large one) is likely to be a chance outcome of the sampling procedure. Non-parametric tests can be used to establish this. If it turns out that this is unlikely to be a chance occurrence, then it is possible to say that there is a small relationship between gender and satisfaction.

*2  Comparison of distributions*  We may notice that there is an apparent difference in the actual distribution of responses (percentages should *not* be used when drawing up a table for statistical analysis), as shown below.

|  | Low career success | High career success |
|---|---|---|
| Strong feelings of control | 13 | 20 |
| Weak feelings of control | 27 | 15 |

*Respondents categorized by feelings of control and perceived career success*

Inspection of the table suggests that there is an association between feeling in control of one's life and career success. However, this distribution could have come about by chance. The Chi-Square ($\chi^2$) test is used to explore the likelihood that this is no more than a chance result of sampling. If that seems unlikely (which is to say, if the distribution is statistically significant), then we can say that there does appear to be an association between the two variables.

*3  Correlation*  Correlation explores the strength of the relationship between two variables. The non-parametric calculation of correlation, the

*continued*

Spearman Rho, runs into difficulty when a lot of cases share a score on any variable, so it is common to calculate the parametric Pearson Product Moment Coefficient. For example, if a sample of 100 can be ranked on their scores on a variable so that there are few ties in rank, then Spearman is the best procedure to use. But if 25 have scored '5', 20 have '4', 17 have '3', 30 have '4' and 8 have '5', then it might be advisable to use the Pearson test.

**Statistical significance**: Many novices make the mistake of looking at data and seeing differences in patterns of response and then assuming that they have got something of importance. Anyone who has tossed a coin ten times will know that there's nothing particularly unusual about getting seven heads and three tails (but it would be unusual to flip 100 times and get a 70/30 split, and exceptional to get a 700/300 split from 1000 tosses of the coin). Statistical tests establish the likelihood of a pattern being the product of chance. If the possibility is just 5 per cent, then we normally say that the results are statistically significant – we're on to something. It needs to be stressed that something can be statistically significant without the difference being very interesting or important. This truth is illustrated by the coin tossing example, where a 7/3 split on a small sample may be quite normal, but is quite exceptional in a larger sample. In other words, the larger the number of cases, the smaller the imbalance **in the ratio** has to be before statistical significance is reached. Work with large samples frequently produces many statistically significant findings, which are small, often uninteresting and frequently of little use; they are statistically significant largely because of the sample size.

**Multivariate analysis** is used where we wish to examine the influence of sets of variables. For example, we may suspect that several variables are closely related and together have an effect. The technique of cluster analysis is used to explore whether there are sets of variables at work.

Statistical techniques can also be used to 'remove' the influence of confounding variables. Take the case of career success and beliefs about control over life. It might be said that career success is related strongly to educational achievement, and that if we really wanted to see how far people's beliefs about their levels of control related to career success, we ought to create a level playing field by only comparing people with equivalent educational attainments. Ideally, the study would have been designed to control for educational attainment, but where that was not done it would be possible to use statistical techniques to allow for the interaction of educational attainment, career success and beliefs about levels of control.

to feed the disparity back to the sample, perhaps through focus groups, and ask for their suggestions and explanations. The wrong approach is to discard data because they are inconvenient. Instead, following our suggestion on page 73, describe and discuss it in the research report.

*Qualitative analysis*

We began the chapter with quotations claiming that the analysis of data is relatively neglected in books on social research methods. There are exceptions (for instance, Dey, 1993; Bryman and Burgess, 1994), but the general neglect of data analysis can give readers the impression that significant ideas, conceptualizations and associations somehow emerge from the data of their own accord. As the first section of this chapter implied, if there are difficulties in seeing meanings in quantitative data, they are far more formidable with qualitative data – if only because of the sheer bulk of a set of interview transcripts.

The analysis of open questions – of qualitative data – usually begins at the design stage (see Figure 11.1) and continues, albeit informally, while the interviews are being done. Figure 11.2 extends the picture in Figure 11.1 by showing the analytical process as it parallels the interviewing and continues after it is done.

Even in the earliest stages of data collection, you can be on the look-out for themes that seem to be especially significant, whether from the perspective of the informants, the research question, current debates, or methodology. Keep notes of your ideas, hunches and insights. If it becomes evident that otherwise unexpected issues are coming to the fore, you may want to tweak the interview schedule in order to pursue them. It is not unknown for a qualitative study to be rethought after the first few interviews, which then take on the status of a second pilot study.

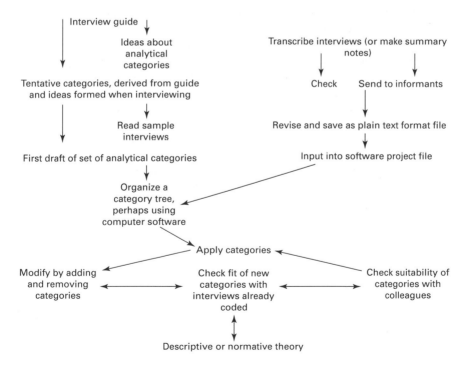

FIGURE 11.2  *Analysing qualitative data (this complements Figure 11.1, so does not show the tacit data analysis that precedes interviewing)*

Neither Figure 11.1 nor Figure 11.2 explains how a researcher gets a purchase on thousands of pages of transcripts, fieldnotes and other documents and turns the opinions, sentiments and thoughts that they contain into a succinct account that offers an answer to the research question. It is to that we now turn.

## Grounded theory

> There is no formula to aid the researcher in interpretation of qualitative research data . . . amongst the most essential [qualities is] to be able to stand back from the problem to get a new perspective; work with contradictions; explore new relationships; turn the problem around, perhaps even upside down; understand basic motivations and apply them; see behind rationalizations; ask and try to answer the question 'what is the meaning of this?' (Mostyn, 1985: 140)

You do not have to read many accounts of research before you come across the term 'grounded theory', an approach that is concerned with 'the discovery of theory from data' (Glaser and Strauss, 1967: 1; see also Strauss and Corbin, 1990). In fact, if citations in research texts or in research reports are anything to go by, grounded theory provides a common methodological framework for qualitative research. Whether grounded theory is actually used as much as it is referred to is another matter. It may well be that some, but not all, of its elements are used.

Essentially, the development of grounded theory involves constantly searching, comparing and interrogating the first few transcripts to establish analytical categories that address the research questions, that are mindful of the research literature, and which will allow the greatest amount of the data to be coded without either forcing them into categories or having categories that are so sprawling as to be virtually meaningless. This first stage of analysis is followed by further rounds of data collection, each of which serves to facilitate the refining of the initial categories in the light of these subsequent investigations. Thus, each time the researcher enters the field, the modified analytical categories are used as sensitizing devices to inform the collection of data. In this way, the researcher is seeking out links between the analytical categories, exploring emerging concepts and theories by seeing how they stand up to further data. In grounded theory, analysis is interwoven with data collection, a process of finding, analysing and theorizing. A variant of this claims that grounded theory is built by analysing data, forming tentative theories, testing them against the data, revising the theories, retesting them, and so on. Turner (1981) offers a detailed discussion of qualitative data analysis, including a series of nine procedural stages to follow when using the grounded theory approach.

The influence of grounded theory now extends as far as qualitative data analysis software. For instance, the designers of the software package NUD*IST (Non-numerical Unstructured Data Indexing, Searching and Theory-building) explicitly state that it supports this approach, allowing analytical categories to be formed, collapsed or subdivided at will. Other programs, such as Ethnograph, ATLAS/ti and HyperResearch, have their own strengths when it comes to analysing qualitative data. Kelle (1995) and Weitzman and Miles (1998) review different software packages, and also discuss the processes and problems of using computers to manage the analysis of qualitative data.

In practice, how does the analysis proceed? How do the ideas that are presented in the final report emerge? It is to the nuts and bolts of the analysis of qualitative data that we now turn.

*Indexing the data* First, the data need to be organized, by producing some manageable, systematic guide to heaps of data – transcripts, your notes and memos, perhaps other materials you have collected. Generally speaking, this implies some form of indexing (sometimes referred to as 'coding' and implying similar but not identical processes – see Bryman and Burgess, 1994) and retrieval. For indexing, which is just like indexing a book, the principle of 'cut and paste' is followed. Essentially, chunks of speech are coded and cut out of the transcript (or marked on the computer file) and pasted with similar items under a category or topic heading, so that like is with like. In the past (and with small data sets today) the researcher would paste the extracts on to cards, making duplicates where a passage of text needed to be indexed under more than one heading. Flexible software packages have speeded up this process and contain sophisticated tools to help the analyst to keep track of the categories and see relationships between them. For many small-scale research projects manual indexing will be sufficient and speedier. Box 11.4 illustrates the indexing (coding) process.

Indexing needs to be carefully done, and it is very desirable to check that your indexing of the data is not eccentric by getting others to use your rules to index a sample of transcripts. We develop this more fully in our discussion of inter-rater agreement in Box 11.5. The point here is that careful and consistent indexing is necessary but it is thwarted if the categories for analysis are inadequate. There has to be a sound basis for choosing to index according to some categories rather than others and the thinking behind it should be set out in the report, thereby consolidating the credibility or trustworthiness of your approach to data analysis.

The first step is to read through a sample of transcripts, which may be the first ones to be transcribed. Here, you are continuing what may have been going through your mind before, during and after these interviews, that is, looking for emerging themes, particular characteristics or qualities, unexpected messages and meanings, fruitful lines of enquiry, or possible foci for deeper study. This thinking will, as Figure 11.1 showed, also be informed by the literature and the overall research objectives, which will have been produced with the readers in mind. Following grounded theory, these categories are checked for adequacy against the new data coming in. Typically, the following questions are asked as the emergent categories are checked against new data:

- Do they cover all of the data that are relevant to the research aims? (It is normal to get a lot of 'background noise' in transcripts that cannot be used. The problem is if categories stop you from recognizing the importance of some data.)
- Are new categories needed?
- Do existing categories need to be split into sub-categories?

- Are there too many categories, so that you are regularly giving the same segments more than one code and finding that the distinctions implied by the different codes do not really describe significant differences in the data?
- Does your emerging sense of what should be included in a category need to be reviewed? (It is quite common to realize that the way a category was applied to early transcripts needs to be changed, which means that those transcripts need to be re-indexed.)
- Are there categories that are suggested by the literature which are not being used and ought to be applied to the data? (It is quite acceptable to find that categories suggested by the literature have no relevance to the data. The mistake is not to check whether that is the case.)

In this way, the categories are 'grounded', rooted empirically in the data and conceptually in the research issues.

There is room for argument about how fine-grained, or detailed, the categories and indexing scheme should be. The finer the grain, the lower the reliability of analysis of 'messy', qualitative data will tend to be (see Box 11.5), the more complex will be the set of rules to use, and the longer it takes. On the other hand, coarse-grained analysis is effectively discarding some of the meanings that could be derived from the data. When the analysis is computer-based, it is easy to change your mind and go from coarse-grained to fine-grained analysis as indexing proceeds.

There is also room for argument about the units of analysis. Plainly we would seldom be looking for the incidence of specific words. Similarly, if each sentence were coded, analysis would be a very long process. As we have said, there are circumstances, notably in discourse analysis, when this level of analysis is needed. It is more usual to index complete segments of meaning (sentences or paragraphs), which can often be organized around responses to questions. So, if the question is about strategies for dealing with unhappy events, it is possible to identify a series of categories, for example 'withdraw', 'stop over-eating', 'see friends', 'buy something', 'rage', etc., and index each segment that refers to one of those categories. Some segments will refer to more than one and should be indexed under each category.

Indexing can be tedious but it is always important. It is often slow, especially in the early stages when you are not familiar with the indexing rules and the process is not 'automated'. While we have suggested that building grounded theory implies that transcripts are analysed throughout the research, we would not recommend indexing transcripts one by one, as they come in. That does not give you much chance to build up speed at indexing and reduces the likelihood that you will make connections between things said in different interviews. We suggest indexing batches of interviews.

Indexing, then, is not straightforward. It is subjective: the analysis involves the exercise of judgement about the meaning and significance of the data. In terms of consistency, this is easiest if there is one researcher involved in the project, but there is a danger with it that your judgements may be eccentric. This problem is discussed in Box 11.5. Besides, since indexing normally takes place over a long

---

**Box 11.4  Coding data**

One hundred and seventy-eight teachers were asked whether they saw teaching as a profession and if so, why. A sample of responses was selected for coding. Each distinct idea was written down, with similar ideas being written alongside each other, and identical responses being tallied. For example, teaching was said to be a profession where teachers:

| | |
|---|---|
| Wear a suit/neat clothes 111111 | (g) |
| Higher education needed 111 | (e) |
| Clean shaven 1 | (g) |
| Mark work regularly 111 | (f) |
| Tidy hair 1 | (g) |
| Decide how to teach a topic 1111 | (d) |

The *full set* of ideas (over a hundred were noted) in the sample of transcripts could be collapsed to form eight main categories, which were:

| | |
|---|---|
| the public standing of teaching | (a) |
| teachers' inter-personal skills | (b) |
| teachers' possession of standards and values | (c) |
| teachers' autonomy and non-routine decision-making | (d) |
| the possession of specialist knowledge | (e) |
| conscientiousness | (f) |
| appearance and self-presentation | (g) |
| others | (h) |

It can be seen that 4 of the ideas in the sample above fell into category (d); 3 into (e); 3 into (f); and 8 into (g).

The categories were discussed by all five researchers, who agreed that they were usable and covered all of the data. Definitions of each category were then written, to make public their meanings and to enable any member of the team to apply them consistently.

The categories were then used to index the complete set of interviews.

---

period, you can face problems remembering on what basis you allocated something to a particular category, or in remembering where examples of particular categories are to be found. This is where notes and memos to yourself are vital, as if you were writing a running commentary on what you are doing for colleagues in a research team. These notes can contain your ideas, hunches, assumptions, thoughts about possible relationships, comments on data, indexing rules, and observations on methodological problems. This not only makes the process of

---

### Box 11.5   Inter-rater agreement

This is sometimes called 'inter-observer reliability'. It is concerned with two things. First, with establishing that your categories are fit for the purpose of analysis and, secondly, with establishing the accuracy of your indexing.

We are aware that it is not always easy for students, who are often working alone, to get others to examine their analytical processes. However, our experience is that most can find a colleague who will spend some time examining categories and indexing. The gesture of getting another opinion on your work may not make a great impact on what you do and how, but it is important in showing that you have taken this part of establishing the trustworthiness of your work as seriously as it is reasonable to expect.

Others should apply your categories and the rules for indexing the data to a selection of transcripts. What you are looking for at this point is confirmation that the categories you have chosen are workable, that they take in all the significant data, that they are not unnecessarily fine-grained, and that no sub-categories are needed. There is usually some disagreement amongst the different people who use the categories and there are no rules for resolving that disagreement. Rather, the disagreements should be regarded as raising points for you to consider and respond to. The aim is to tune your system of categories, leading to a final set that, informed by others' comments, is defensible, or plausible.

When the categories have been fixed in their final version, at least one other person should index a sample of transcripts. At issue is the closeness of fit of their coding with yours. It is possible to calculate the degree of agreement between you and other coders, which is usually expressed as a percentage. However, this is not easily done with complex qualitative data, when it is seldom clear what the unit of analysis should be (phrase, sentence, paragraph).

In the study of teachers' professional cultures, it was found that the five researchers agreed on the themes to be found in the data and agreed on the relative weightings of the different themes. When the data were analysed by tallying the ideas that respondents used to support different positions, the different researchers reached similar conclusions. However, there was disagreement at the level of fine-grained analysis, especially as some researchers only indexed answers given to the designated prompt question, while others indexed relevant material from elsewhere in the interview, recognizing that 'speech . . . is usually grammatically primitive, full of redundancies and back-loops, empathetic and subjective, tentative, repeatedly returning to the same words and catch-phrases' (Thompson, 1988: 243). Armstrong and colleagues (1997) report a similar experience in coding focus group data on cystic fibrosis sufferers.

The team concluded that formal measures of inter-observer reliability were inappropriate. They substituted the notion of plausibility, which was

*continued*

> based on an understanding of the way historians establish claims in their work. They argued that analyses of the data had to be plausible and defensible with reference to the substantial archive of transcripts. The interpretations had to convince all five members of the team and be open to public scrutiny. However, there was no point in trying to get agreement on the fine-grained analysis of any one transcript, since, following both postmodern thought and historians' research methods, it was accepted that transcripts were open to multiple readings. The important thing was to produce readings that could convince colleagues in the team and be publicly supported by detailed reference to the archive of transcripts.

indexing transparent to others (see Chapter 4), it is also helpful when writing up the account of the analytical procedures, and valuable when you need to remind yourself about how you are indexing and why – which can be surprisingly often. If you are a part of a research team, this sharing of assumptions, definitions and ideas is essential if there is to be anything close to a common approach to indexing and analysis.

*Retrieval* Having organized the data in this way, the next step is to retrieve them, in other words to search for all the information about a particular topic or theme that has been indexed under the same code. This is the time when the computer is really useful, since not only can the appropriate text segments be swiftly retrieved, key quotations can also be transferred into the relevant section of the draft report. It is also easy to investigate sub-groups so that, for example, the material in a category that comes from men can be compared with that from women. Systematic software-based retrievals offer the possibility of carrying out complex searches. Depending on the particular package, this can include searching for co-occurrences of codes in the text. The co-occurrence of codings may be:

- Overlapping (text coded A overlaps with text coded B).
- Nested (text coded A is contained – or nested – within text coded B).
- Sequential (text coded A is followed by text coded B).
- Proximity (text coded A is followed within a specified space by text coded B).

Many programs have search systems that include the Boolean operators 'and', 'or' and 'not' to link text segments together. In this way, relationships between material can be examined:

- Text coded A *and* text coded B.
- Text coded A *or* text coded B.
- Text coded A *not* text coded B.

For more comprehensive information on computer-aided search and retrieve operations, see Prein, Kelle and Bird (1995).

Retrieval presents you with information taken out of context. Some writers, notably Briggs (1986), see this as a major problem, arguing that interviews are special social situations whose meanings are only intelligible in that social context: they are 'linguistic forms that are unavoidably referential, surface segmentable and relatively presupposing' (p. 116). 'The interview', he argues, 'is a unique speech event that is patterned by a complex array of communicative features, many of which are not shared by "ordinary" conversation' (p. 26), so that ' . . . this hiatus between the communicative norms of the interviewee and researcher can greatly hinder the research . . . and lead the researcher to mis-construe [interviewees'] meanings' (p. 3). He writes as an anthropologist who is very concerned that the interview is a special, Western cultural artefact. Without rejecting his point, we observe that many social research interviews are done with people who are familiar with them and that the 'communicative norms' that they apply need not be far removed from those understood by the interviewer. However, his advice, that 'a few hours of auditing tapes, reading notes and transcripts, and thinking about the interview places one in the best position for discerning the broad significance of the results' (p. 105), is advice that we endorse. We are less convinced that it is always useful to read transcripts that contain hesitations, pauses and false starts, and while we agree that it is ideal to use video recording to capture informants' body language, we are not convinced that it adds much of significance to many research projects. Certainly both recommendations have value when close analysis is needed and where there is a suspicion that there is a gap between the 'metacommunicative norms' of the interviewer and the interviewed. But in many projects, the decontextualization issue is not a pressing one, always given that the researcher is alert to the sub-cultures and cultures from which respondents are drawn, and has a good understanding of the interviews as complete texts (Lucas, 1997), as well as a cut-and-paste assemblage of fragments. In such cases, the decontextualization problem can often be laid aside, but always in the knowledge that a reading of the text that is more alert to contextual variables *might* lead to a different interpretation. Researchers should be alert to this possibility, but not paralysed by it.

There is one case in which the problem of decontextualization is especially prominent. It is possible for researchers to analyse data collected by others. For example, in England, the Economic and Social Research Council maintains an archive of qualitative data known as QUALIDATA (Corti et al., 1995). While there is enormous potential in researchers' being able to analyse data collected by others, there are difficulties, which may be more or less serious, depending on the purpose of the re-analysis. Researchers working on the archive may not know the original research aims and are unlikely to understand fully the ways in which those aims led to the exact research design. Furthermore, since they did not do the interviews, they do not have the 'second record', or the contextual knowledge, that those who did the interviews had about the respondents and the setting. For many enquiries, this problem with re-analysis will not be significant, but it is easy to see how other enquiries, especially those that seek a deep understanding of the respondents and their settings, can be hamstrung by this lack of contextual awareness.

One way of addressing this issue has been mentioned previously, namely sharing interpretations with others, such as supervisors, colleagues and respondents. This is a useful check on becoming too close to the data, with the result that you can overlook certain aspects of the evidence, as well as a check on the general plausibility of the interpretation.

*Interpreting the data* We have suggested that interpretation is a process that inevitably pervades the whole research process, from conception to reporting. It should be stressed that we are not saying that interpretations remain unchanged throughout this process. It is an elusive process to capture in writing, but over and above a carefully crafted index scheme, it takes creativity, imagination and a degree of luck (Richards and Richards, 1994). The key factors are to work with the data and to keep in mind the goals of the project. So, if the project is intended to help to improve practice in an area, then it makes sense to read the data with an eye to see, amongst other things, ways in which policy and practice might be changed in order to improve matters as they are seen through the eyes of one set of stakeholders.

That said, Huberman and Miles (1994) have listed 13 useful tactics for generating meaning, of which some of the most easily used are:

- Note patterns and themes.
- Look for concepts that describe related observations.
- Try counting to see whether something is as common (or as rare) as it seems.
- Compare and contrast to see whether categories are distinctive, and whether they need to be split.
- Explore relationships between variables, in the process asking whether there might be 'hidden variables' that you have missed.
- Check whether your analysis can be put together in a story that is plausible to you and that can be related to the picture you drew in the literature review.

As you search the categories, one dimension to examine is the extent to which the responses of different sub-groups vary, one to another. From a sociological point of view, even though differences in terms of gender, social class and race are standard ones to explore, they are nevertheless a convenient point of departure in analysis. Are there associations between these variables and, say, occupational position, attitudes, motivations, beliefs, reported behaviours or reactions to change? And, if there appear to be differences, can they be plausibly substantiated with as much confidence as is the case with the quantitative researcher who has established statistical significance? Naturally, it is important to look for disconfirming as well as confirming evidence. Where it is found, your interpretation might be:

- That the original hunch cannot plausibly be sustained.
- That the original idea needs modifying, perhaps by introducing a new variable to divide the group into two. For example, while most of the school teachers interviewed felt oppressed by the National Curriculum, a group felt less intimidated. Younger teachers were over-represented in that group.

- That situational or site-specific factors should be considered. In the study of teachers, reactions to change varied according to the 'organizational health' of their place of work. It was vital to know the whole set of interviews, as complete interviews, to reach this understanding.
- Further research is needed.

In many ways, anomalies and disconfirming evidence are irritating, since they slow the process of interpretation and keep us from the tidy findings that appeal to many audiences. However, as we noted in Chapter 2, trying to understand the anomalies often provokes new insights or theories which, even if they cannot be well worked out in the present study (which was not designed with those theories in mind) can be influential in your later research work. And, to repeat a point, your credibility is strengthened when you report and discuss such anomalies.

As analysis and interpretation proceed, be imaginative and adventurous. How, for instance, might these data be interpreted by a Marxist? A feminist? A post-modernist? A behaviourist? Equally, as you move back and forth between the data and the literature, keep looking for interpretations buried in the data themselves.

Analysis and interpretation stop when time runs out, or, ideally, when you see nothing fresh as you read the data, even if you try reading it as you wear an unfamiliar hat.

*Criticisms of approaches to the qualitative analysis of data*   Data from closed questions, subjected to the 'scientific' process of statistical analysis, appear to be objective and unobjectionable, although we have reviewed some of the ways in which their meanings are more ambiguous and contestable than is often recognised. Data from open questions lead to interpretations that are more provisional and contentious, and for some people they have a strong flavour of subjectivity about them. To the postmodernist this is the way the world is, but others, especially practitioners and policy-makers, look for unequivocal reports that show them what to do better and how to do it. For this reason, they can be frustrated with the tenuousness, provisionality and complexity of reports based on qualitative data. This is the main criticism of qualitative data and the way they are analysed, although it is also a criticism directed at those who ask of this research things which it cannot provide.

However, we have reviewed ways in which researchers can check that their interpretations are neither quixotic, nor eccentric. Our suggestions do have problems, though. First, when looking for colleagues to appraise our analyses, we are likely to choose people to review our indexing and interpretations who share our research stance, which can be a closed, self-confirming loop. In this way, groups of researchers of the same ilk can end up grooming each other while failing to recognize the scepticism that those outside of the côterie may have for their research stance and methods.

Secondly, inviting comments and feedback can be double-edged. Respondents and critical friends may confirm the plausibility of the account and agree that the research has been carefully done. Yet, interviewee feedback can be problematic (Hammersley and Atkinson, 1995). If the interpretation conflicts with what the respondents believe, or if the methods do not match their ideas about the nature of rigorous enquiry, and especially if the interpretations cast respondents in a poor light, then they will question the validity and integrity of the work. Here, they may be representing their vested interests (see also Chapter 9). You may, nevertheless, wish to modify the analysis in the light of their criticisms and advice, but not to the point of watering down the findings so that they are no longer meaningful. Equally, it is important to appreciate that the responses themselves are data that say a lot about the people you have interviewed, about their beliefs and myths (Thompson, 1988; Hammersley and Atkinson, 1995).

Our view is that the criticisms of qualitative research are mainly based on theories of social science that want this approach to research to deliver what it cannot (and which some would say that other approaches cannot deliver either). An important way of responding to those criticisms is by making it clear what the research is able to do, what it is not able to do, and why. Furthermore, given the difficulty that some expert researchers have in warranting the trustworthiness, plausibility and credibility of the processes of data analysis and interpretation, it should also be emphasized that all research is a compromise. It is a compromise between what we would wish to do and what we can do; between ideals and the need to get the work done; and between the search for the best possible interpretations and the ethical need to be mindful and respectful of research subjects. Where these compromises mean that what we publish falls short of what we would have wished to publish, then it is good practice to address that in print.

## Conclusion: from analysing to writing

The next chapter concentrates on writing the final report. Here, we make the point that the process of analysis has seen a lot of the 'Results' chapter of the report written. Analysis of closed questions will have produced tables, charts and graphs, while analysis of open questions will have identified those particularly telling quotations that will dominate the report of the results. If a journal has been kept throughout the analysis, then a lot of material will also have been generated that will appear in the 'Discussion' section.

In order to illustrate how the products of these processes of analysis percolate into the research report, we present in Box 11.6 an extract from an article based on interviews with a range of stakeholders in a new vocational qualification for 18-year-olds (Helsby et al., 1998). It gives a flavour of the ways in which data from qualitative analysis can be integrated into the writing of the final report. You might particularly notice how much space the data take up, which is a problem for those of us (almost all of us) who have to write to word limits. Appreciate, too, how little of the raw data makes it into the final report. And, finally, consider the way that quotations are used purposefully, blended as neatly as possible into the flow of the text.

---

**Box 11.6   Reporting the outcomes of qualitative interview research
(from Helsby et al., 1998: 71–72)**

[ . . . ] As already indicated, evidence from the interviews suggests that factors within the General National Vocational Qualifications [GNVQs] framework may in practice severely restrict the 'empowerment' of both teachers and students. In particular, the atomisation of content which is encouraged by the complex course specification and exacerbated by the introduction of end of unit tests may militate against holistic understanding by students and coherent course planning by teachers. In other words, their power to create connections and meanings is, in practice, constricted by atomised specifications. Certainly there were suggestions from some of the college lecturers interviewed that GNVQs made it more difficult to continue with the integrated assignments that had been used with the BTEC National Diploma :

> One of its problems is that it is very bitty, it is hard to get a theme running through when you are distracted by performance criteria. Also, it is almost impossible to have an integrated approach because of the end tests.(Lecturer in GNVQ Business)

Similarly, one of the schoolteachers criticised the lack of realism implied in teaching different elements separately:

> The assessment system forces you to teach the Units as discrete units, which is not true to real life businesses where areas overlap. (Business Studies teacher)

The point is not that such integration is forbidden by GNVQ requirements, but rather that, in practice, it becomes more difficult to implement it whilst at the same time ensuring complete coverage of all of the discrete elements.

This 'atomisation' can be related to Bernstein's (1971) concept of classification. Whereas Bernstein was referring to the strength of boundary maintenance between different academic subjects, the term may also be relevant to this effective separation of different aspects of the same (vocational) subject matter within a GNVQ course. Although the course is ostensibly 'integrated' across a broad vocational area, the fact that, in practice, it is parcelled into separate units of learning and assessment makes it more difficult for both teachers and students to make the interconnections between various elements that might lead to a richer and deeper appreciation of the area and enhance critical understanding:

> It is difficult to look at wider contexts with GNVQ, it is limiting. It is a mechanistic approach that is not concerned with concepts, ideas or abstractions, it is not looking at interconnections or at the context in which things occur, how it might be different. It is not making them think. (Business Studies teacher)

*continued*

At the same time, Bernstein's notion of 'framing' is also potentially relevant to our understanding of the power dynamics within GNVQ courses. Despite the apparent freedom promised for both teachers and students by the GNVQ system, in reality it tends to encourage practices . . . which suggest relatively little control over the selection, organisation, pacing and timing of the knowledge generated in the learning process:

It is much more assessment-led, there's more time filling in paper, a significant amount of tutorial time for portfolio-building and less time for teaching. (Lecturer in Leisure and Tourism)

# 12 Writing the Report, Disseminating the Findings

> In the mind, as well as in the body, there is the necessity of getting rid of waste, and a man of literary habits will write for the fire as well as for the press. (Jerome Cardan, 1501–1576)

The main theme of this chapter is that writing is a process of drafting, throwing the draft on the fire, redrafting, feeding the fire, and . . . Most chapters of this book have been redrafted four times, some more. All have been regularly polished, tuned and tweaked. On this view, writing is a continuous process that runs in parallel with other research activities. It is not an end-of-research event.

The experience of writing many essays, term papers and reports is some preparation for writing a research report, dissertation or thesis, but it is seldom sufficient. A report certainly requires all the skills that essay writing develops, notably reviewing and criticizing other people's ideas and evidence, while developing an argument in response to a question or problem. However, it also requires the ability to describe clearly and convincingly the choice of methods and to handle a substantial body of evidence in a way that is fair, persuasive and uncluttered. Because the research report will often be longer than a term paper or essay, it can be daunting, which can lead some people to make the serious mistake of putting off the writing for as long as possible. In addition, the length itself poses problems of organization, structure and coherence that are more acute than in essays.

Although a conventional academic report is the most common product of research, there is growing interest in creative expressions of research findings in the form of broadcasts, narrative, story and film. It is worth recalling that Balzac's *Comédie Humaine*, Dickens' *Hard Times* and Zola's the *Rougon-Macquart* are works of social analysis that could, especially in Zola's case, be located within critical theory. In Britain today, writers such as Peter Ackroyd and Pat Barker show the power that fiction has authentically to represent a past, and to do more besides. These are interesting, exciting developments, but we will not explore them here, concentrating instead on mainstream report writing.

## Starting Writing

This section is influenced by two books. The first, Boice's report (1992) of a well-thought-out programme to support new members of academic staff, may seem to be an odd inspiration. Undergraduate and postgraduate students writing reports are not in the same business as full-time academic staff: students are novices, staff are experts; students strain to write, but lecturers' fingers fly across the keyboard, with neat phrases smoothly appearing and complex concepts rolling across the pages. Or so those who are not members of academic staff might think.

One of the striking things about Boice's research is that he showed how difficult people find writing, even when they have already produced their PhD theses. Investigating further, he found that the academics who were the most productive writers were not those who waited until they had clear days when they could 'binge' on writing. Those days disappear under tides of other tasks. The productive writers were those who tried to write a little regularly, or even daily.

That is our first message: write regularly and throughout the project. Do not try to write the report in one go. It is better to draft an introduction (which will certainly be rewritten later) very early in the research. There was advice on doing the literature review in Chapter 4, which should be referred to as the writing continues. The suggestion here is that the review is best written up while the research and thinking are in progress, again in the knowledge that it will be reshaped when the research is done. Likewise, it is a good idea to write the section on the research methods when decisions are made about the research design and while piloting takes place. Field notes and memos you wrote to yourself will often provide draft material for incorporation in the report.

That is one of the strongest themes in Becker's book (1986), which is the second that influences this section. Keep drafting, editing, shaping, changing. That is the best way of beating writer's block. The trick is to write *something*, if only as a way of helping you to get to something better. Remember that not everything that is written is 'good' writing (whatever that is). This chapter bears few traces of draft 1, although it is recognizably close to drafts 2 and 3. Without the experimentation of draft 1, drafts 2 and 3 would not have been possible. Key meanings emerged in the course of doing that first draft, and if many of its devices and phrases have gone, the ideas remain.

However, it is important to be able to look later at this quick-writing with a fresh, appraising eye so as to be able to edit and revise it. Three ways of bringing a fresh eye to your draft are:

- Re-read what you have written with a style book beside you.
- Put the draft away for a couple of weeks or so, and come back to it as an unfamiliar piece of writing.
- Get friends to look at it.

The first strategy is good for improving style, but it is not much help with evaluating the ideas, evidence and structure. The second is a good strategy if the time is available. For example, the first draft of this section was laid aside for five weeks, which meant that it could be re-read with more detachment and with a sharper critical intent. The third strategy is the best, although you need to be prepared for criticism and suggestions that may not be entirely welcome.

Most of us have feelings of unease, unworthiness and risk when we show others our drafts. These feelings are well described by Pamela Richards in Becker's book. Many people try to minimize these feelings by spending ages on the first, 'quick' drafts, wrestling with getting their prose 'in a fit state to be seen' – putting it in its academic 'Sunday best'. Yet, friends' comments on these early dabblings could show us what we do not see, highlight the strengths and provide pointers about where ideas should be developed, where reconsideration is necessary, and where serious repair work must be done.

## A language for the report

People often find academic writing difficult. One reason is that the common style of academic writing is virtually a new language to novices, who struggle and falter, as do people learning any new language. For example, we may casually use sexist and discriminatory language in daily speech with friends. Undesirable in itself, it is quite unacceptable in print. The British Sociological Association is just one of the professional bodies that publishes helpful guides to writing in non-discriminatory language (see p. 94).

There is also an assumption that academic writing has to be ghastly, and there certainly is a lot of ghastly academic writing – bloodless prose that has no hint that the subject of study is people. Long sentences. Long words and technical terms (jargon, if you prefer). The passive voice. Otiosity, meretriciousness and a predilection for impressive Latinate words.

It does not have to be like that. The best academic writing is direct, simple and clear, as in Becker's book. Plain and direct writing is easier on the reader and encourages precision and clarity of thought. Here it would be worth reading the classic essay on this point, George Orwell's *Politics and the English Language* (1954).

Why is so much academic writing so bad? One reason is that there is a belief that the passive voice is better, since it appears so much more scientific to say 'subjects were asked' rather than 'we asked them', and that goes with the assumption that long words are a sign of learning. Unfortunately, academics often perpetuate these peculiar notions, leaving students little choice but to ape this bad writing if they want to get good grades. Students also often act on the basis of subliminal beliefs about good writing, even though these are often, in effect, beliefs that describe bad writing. It sometimes makes no difference when a tutor makes it clear that long words are not better than short ones and that making the meaning clear is the first task of the writer. Other advice that frequently gets ignored is that writing needs to be 'reader-friendly', so that the reader knows why something is being covered in a certain way and where the argument is going.

If the report is for practitioners and other interested people, bear in mind that they will not usually like a dull academic style and will complain that academics' technical terms baffle them: that the report is littered with jargon. One way of checking whether your writing is suitable for a lay audience is to give it to friends who do not know your subject, let alone your research. Listen very carefully to their comments. If they have difficulty with *any* part, the best advice is to assume that you have not written clearly enough *for that audience*. Change it.

It is common, when writing for practitioners and others who are not in mainstream academic life, to begin with an executive summary. This should set out the main findings and any recommendations. It should convey the essence of the research and say why it is significant so that the busy person who reads nothing more than the summary has a full understanding of what the report is saying. The summary is often put in bullet point form with cross-references between each point and the body of the report.

The difference between writing for academic and other audiences can be highlighted by looking at the way references are given. Academic writing is full – usually far too full – of references, even to the extent of giving references to material that no one is going to be able to locate, let alone wish to read. We all often fall short of the ideal of giving references only when:

* We are summarizing distinctive views or findings.
* We are quoting directly.
* We wish to indicate where differing views may be found.
* They direct readers to useful sources of further information.

When writing a report for a non-academic audience, it is advisable to keep references to a minimum. In this situation, it may be helpful to provide an annotated bibliography at the end of the report. Since there will be few references, it takes little space to write a short (up to 50 words) commentary on each one, summarizing what it says and indicating its significance in the context of the report.

### Criteria for judging research reports

Near the beginning of good programmes of study academic staff will set out the criteria by which research reports are to be judged. Better still, they may spend time working through the criteria, perhaps by having students grade one or two anonymous reports, so that the criteria are not just available but are also understood. While criteria will vary by institution, subject and level of study, there are some things that are generally valued and others that signify an inferior report. Box 12.1 offers a view of these characteristics.

### Organizing the report

It is easiest to organize the report around one of the conventions. Scientific reports, such as those found in most psychology journals, tend to have a very formal structure, which may be quite suitable for the presentation of survey findings to audiences who expect reports to follow that form. Conventions are less binding when writing in other disciplines and for other audiences.

The difference between a good and an acceptable report does not usually depend on how good the research was. The coherence of the report and the

**Box 12.1  General criteria for judging a research report**

## Outstanding report

- Problem or issue is clearly stated.
- The findings or argument are stated early in the report and it is easy to see in the body of the report that they are the best conclusions from the investigation.
- Links are made to other work in the field and the issue of significance ('who cares?') is addressed.
- The research methods are explained and justified and are appropriate to the issues raised in the literature review.
- The design can be justified as an appropriate way of investigating the problem and, within the limits of time and resources, promises a plausible answer to the questions raised in the literature review. The findings are readily understood.
- In reports of survey research, graphs and tables summarize the data and statistical tests are used. In qualitative research, relevant quotations are used to illustrate the general points being made.
- The conclusions are related to the findings and to the literature review.
- Unresolved issues are explored and directions for further research are indicated.
- Realistic suggestions for action are made where this is appropriate.
- There are signs of originality or of intellectual excitement.
- The report makes a useful and secure contribution to understanding of the field.

## Acceptable report

An acceptable report will have many of the characteristics of an outstanding report but not all of them. The last criterion is unlikely to have been met. Rewriting each criterion at the acceptable level produces the following profile.

- The problem or issue is stated.
- The findings or argument may or may not be stated early in the report.
- Where they are, it is not easy to see in the body of the report that they are the best conclusions from the investigation.
- Links are made to other work in the field but they are not sufficiently full.
- The issue of significance ('who cares?') gets passing attention.
- The research methods are described.
- It is often not shown that they are the best ways of investigating the issues raised in the literature review.
- Within the limits of time and resources, the research design promises to shed some light on the questions raised in the literature review.

*continued*

- The findings are comprehensible with some effort by the reader.
- The conclusions are not strongly related to the findings and to the literature review.
- Unresolved issues may not be explored and directions for further research may not be indicated.
- There may not be any realistic suggestions for action, even where that would have been appropriate.

**Unacceptable report**

The acceptable/unacceptable borderline is very much one of local custom and practice. In some cases, falling short on one of the criteria of acceptability is enough to ensure failure. In others, there may need to be weakness on several counts before a report is regarded as unacceptable. There is little point, then, in repeating the criteria of acceptability, but casting them in the language of failure. What follows is a list of some distinctive features of poor reports. However, some of these features are to be found in work that is otherwise acceptable:

- The prose hurts. This may involve poor spelling; the grocer's apostrophe ('the informant's said that . . .'); highfalutin writing that fails ('the problematic in this issue is comprised of . . .'); long and pompous sentences; difficulty in understanding what the writer is getting at.
- The literature review is too short. That does not mean that there are insufficient references; it means that the writer has not really got the essence of the sources that have been used. In these cases, the review is often organized as first a summary of *this* book and then of *that* article. It is like reading a shopping list. Good reviews are organized around issues and themes.
- It is hard to understand what the findings are. This section is often confused and frequently is organized as a question-by-question report of the findings: far better to present the findings in terms of the questions posed at the beginning of the report and developed in the literature review.
- Poor reports often seem to produce conclusions like a conjurer pulling rabbits from a hat, avowing that what has gone before self-evidently leads to those conclusions. The conclusions are disconnected from the rest of the report and no amount of insistence that 'it has been shown that . . .' can hide it. In short, there may be some information in the report but it is not organized so as to help the reader know what it is supposed to signify.
- References are a mess. Few people are failed on the basis of bogus, incomplete, or poorly presented references. However, these faults can make readers suspicious of the rest of the report.

evidence in it of critical, analytical and evaluative thinking are as important, or more important.

## A framework for the report

Undergraduate reports are likely to be 5,000–10,000 words long, and dissertations will tend to be 10,000–20,000 words long. PhD theses usually fall in the range of 80,000–100,000 words. First drafts are usually too long (ours are). Edit by cutting out material that neither develops the argument nor advances the conclusions. That may mean departing from the balance between the sections of the report that we suggest below. That is perfectly reasonable, particularly as our suggestions are precisely that – suggestions, not prescriptions.

In all cases, you should make clear and strong connections between each section and chapter and summarize what has been shown or argued in each section or chapter. Do plenty of signposting, summarizing what you've argued and explaining why the next batch of information is significant, and letting the reader know where your argument is going.

The following elements generally need to be present in a report, although in longer reports any of them may be divided into several chapters.

*Introduction*  This should say what the problem is, why it is of any interest or importance and set out the main conclusions of the research. It may include or take the form of an executive summary. Avoid an introduction that says that certain methods were used to investigate the problem, which led to unspecified conclusions. That is weak and makes it seem as if you do not know what you are trying to say. Keep this section short, allowing perhaps 5 per cent of the overall word count for it.

*Background*  This section may not be needed, since the literature review may effectively provide the background. Where it is necessary to supply some background that cannot be presented elsewhere, keep it brief and to the point. Historical backgrounds often contain a lot of information that is not needed in order to understand what is being investigated or claimed. Remove it.

*Literature review*  Discussed in Chapter 4, this is one of the most important parts of the report. It should set out the state of thinking about the problem or issue that you have investigated; identify gaps in existing knowledge, or flaws and problems with it; note methods of enquiry that have been used in this area; and conclude by identifying the key questions that will be studied and the methods of enquiry that are likely to be productive. This can take 20–25 per cent of the report, where it is a report for an academic readership. It can also be a lot shorter.

*Research design*  Show that the methods used were the best of all those that might have been used (see Chapter 6 for an example). Details of the development and piloting of interview schedules should be included, ideally showing how each question or planned prompt was designed to explore an aspect of a research question listed in the previous chapter. In the best reports, there is a clear and strong link between the design and the literature review. Include details of sampling and discussions of credibility and generalizability. This is also the place to give serious attention to something that is frequently side-lined, namely the analysis of the data. Methods of data analysis should be discussed and there should be some evaluation of the confidence that can be placed in the outcomes of this analysis. Finally, consider the strength of the design overall, if need be, indicating how more time or resources would have allowed for improvements. Allow up to 20 per cent of the report for this important section.

*Results* Say what you found. Some writers like to interweave reporting the results and commenting upon them, in which case this section will be combined with the next, and probably be organized into several shorter chapters. Each one will address a key theme in the data, describing what was found and commenting upon it. Other writers like simply to present the data, perhaps using the end-of-chapter summary to indicate the themes that will be pursued in the discussion. Where the results are presented without commentary, give no more than 30 per cent of the report over to them.

*Discussion* This section is one of the most important in a report and the one that often does more than any other to determine how well it is received. It needs to appraise the results and their meaning mainly in terms of the themes raised in the literature review, making it quite clear how these results confirm or change thinking about the problem or issue. It is here that the argument is most developed and it is here that the claim to having found something of interest is laid. It can take about 20 per cent of the report.

*Conclusion (and recommendations)* The conclusions should already be clear. They can be restated, but doing only that makes a dull ending. This is a good place to speculate on the significance of these conclusions – what are their implications, whether for views of the field, for research methods, or for policy and practice? The conclusion is a good place to connect your research, which will usually be small in scale, with far larger issues. Yet the conclusion does not need to be much longer than 5 per cent of the whole.

*References* Find out if there is a style that you are expected to use, or choose a referencing style, and then stick rigorously to it.

*Appendices* Appendices are not always counted within the length limit. They are an ideal place to put research instruments, some of the data and a limited number of other documents of importance. Number them as Appendix 3.1, 4.2 etc. (the first appendix for Chapter 3, which might be an interview schedule, and the second appendix for Chapter 4, which might be a particularly interesting transcript). That said, keep appendices to the minimum. Too many appendices can be taken as a sign that the writer lacks the power to select what is really important.

## Dissemination

Many students, particularly undergraduates, do not see disseminating research findings as a priority, so this section is brief.

Undergraduate reports are not usually disseminated beyond the tutor and examiners. One exception is when the report comes from an action research project, where the whole point is to try to affect practice and where collaboration is the norm. In such circumstances, the report may be written primarily for practitioners and the style should reflect that. In rare cases, undergraduates are encouraged to summarize their report for publication, often in practitioner-focused journals, where readability, concision and practicability are, again, at a premium. Reports of postgraduate research tend to be more widely disseminated, and may be published in academic journals, in which case the rules for writing are more formal.

### Report to participants

Where participants are literate, there is almost an ethical, as well as a practical, case for disseminating findings to them. This can be a two-stage process. Findings are disseminated when transcripts are sent to informants for checking and again when a report to participants is circulated. In this report cover what will be of interest and significance to them in comprehensible language. Normally, you will omit references.

In response, you may be told about factual errors. Also, this report gives participants the opportunity to confirm that the findings are, at face value, a valid representation of what they believe and understand, which is a helpful confirmation of the study's validity. Alternatively, where participants have reservations, these should cause re-thinking (Hammersley and Atkinson, 1995). However, this is not saying that participants should have the last word on what your results mean. The point is that their interpretations should lead you to consider your interpretation. Once your study is completed, you might wish to distribute a final report to participants.

### Practitioner journals

These are good channels of dissemination. They tend to appear frequently, to have a need for interesting copy, and to prefer short, clear, practice-focused pieces. If an article can be linked with a forthcoming anniversary of interest (50 years of the NHS, for example), it has greater appeal on the grounds of topicality. The cardinal rule for getting published in these journals is to find out what the journal looks for in terms of style, typical length and referencing conventions. The second rule is to write with the journal's readership in mind. This is not only a matter of style, but one of messages too: readers are likely to be preoccupied with the 'so what?' question, and this must not only be answered (preferably in the first paragraph) but also answered in terms of the practical implications of your research. Editors of these journals can be swayed where there are good, human-interest pictures accompanying the text.

*Academic journals*

The cynic might wonder whether this counts as dissemination, since the number of people getting beyond the abstract of most articles is surprisingly low (and estimates of fewer than ten people have been made for some fields and journals). However, publication in these journals is a prerequisite for consideration for an academic post and can be helpful in applying to do research or when going for other sorts of employment. Most journals contain guidelines on what they publish and the preferred style.

Editors of academic journals will send your article out to experts in the field for refereeing. Ideally, the referees will not know who wrote the article, so they should judge it on its merits alone. Good referees provide helpful suggestions for improving your article and do so quickly. Others take months and provide vague, unhelpful and sometimes hurtful comments. Whether the process is fast or slow, helpful or hurtful, it is something that happens to all of us in academic life. The points to heed here are that it may take a long time to get your paper accepted; acceptance may only happen after one, two, or even three revisions; and so your paper may not be published until two years after you first submitted it.

If your paper is rejected, take account of the reasons, revise with the help of friends, colleagues and supervisors, and try another journal.

Do not make the mistake of assuming that readers will instantly see the significance of your work. Unless that is clear, from the beginning and in the abstract, it is unlikely that most readers of the journal will read your article. For that reason, editors may be reluctant to consider it for publication. This is especially true of case studies. If, for example, you have done research on midwifery in Hong Kong, editors of an international journal will want you to be clear about the implications of the study *for an international readership*. If no implications are drawn out, or if they relate to Hong Kong alone, then publication is unlikely.

*Conference presentation*

It is usually easy to get a proposal accepted to present your work, usually orally or in a poster presentation. With oral presentations, performance skills are very important. The main advice is never read a paper, although it is good practice to give participants a paper to take away, or to direct them to the web site where it may be found. Instead, make up six or so overhead projector slides, each containing about six points. Talk to those points, using presentational skills to best effect (Gelb, 1988, is excellent on doing presentations). As always, make sure that the main implications of the research that are relevant to this audience stand out: in the old adage, tell them what those points will be, tell them the points, and then tell them that you've told them. Allow time for questions, always in the knowledge that you will invariably *ad lib* to your slides for longer than you had expected. If, as happens in the best presentations, there are activities that involve the audience, recognize that these also take longer than is usually assumed.

*Bulletin boards*

Sharing your findings electronically is a good way of getting quick reactions from international audiences. It is important to keep electronic postings short. One strategy is to post the main points electronically and direct interested recipients to a web site containing the complete article (or invite them to e-mail you for a copy of it). Publishing in this way does not yet receive much credit in academic circles.

*A book*

Print runs for academic books are normally in the hundreds, which means that books will not reach large audiences, seldom make your reputation, and certainly will not make you rich. They are, though, a good way for would-be academics to start building a reputation.

There is an art to identifying publishers who will be interested in your work and in convincing them of the value of your book proposal (and it is far better to get a proposal accepted and then write than to send a completed typescript to a publisher). Most publishers will supply guidelines on making a proposal. They will be looking for an idea that has the edge over other books in the field and that will have reasonable sales. Many academic book proposals have very poor sales prospects and will be rejected on that ground alone. Poor sales prospects mean that publishers are seldom interested in publishing theses. One of us has written a book based on a PhD thesis, but substantial presentational changes were made to the thesis to produce a marketable book.

**Conclusion**

It would be nice to think that this book is completed as these words are written. Nice, and unrealistic. Before this draft makes it to print, there will be revisions, and revisions of revisions, and the references will need to be got into order, which is always a long and tiresome task. That work will continue alongside our on-going work on our own interview-based research projects. For Peter, that means coding up interview data. In some ways a tedious activity, in this case there is added spice to it, since the two researchers involved are quite independently devising indexing systems and coding up the data in order to explore the multiple ways in which the same archive can be read. For Hilary, it means setting up interviews for the Carers' Act project, refining the research design as the first couple are done, and beginning to see themes in the data and lines of analysis. These fluid, overlapping processes neatly illustrate the nature of interview-based research in the qualitative tradition.

# Appendix
# An Interview Research Checklist

This checklist summarizes key issues discussed in the text which you may need to think about in your research. However, we have consistently emphasized that the research design has to be fit for the purpose, and that research practice is about making the best choices in situations that are not ideal. The implication of this insistence is that it will be quite reasonable to give a 'No' answer to some of the questions we have raised.

However, since a research report to academic audiences will need to give an account of your choice of methods and the way you carried them out, you might wish to say something in your report about the questions to which you have answered 'No'.

Some questions you will repeatedly revisit, for we have argued that research 'stages' overlap and that certain issues have to be repeatedly addressed during the work. We saw no better way of asking these questions than in this form, but the form itself does tend to suggest that research is a 'when you've done that, do this' process, which is not what we have been trying to say.

| Question | Yes? | No? | Comment | Suggestion |
|---|---|---|---|---|
| You've got a research problem, but have you got something that's researchable – research questions, in other words? | | | Typical difficulties are wanting to explore problems that are loose, poorly defined and lead to too many research questions | Refer back to Chapter 4 and keep asking whether your research questions are too broad, too ambitious |
| Can you write out the research question(s) that your study will investigate? | | | Getting a problem into a more defined and limited form is vital. Big questions are answered in many, small bites of research | Time to talk with your tutor, supervisor, or friends. The importance of getting regular supervision sessions cannot be exaggerated |
| Do you know what your research stance is (positivist or qualitative) and what its implications are? Is your stance appropriate for the problem you're going to work on? | | | Different stances have very different implications for the methods you would choose, the claims you would want to make, and for what you could say about their generalizability | Better to be clear now about your stance and its implications, rather than later to try to make claims that are beyond the methods used. Have another look at Chapters 1 and 3 |
| Is your reading making it clear what are the key issues (methodological, conceptual and empirical) attaching to this problem? | | | The reading – or literature review – is important as it provides one way of answering the 'so what?' question. It also helps you focus in on a researchable and manageable aspect of the general problem | Time to talk – with friends and academic staff. It might be that there is no problem of interest to investigate. Or they might be able to help you sort what matters from the mass of information in the literature |

| Question | Yes? | No? | Comment | Suggestion |
|---|---|---|---|---|
| Have you begun a first draft of the literature review? | | | If you start now, it should focus your attention on the fit between the research questions and the methods | If at all possible, find time to draft, even in outline, a summary of the literature (see Chapter 4) |
| Are your intended methods going to tell you enough about your research question? | | | Some methods tell you too much (collecting too much data is a common mistake), others are simply not up to answering the question you set | A reality check is needed. Imagine you are a critical reviewer of your planned study. Think of all the fair objections that could be made on methodological grounds, and of answers to them. Now ask if your methods need changing |
| Is there some form of triangulation in the methods you are thinking about using? | | | Triangulation helps you and the reader to be more confident that your work is systematic and serious | Different problems and stances have different implications for triangulation: chcck back to Chapter 2 |
| Have you started writing an account of the methods you have chosen, explaining why they are appropriate, trustworthy and credible? | | | It is much harder to draft this section of your report later. Doing it now is also a good check that your intended methods are credible, trustworthy and appropriate | |

| Question | Yes? | No? | Comment | Suggestion |
|---|---|---|---|---|
| Have you been able to negotiate access to a research site and study sample? | | | It is quite common to find difficulties in getting this access. Before going further, you ought to be sure that you'll get the access you need | You will need to be able to convince people you hope to involve in your study that there is some pay-off for them, and no risk of harm to them |
| Are your sampling strategy and projected sample size fit for the purpose? | | | Assuming they are, have you allowed for high non-response rates from those you ask to be interviewed? | Plan your sampling strategy around high non-response/non-availability rates. And ask whether you need to be interviewing so many |
| Will the interviewer be safe? | | | See Chapters 5 and 9 | **If you have doubts on this count, do not go ahead** |
| Have you got the resources to do what you plan? | | | We have all underestimated how long fieldwork *and* analysis will take | Again, the only suggestion is to look critically at what you say you can do, *bearing in mind your other commitments* |
| Is this study ethically sound? | | | See Chapters 7–9 | You must revise your study if you have doubts, taking advice from your tutors or supervisors |

| Question | Yes? | No? | Comment | Suggestion |
|----------|------|-----|---------|------------|
| Have you piloted the methods you'll use, even if they will take the form of largely unstructured conversations? | | | Piloting allows you to find glitches in your performance, as well as showing you which questions, prompts, or topics of enquiry may be problematic, sterile, or need different research methods | You should do at least a couple of dummy interviews (more with surveys) with people who will not be in your final sample. Analyse the data you get to check that analysis is possible and that you've not underestimated the time involved |
| Are practical arrangements – for example, for taping, even where there is no mains power, and for storing data so that confidentiality is maintained – in place? | | | Here, remember that the Data Protection Act regulates the storage of personal information on computers in the UK (and is likely to be extended to other personal data records) | |
| Have you sorted out a dependable and affordable way of getting interview data recorded ready for transcription? | | | This is only repeating the theme of Chapter 10 that transcription is far more problematic a process than novices might expect | If transcription is going to be a problem, consider whether your research would be significantly weakened if you summarized the interview in note form |

| Question | Yes? | No? | Comment | Suggestion |
|---|---|---|---|---|
| Are you analysing the transcriptions as they begin to come in? (And, of course, you were doing informal interpretation and analysis when you did the interviews, weren't you?) | | | This is less of an issue for survey researchers but even there, it is a good idea to see if the research is actually getting at your question. It is vexing to find out when the fieldwork is done that it has not given data that help you to answer the research questions | If early data analysis suggests there is a problem, change the research design to deal with it. The cost is that you have to treat these early data as coming from a second pilot. That's a lot better than finding the problem too late |
| What have you done to demonstrate that your data are being analysed in a trustworthy way? | | | You should consider whether you need to demonstrate inter-observer reliability, or whether other means of establishing the credibility of analysis are preferable | |
| Are there anomalies and unexpected patterns within the data? | | | Good analysis should show these unexpected features (and not just 'sweep them under the carpet') | Another look at the literature may give hints about what lies behind these unexpected findings. On the other hand, you may have to conclude that 'further research is needed' |

| Question | Yes? | No? | Comment | Suggestion |
|---|---|---|---|---|
| Have you left plenty of time for revising draft sections of your report and for writing a piece that does justice to all the time the research has taken? | | | See Chapter 12 for reminders about the amount of time this can take; also for notes on style and structure (and a good structure is very important) | If time is too limited, it's always worth trying to get the deadline extended: sometimes it works |

# References

Acker, J., Barry, K. and Esseveld, J. (1983) 'Objectivity and truth: problems in doing feminist research', *Women's Studies International Forum*, 6(4): 423–35.

Adler, P.A. and Adler, P. (1991) *Membership Roles in Field Research*, 2nd edn. London: Sage Publications (1st edn, 1987).

Alderson, P. (1995) *Listening to Children: Children, Ethics and Social Research*. Ilford: Barnardos.

Allan, G. (1980) 'A note on interviewing spouses together', *Journal of Marriage and the Family*, 42: 205–10.

Altheide, D. L. and Johnson, J. M. (1994) 'Criteria for assessing interpretive validity in qualitative research', in N.K. Denzin and Y.S. Lincoln (eds), *Handbook of Qualitative Research*. London: Sage Publications. pp. 485–99.

Amato, P.R. and Ochiltree, G. (1987) 'Interviewing children about their families: a note on data quality', *Journal of Marriage and the Family*, 49(3): 669–75.

Anderson, J. (1998) 'Transcribing with voice recognition software: a new tool for qualitative researchers', *Qualitative Health Research*, 8(5): 718–23.

Andreasen, A.R. (1983) 'Cost-conscious marketing research', *Harvard Business Review*, 83 (4): 74–9.

Arksey, H. (ed.) (1992) *How to Get a First Class Degree*. Lancaster: Unit for Innovation in Higher Education, University of Lancaster.

Arksey, H. (1994) 'Expert and lay participation in the construction of medical knowledge', *Sociology of Health & Illness*, 16(4): 448–68.

Arksey, H. (1996) 'Collecting data through joint interviews', *Social Research Update*, issue 15. Guildford: Department of Sociology, University of Surrey.

Arksey, H. (1998) *RSI and the Experts: The Construction of Medical Knowledge*. London: UCL Press.

Arksey, H., Heaton, J. and Sloper, P. (1997) *Carers' Perspectives on Hospital Discharge Procedures for Young Adults with Physical and Complex Disabilities*. York: Social Policy Research Unit, University of York.

Armstrong, D., Gosling, A., Weinman, J. and Marteau, T. (1997) 'The place of inter-rater reliability in qualitative research', *Sociology*, 31(30): 597–606.

Backett, K. (1990) 'Image and reality: health enhancing behaviours in middle class families', *Health Education Journal*, 49(2): 61–3.

Backett, K. and Alexander, H. (1991) 'Talking to young children about health: methods and findings', *Health Education Journal*, 50(1): 34–8.

Ball, S.J. (1981) *Beachside Comprehensive*. Cambridge: Cambridge University Press.

Barker, P. (1996) *The Ghost Road*. London: Penguin.

Barnes, J.A. (1979) *Who Should Know What? Social Science, Privacy and Ethics*. Harmondsworth: Penguin.

Becker, H. (1986) *Writing for Social Scientists*. Chicago: University of Chicago Press.

Bell, C. and Newby, H. (eds) (1977) *Doing Sociological Research*. London: George Allen & Unwin.

Belson, W.A. (1986) 'Testing the accuracy of survey-based claims about purchases: purchases of different brands of chocolate confectionery in the last seven days', in W.A. Belson (ed.), *Validity in Survey Research*. Aldershot: Gower. pp. 39–86.

Benney, M. and Hughes, E.C. (1956) 'Of sociology and the interview', *American Journal of Sociology*, 62: 137–42.

Beresford, B. (1997) *Personal Accounts: Involving Disabled Children in Research*. London: Stationery Office.

Bernstein, B. (1971) 'On the classification and framing of knowledge', in M.E.D. Young (ed.), *Knowledge and Control: New Directions for the Sociology of Education*. London: Collier–Macmillan. pp. 47–69.

Blackmore, J. (1996) 'Breaking the silence: feminist contributions to educational administration and policy', in K. Leithwood, J. Chapman, D. Corson, P. Hallinger and A. Hart (eds), *International Handbook of Educational Leadership and Administration*. Dordrecht: Kluwer. pp. 997–1042.

Blaikie, N.W.H. (1991) 'A critique of the use of triangulation in social research', *Quality and Quantity*, 25: 115–36.

Blaxter, L., Hughes, C. and Tight, M. (1996) *How to Research*. Buckingham: Open University Press.

Boice, R. (1992) *The New Faculty Member*. San Francisco: Jossey–Bass.

Booth, T. and Booth, W. (1994) 'The use of depth interviewing with vulnerable subjects: lessons from a research study of parents with learning difficulties', *Social Science and Medicine*, 39(3): 415–24.

Booth, T. and Booth, W. (1996) 'Sounds of silence: narrative research with inarticulate subjects', *Disability & Society*, 11(1): 55–69.

Booth, T., Simons, K. and Booth, W. (1990) *Outward Bound: Relocation and Community Care for People with Learning Difficulties*. Buckingham: Open University Press.

Boyle, M. and Woods, P. (1996) 'The composite head: coping with changes in the primary headteacher role', *British Educational Research Journal*, 22(5): 549–68.

Brannen, J. (1988) 'The study of sensitive subjects', *Sociological Review*, 36(3): 552–63.

Brenner, M., Brown, J. and Canter, D.V. (eds) (1985) *The Research Interview: Uses and Approaches*. London: Academic Press.

Briggs, C. L. (1986) *Learning to Ask: A Sociolinguistic Appraisal of the Role of the Interview in Social Science*. Cambridge: Cambridge University Press.

British Sociological Association (1997) *Guidelines for Good Professional Conduct and Statement of Ethical Practice*. Durham: British Sociological Association.

Brown, H. and Smith, H. (eds) (1992) *Normalization: A Reader for the Nineties*. London: Tavistock/Routledge.

Bruner, J. (1990) *Acts of Meaning*. Cambridge, MA: Harvard University Press.

Bryman, A. (1988) *Quantity and Quality in Social Research*. London: Routledge.

Bryman, A. and Burgess, R.G. (eds) (1994) *Analyzing Qualitative Data*. London: Routledge.

Bryman, A. and Cramer, D. (1997) *Quantitative Data Analysis with SPSS for Windows: A Guide for Social Scientists*. London: Routledge.

Buckeldee, J. (1994) 'Interviewing carers in their own homes', in J. Buckeldee and R. McMahon (eds), *The Research Experience in Nursing*. London: Chapman & Hall. pp. 101–13.

Bulmer, M. (ed.) (1982) *Social Research Ethics: An Examination of the Merits of Covert Participant Observation*. London: Macmillan.

Burgess, J., Goldsmith, B. and Harrison, C. (1990) 'Pale shadows for policy: reflections on the Greenwich Open Space project', in R.G. Burgess (ed.), *Studies in Qualitative Methodology* (Vol. 2): *Reflections on Field Experience*. London: JAI Press. pp. 141–67.

Campbell, D.T. and Stanley, J.C. (1963) *Experimental and Quasi-experimental Designs for Research*. Boston, MA: Houghton Mifflin.

Cannon, S. (1989) 'Social research in stressful situations: difficulties for the sociologist studying the treatment of breast cancer', *Sociology of Health and Illness*, 11(1): 62–77

Cannon, S. (1992) 'Reflections on fieldwork in stressful situations', in R.G. Burgess (ed.), *Studies in Qualitative Methodology* (Vol. 3): *Learning about Fieldwork*. London: JAI Press. pp. 147–82.

Cohen, L. (1976) *Educational Research in Classrooms and Schools: A Manual of Materials and Methods*. London: Harper & Row.

Collinson, D.L. (1992) 'Researching recruitment: qualitative methods and sex discrimination', in R.G. Burgess (ed.), *Studies in Qualitative Methodology* (Vol. 3): *Learning about Fieldwork*. London: JAI Press. pp. 89–121.

Conroy, J. and Bradley, V. (1985) *The Pennhurst Longitudinal Study: A Report of Five Years of Research and Analysis*, Philadelphia, PA: Temple University Developmental Disabilities Centre/Boston: Human Services Research Institute.

Cooper, H. (1998) *Synthesizing Research: a Guide for Literature Reviews*, 3rd edn. Thousand Oaks, CA: Sage Publications.

Cornwell, J. (1984) *Hard-Earned Lives: Accounts of Health and Illness from East London*. London: Tavistock Publications.

Corti, L., Foster, J. and Thompson, P. (1995) 'Archiving qualitative research data', *Social Research Update*, issue 10. Guildford: Department of Sociology, University of Surrey.

Cotterill, P. (1992) 'Interviewing women: issues of friendship, vulnerability, and power', *Women's Studies International Forum*, 15(5/6): 593–606.

Cramer, D. (1997) *Basic Statistics for Social Research: Step-by-step Calculations and Computer Techniques using Minitab*. London: Routledge.

Cronbach, L.J. (1975) 'Beyond the two disciplines of scientific psychology', *American Psychologist*, 30(2): 116–27.

Cunningham-Burley, S. (1985) 'Rules, roles and communicative performance in qualitative research interviews', *International Journal of Sociology and Social Policy*, 5: 67–77.

Data Protection Registrar (1997) *The Data Protection Act 1984: Student Information*. Wilmslow: Data Protection Registrar.

Denzin, N.K. (1970) *The Research Act in Sociology: A Theoretical Introduction to Sociological Methods*. London: Butterworths. 1st edn.

Denzin, N.K. (1989) *The Research Act: A Theoretical Introduction to Sociological Methods*. London: Prentice Hall. 3rd edn.

Denzin, N.K. (1992) 'Whose Cornerville is it anyway?', *Journal of Contemporary Ethnography*, 21(1): 120–32.

Denzin, N.K. and Lincoln Y.S. (eds) (1994) *Handbook of Qualitative Research*. London: Sage Publications.

Devault, M.L. (1990) 'Talking and listening from women's standpoint: feminist strategies for interviewing and analysis', *Social Problems*, 37(1): 96–116.

de Vaus, D.A. (1996) *Surveys in Social Research*, 4th edn. London: UCL Press (1st edn, 1985).

Dey, I. (1993) *Qualitative Data Analysis: A User-Friendly Guide for Social Scientists*. London: Routledge.

Dijkstra, W., van der Veen, L. and van der Zouwen, J. (1985) 'A field experiment in interiewer–respondent reaction', in M. Brenner, J. Brown and D. V. Canter (eds), *The Research Interview: Uses and Approaches*. London: Academic Press. pp. 37–64.

Donmoyer, R. (1996) 'Educational research in an era of paradigm proliferation: what's a journal editor to do?', *Educational Researcher*, 25(2): 19–25.

Douglas, J. D. (1985) *Creative Interviewing*. Beverly Hills, CA: Sage Publications.

Drummond, N. and Mason, G. (1990) 'Diabetes in a social context: just a different way of life in the age of reason', in S. Cunningham-Burley and N.P. McKeganey (eds), *Readings in Medical Sociology*. London: Routledge. pp. 37–54.

Dunn, L. (1991) 'Research alert! Qualitative research may be hazardous to your health', *Qualitative Health Research*, 1(3): 388–92.

Easterby-Smith, M., Thorpe, R. and Lowe, A. (1991) *Managing Research: An Introduction*. London: Sage Publications.

Economic and Social Research Council (ESRC) (1997) *ESRC Studentship Handbook 1997: A Guide for Postgraduate Award Holders*. Swindon: ESRC.

Erlandson, D.A., Harris, E.L. Skipper, B.L and Allen, S.D. (1993) *Doing Naturalistic Inquiry: A Guide to Methods*. Newbury Park, CA: Sage Publications.

Farrall, S., Bannister, J., Ditton, J. and Gilchrist, E. (1997) 'Open and closed questions', *Social Research Update*, issue 17. Guildford: Department of Sociology, University of Surrey.

Fielding, N.G. (1990) 'Mediating the message: affinity and hostility in research on sensitive topics', *American Behavioral Scientist*, 33(5): 608–20.

Fielding, N.G. and Fielding, J.L. (1986) *Linking Data*. London: Sage Publications.

Finch, J. (1984) 'It's great to have someone to talk to: the ethics and politics of interviewing women', in C. Bell and H. Roberts (eds), *Social Researching: Politics, Problems, Practice*. London: Routledge & Kegan Paul. pp. 70–87.

Finch, J. (1987) 'The vignette technique in survey research', *Sociology*, 21(1): 105–14.

Fine, G.A. and Sandstrom, K.L. (1988) *Knowing Children: Participant Observation with Minors*. London: Sage Publications.

Firestone, W.A. (1993) 'Alternative arguments for generalizing from data as applied to qualitative research', *Educational Researcher*, 22(4): 16–23.

Flynn, M.C. (1986) 'Adults who are mentally handicapped as consumers: issues and guidelines for interviewing', *Journal of Mental Deficiency Research*, 30: 369–77.

Frey, J.H. (1989) *Survey Research by Telephone*, 2nd edn. London: Sage Publications (1st edn, 1983.)

Gage, N. L. (1989) 'The paradigm wars and their aftermath; a 'historical' sketch of research on teaching since 1989', *Educational Researcher*, 18(7): 4–10.

Gelb, M. (1988) *Present Yourself*. Torrance, CA: Jaimar Press.

Glaser, B.G. and Strauss, A.L. (1967) *The Discovery of Grounded Theory: Strategies for Qualitative Research*. Chicago: Aldine Publishing.

Goffman, E. (1959) *The Presentation of Self in Everyday Life*. Harmondsworth: Penguin.

Grasha, A.F. (1996) *Teaching with Style*. Pittsburgh, PA: Alliance Publishers.

Greenbaum, T.L. (1998) *Handbook for Focus Group Research*, 2nd edn. London: Sage (1st edn, 1987).

Guba, E.G. and Lincoln, Y.S. (1989) *Fourth Generation Evaluation*. London: Sage Publications.

Guba, E.G. and Lincoln, Y.S. (1994) 'Competing paradigms in qualitative research', in N.K. Denzin and Y.S. Lincoln (eds), *Handbook of Qualitative Research*. London: Sage Publications. pp. 105–17.

Gurney, J.N. (1985) 'Not one of the guys: the female researcher in a male-dominated setting', *Qualitative Sociology*, 8(1): 42–62.

Hammersley, M. and Atkinson, P. (1995) *Ethnography: Principles in Practice*, 2nd edn. London: Routledge (1st edn, 1983).

Hazel, N. (1995) 'Elicitation techniques with young people', *Social Research Update*, issue 12. Guildford: Department of Sociology, University of Surrey.

Helsby, G., Knight, P. and Saunders, M. (1998) 'Preparing students for the new work order', *British Educational Research Journal*, 24(1): 63–78.

Hesketh, A.J. and Knight, P.T. (1997) 'Rationality and quality in postgraduates' choice of course'. Paper presented to the Society for Research in Higher Education Annual Conference, Warwick University, December 1997.

Holden, C. (1979) 'Ethics in social science research', *Science*, 206(1418): 537–40.

Holden, G., Rosenberg, G., Barker, K., Tuhrim, S. and Brenner, B. (1993) 'The recruitment of research participants: a review', *Social Work in Health Care*, 19(2):1–44.

Holland, J. and Ramazanoglu, C. (1994) 'Coming to conclusions: power and interpretation in researching young women's sexuality', in M. Maynard and J. Purvis (eds), *Researching Women's Lives from a Feminist Perspective*. London: Taylor & Francis. pp. 125–48.

Homan, R. (1991) *The Ethics of Social Research*, London: Longman.

Huberman, A.M. and Miles, M.B. (1994) 'Data management and analysis methods', in N.K. Denzin and Y.S. Lincoln (eds), *Handbook of Qualitative Research*. London: Sage Publications. pp. 428–44.

Hughes, R. (1998) 'Considering the vignette technique and its application to a study of drug injecting and HIV risk and safer behaviour', *Sociology of Health and Illness*, 20(3): 381–400.

Hughes, R. (1999) 'Why do people agree to participate in social research? The case of drug injectors', *International Journal of Social Research Methodology*, 1(4): 315–24.

Jacob, E. (1987) 'Qualitative research traditions: a review', *Review of Educational Research*, 57(1): 1–50.

Jick, T.D. (1983) 'Mixing qualitative and quantitative methods: triangulation in action', in J. van Maanen (ed.), *Qualitative Methodology*. London: Sage Publications. pp. 135–48.

Jordan, B. and Henderson, A. (1995) 'Interaction analysis: foundations and practice', *Journal of the Learning Sciences*, 4(1): 39–103.

Jordan, B., James, C., Kay, H. and Redley, M. (1992) *Trapped in Poverty? Labour-Market Decisions in Low-Income Households*. London: Routledge.

Kelle, U. (ed.) (1995) *Computer-aided Qualitative Data Analysis*. London: Sage Publications.

Kelly, L., Burton, S. and Regan, L. (1994) 'Researching women's lives or studying women's oppression? Reflections on what constitutes feminist research', in M. Maynard and J. Purvis (eds), *Researching Women's Lives from a Feminist Perspective*. London: Taylor & Francis. pp. 27–48.

Kinsey, A.C., Pomeroy, W.B. and Martin, C.E. (1948) *Sexual Behavior in the Human Male*. London: W.B. Saunders.

Kinsey, A.C., Wardell, B.P., Clyde, E.M. and Gebhard, P.H. (1953) *Sexual Behavior in the Human Female*. Bloomington, IN: Indiana University Institute for Sex Research.

Kitson, G.C., Clark, R.D., Rushforth, N.B., Brinich, P.M., Sudak, H.S. and Zyzanski, S.J. (1996) 'Research on difficult family topics: helping new and experienced researchers cope with research on loss', *Family Relations*, 45: 183–8.

Knafl, K.A. and Breitmayer, B.J. (1991) 'Triangulation in qualitative research: issues of conceptual clarity and purpose', in J.M. Morse (ed.), *Qualitative Nursing Research: A Contemporary Dialogue*. London: Sage Publications. pp. 226–39.

Knight, P. and Saunders, M. (1999) 'Understanding teachers' professional cultures through interview: a constructivist approach', *Evaluation and Research in Education*, 13(2): 61–72.

Krueger, R.A. (1994) *Focus Groups: A Practical Guide for Applied Research*, 2nd edn. Thousand Oaks, CA: Sage Publications.

Krueger, R.A and Morgan, D. L. (eds) (1998) *Focus Group Kit*, Vols 1–6. Thousand Oaks, CA: Sage Publications.

Lather, P. (1986) 'Issues of validity in openly ideological research', *Interchange*, 17(4): 63–84.

Lavrakas, P.J. (1987) *Telephone Survey Methods: Sampling, Selection and Supervision*. Beverly Hills, CA: Sage Publications.

Lee, R.M. (1981) 'Interreligious courtship and marriage in Northern Ireland'. PhD dissertation, University of Edinburgh.

Lee, R.M. (1992) 'Nobody said it had to be easy: postgraduate field research in Northern Ireland', in R.G. Burgess (ed.), *Studies in Qualitative Methodology* (Vol. 3): *Learning about Fieldwork*. London: JAI Press. pp. 123–45.

Lee, R.M. (1993) *Doing Research on Sensitive Topics*. London: Sage Publications.

Lee, R.M. and Renzetti, C.M. (eds.) (1990) 'The problems of researching sensitive topics: an overview and introduction', *American Behavioral Scientist*, 33(5): 510–28.

Lever, J. (1974) 'Games children play: sex differences and the development of role skills.' PhD dissertation, Yale University.

Lever, J. (1981) 'Multiple methods of data collection: a note on divergence', *Urban Life*, 10(2): 199–213.

Lincoln, Y.S. and Guba, E.G. (1985) *Naturalistic Inquiry*. London: Sage Publications.

Locke, L.F., Silverman, S. J. and Spirduso, W.W. (1998) *Reading and Understanding Research*. Thousand Oaks, CA: Sage Publications.

Lofland, J. (1971) *Analyzing Social Settings: A Guide to Qualitative Observation and Analysis*. Belmont, CA: Wadsworth Publishing.

Lucas, J. (1997) 'Making sense of interviews: the narrative dimension', *Social Sciences in Health*, 3(2): 113–26.

Lummis, T. (1987) *Listening to History*. London: Hutchinson.

Mason, J. (1994) 'Linking qualitative and quantitative data analysis', in A. Bryman and R.G. Burgess (eds), *Analyzing Qualitative Data*. London: Routledge.

Mason, J. (1996) *Qualitative Researching*. London: Sage Publications.

May, T. (1997) *Social Research: Issues, Methods and Process*, 2nd edn. Buckingham: Open University Press (1st edn, 1983).

McCracken, G. (1988) *The Long Interview*. London: Sage Publications.

McCulloch, G., Helsby, E. and Knight, P. (2000, forthcoming) *The Politics of Professionalism*. London: Cassell.

McKee, L. and O'Brien, M. (1983) 'Interviewing men: taking gender seriously', in E. Gamarnikow, D. Morgan, J. Purvis and D. Taylorson (eds), *The Public and the Private*. London: Heinemann. pp. 147–61.

Measor, L. (1985) 'Interviewing: a strategy in qualitative research', in R.G. Burgess (ed.), *Strategies of Educational Research: Qualitative Methods*. London: Falmer Press. pp. 55–77.

Medhurst, K. and Moyser, G. (1987) 'Studying a religious élite: the case of the Anglican episcopate', in G. Moyser and M. Wagstaffe (eds), *Research Methods for Élite Studies*. London: Allen & Unwin. pp. 89–108.

Merriam, S.B. (1998) *Qualitative Research and Case Study Applications in Education*. San Francisco: Jossey–Bass.

Milgram, S. (1963) 'Behavioural study of obedience', *Journal of Abnormal and Social Psychology*, 67: 371–8.

Minkes, J., Robinson, C. and Weston, C. (1994) 'Consulting the children: interviews with children using residential respite care services', *Disability & Society*, 9(1): 47–57.

Mishler, E.G. (1991) 'Representing discourse: the rhetoric of transcription', *Journal of Narrative and Life History*, 1(4): 255–80.

Morgan, D.H.J. (1972) 'The British Association scandal: the effect of publicity on a sociological investigation', *Sociological Review*, 20 (2): 185–206.

Morgan, D.L. (1988) *Focus Groups as Qualitative Research*. Newbury Park, CA: Sage Publications.

Morse, J.M. (1991) 'Strategies for sampling', in J.M. Morse (ed.), *Qualitative Nursing Research: A Contemporary Dialogue*, London: Sage Publications. pp. 127–45.

Mostyn, B. (1985) 'The qualitative analysis of research data', in M. Brenner, J. Brown and D.V. Canter (eds), *The Research Interview: Uses and Approaches*. London: Academic Press. pp. 114–45.

Murphy, E., Dingwall, R., Greatbatch, D., Parker, S. and Watson, P. (1998) *Qualitative Research Methods in Health Technology Assessment*: A review of the literature. Southampton: National Coordinating Committee for Health Technology Assessment.

Oakley, A. (1981) 'Interviewing women: a contradiction in terms', in H. Roberts (ed.), *Doing Feminist Research*. London: Routledge & Kegan Paul. pp. 30–61.

Oakley, A., Benedelow, G., Barnes, J., Buchanan, M. and Husain, O.A.N. (1995) 'Health and cancer prevention: knowledge and beliefs of children and young people', *British Medical Journal*, 310: 1029–33.

Oldman, C. and Beresford, B. (1998) *Homes Unfit for Children: Housing, Disabled Children and Their Families*. Bristol: Policy Press.

Oppenheim, A. N. (1992) *Questionnaire Design, Interviewing and Attitude Measurement*. London: Pinter.

Orwell, G. (1954) 'Politics and the English Language', in *A Collection of Essays*. Garden City, NY: Doubleday. pp. 162–77.

Ostrander, S.A. (1993) '"Surely you're not in this just to be helpful": access, rapport, and interviews in three studies of élites', *Journal of Contemporary Ethnography*, 22(1): 7–27.

Owens, D. (1996) 'Men, emotions and the research process: the role of interviews in sensitive areas', in K. Carter and S. Delamont (eds), *Qualitative Research: The Emotional Dimension*. Aldershot: Avebury. pp. 56–67.

Pahl, J. (1989) *Money and Marriage*. Basingstoke: Macmillan.

Parry, O. (1992) 'Making sense of the research setting and making the research setting make sense', in R.G. Burgess (ed.), *Studies in Qualitative Methodology* (Vol. 3): *Learning about Fieldwork*. London: JAI Press. pp. 63–87.

Patton, M.Q. (1990) *Qualitative Evaluation and Research Methods*, 2nd edn. Newbury Park, CA: Sage (1st edn, 1980).

Piaget, J. (1929) *The Child's Conception of the World*. London: Kegan Paul.

Pines, M. (ed.) (1983) *The Evolution of Group Analysis*. London: Routledge & Kegan Paul.

Platt, J. (1981) 'On interviewing one's peers', *British Journal of Sociology*, 32(1): 75–91.

Poland, B.D. (1995) 'Transcription quality as an aspect of rigour in qualitative research', *Qualitative Inquiry*, 1(3): 290–310.

Polsky, N. (1967) *Hustlers, Beats and Others*. Chicago: Aldine Publishing.

Potter, J. (1996) 'Discourse analysis and constructivist approaches', in J.T.E. Richardson (ed.), *Handbook of Qualitative Research Methods for Psychology and the Social Sciences*. Leicester: British Psychological Society. pp. 125–40.

Powney, J. and Watts, M. (1987) *Interviewing in Educational Research*. London: Routledge & Kegan Paul.

Prein, G., Kelle, U. and Bird, K. (1995) 'An overview of software', in U. Kelle (ed.), *Computer-Aided Qualitative Data Analysis*. London: Sage Publications. pp. 190–210.

Procter, I. and Padfield, M. (1998) 'The effect of the interview on the interviewee', *International Journal of Social Research Methodology*, 1(2): 123–36.

Punch, M. (1986) *The Politics and Ethics of Fieldwork*. London: Sage Publications.

Radley, A. (1988) *Prospects of Heart Surgery: Psychological Adjustment to Coronary Bypass Grafting*. London: Springer-Verlag.

Ramsay, K. (1996) 'Emotional labour and qualitative research: how I learned not to laugh or cry in the field', in E.S. Lyon and J. Busfield (eds), *Methodological Imaginations*. Basingstoke: Macmillan. pp. 131–46.

Reinharz, S. with the assistance of L. Davidman (1992) *Feminist Methods in Social Research*. Oxford: Oxford University Press.

Ribbens, J. (1989) 'Interviewing – an "unnatural situation"?', *Women's Studies International Forum*, 12(6): 579–92.

Richards, L. and Richards, T. (1994) 'From filing cabinet to computer', in A. Bryman and R.G. Burgess (eds), *Analyzing Qualitative Data*. London: Routledge. pp. 147–72.

Richards, P. (1986) 'Risk', in H. Becker (ed.), *Writing for Social Scientists*. Chicago: University of Chicago Press. pp. 108–20.

Richardson, L. (1992) 'Trash on the corner', *Journal of Contemporary Ethnography*, 21(1): 103–19.

Riessman, C.K. (1987) 'When gender is not enough: women interviewing women', *Gender and Society*, 1(2): 172–207.

Robinson, V. (1996) 'Critical theory and the social psychology of change', in K. Leithwood, J. Chapman, D. Corson, P. Hallinger and A. Hart (eds), *International Handbook of Educational Leadership and Administration*. Dordrecht: Kluwer. pp. 1069–96.

Robson, C. (1993) *Real World Research: A Resource for Social Scientists and Practitioner-Researchers*. Oxford: Blackwell.

Rubin, H.J. and Rubin, I.S. (1995) *Qualitative Interviewing: the Art of Hearing Data*. London: Sage Publications.

Selwyn, N. and Robson, K. (1998) 'Using e-mail as a research tool', *Social Research Update*, issue 21. Guildford: Department of Sociology, University of Surrey.

Sherlock, J. (1992) *Examining Independence: A Study of Forensic Science Evidence in the Pre-Trial Process*. Unpublished PhD thesis. Lancaster University.

Sigelman, C.K., Budd, E.C., Spanhel, C.L. and Schoenrock, C.J. (1981a) 'Asking questions of mentally retarded persons: a comparison of yes–no and either–or formats', *Applied Research in Mental Retardation*, 2: 347–57.

Sigelman, C.K., Budd, E.C., Spanhel, C.L. and Schoenrock, C.J. (1981b) 'When in doubt, say yes: acquiescence in interviews with mentally retarded persons', *Mental Retardation*, 19: 53–8.

Sigelman, C.K., Budd, E.C., Winer, J.L., Schoenrock, C.J. and Martin, R.W. (1982) 'Evaluating alternative techniques of questioning mentally retarded persons', *American Journal of Mental Deficiency*, 85(5): 511–18.

Silverman, D. (1985) *Qualitative Methodology and Sociology: Describing the Social World*. Aldershot: Gower.

Silverman, D. (1993) *Interpreting Qualitative Data: Methods for Analysing Talk, Text and Interaction*. London: Sage Publications.

Skeggs, B. (1994) 'Situating the production of feminist ethnography', in M. Maynard and J. Purvis (eds), *Researching Women's Lives from a Feminist Perspective*. London: Taylor & Francis. pp. 72–92.

Social and Community Planning Research (1998) *Respondent Incentives in Surveys*, 18(2): 1–20.

Spector, M. (1980) 'Learning to study public figures', in W.B. Shaffir, R.A. Stebbins and A. Turowetz (eds), *Fieldwork Experience: Qualitative Approaches to Social Research*. New York: St Martin's Press. pp. 98–109.

Stenhouse, L. (1980) 'The study of samples and the study of cases', *British Educational Research Journal*, 6(1): 1–7.

Strauss, A.L. and Corbin, J. (1990) *Basics of Qualitative Research: Grounded Theory Procedures and Techniques*. London: Sage Publications.

Sudman, S. and Bradburn, N.M. (1982) *Asking Questions: A Practical Guide to Questionnaire Design*. San Francisco: Jossey–Bass Publishers.

Summerfield, P. (1998) *Reconstructing Women's Wartime Lives*. Manchester: Manchester University Press.

Taraborrelli, P. (1993) 'Becoming a carer', in N. Gilbert (ed.), *Researching Social Life*. London: Sage Publications. pp. 172–85.

Thomas, R.J. (1993) 'Interviewing important people in big companies', *Journal of Contemporary Ethnography*, 22(1): 80–96.

Thompson, P. (1988) *The Voice of the Past*. Oxford: Oxford University Press.

Turner, B.A. (1981) 'Some practical aspects of qualitative data analysis: one way of organising the cognitive processes associated with the generation of grounded theory', *Quality and Quantity*, 15: 225–47.

Van Maanen, J., Manning, P.K. and Miller, M.L. (1988) 'Editors' Introduction', in C.A.B. Warren (ed.), *Gendered Issues in Field Research*. London: Sage Publications. pp. 5–6.

Walker, R. (1983) 'Three good reasons for not doing case study', *Journal of Curriculum Studies*, 15(2): 155–65.

Warren, C.A.B. (1988) *Gender Issues in Field Research*. London: Sage Publications.

Webb, E.J., Campbell, D.T., Schwartz, R.D. and Sechrest, L. (1966) *Unobtrusive Measures: Nonreactive Research in the Social Sciences*. Chicago: Rand McNally.

Weitzman, E.A. and Miles, M.B. (1998) *Computer Programs for Qualitative Data Analysis. A Software Sourcebook*. Thousand Oaks, CA: Sage Publications. 2nd edn.

West, P. (1990) 'The status and validity of accounts obtained at interview: a contrast between two studies of families with a disabled child', *Social Science and Medicine*, 30(11): 1229–39.

Whyte, W.F. (1943) *Street Corner Society: The Social Structures of an Italian Slum*. Chicago: University of Chicago Press.

Wilkinson, S. (1998) 'Focus group methodology: a review', *International Journal of Social Research Methodology*, 1(3): 181–203.

Wilson, A. (1998) *Managing Your Research Project: Targets, Tasks and Techniques*. Oxford: Staff Development Office, University of Oxford.

Winkler, J. (1987) 'The fly on the wall of the inner sanctum: observing company directors at work', in. G. Moyser and M. Wagstaffe (eds), *Research Methods for Élite Studies*. London: Allen & Unwin. pp. 129–46.

Woods, P.A., Bagley, C. and Glatter, R. (1998) *School Choice and Competition: Markets in the Public Interest?* London: Routledge.

# Index